Don DeLillo

The University of Georgia Press   Athens and London

David Cowart

Don DeLillo The Physics of Language

Printed in the United States of America

06   05   04   03   02   C   5   4   3   2   1

Library of Congress Cataloging-in-Publication Data

Cowart, David, 1947–
Don DeLillo : the physics of language / David Cowart.
    p. cm.
Includes bibliographical references and index.
ISBN 0-8203-2320-9 (alk. paper)
1. DeLillo, Don—Criticism and interpretation.
2. Postmodernism (Literature)—United States.   I. Title.
PS3554.E4425 Z59 2002
813'.54—dc21   2001045070

British Library Cataloging-in-Publication Data available

The chapter "For Whom Bell Tolls: *Americana*" was first
published in slightly different form as "For Whom Bell
Tolls: Don DeLillo's *Americana*." *Contemporary Literature*,
37, no. 4 (winter 1996): 602–19. Copyright © 1996 The
University of Wisconsin Press. Reprinted with permission.

The chapter "More Advanced the Deeper We Dig: *Ratner's
Star*" was first published under the same title but in slightly
different form in *Modern Fiction Studies*, 45, no. 3 (fall
1999): 600–620. Copyright © 1999 The Purdue Research
Foundation.

For Chase

Language is the house of Being. In its home man dwells.
Heidegger

I began to suspect that language was a subject as well as an instrument in my work.
Don DeLillo

Contents

vii

Part Two: "Before everything, there's language"

Part Three: "The word beyond speech"

Acknowledgments

I have many colleagues and friends to thank for their generous support during my work on this project: those in the Department of English at the University of South Carolina include Amitai Aviram, Meili Steele, and Ed Madden, who shared their knowledge of theory. When I was living abroad and facing a long wait for a newly translated piece by Walter Benjamin, Professor Aviram took the trouble to Xerox his copy and mail it to me. Professor Madden has on more than one occasion saved me a trip to the library by lending me his personal copies of theoretical books I do not own myself. I am grateful to other colleagues who were instrumental in my receiving a research grant in the summer of 1998 — and to Robert Newman, the department chair, who found money to allow me to attend the premiere of DeLillo's play *Valparaiso* in Cambridge, Massachusetts.

On a Fulbright fellowship at Syddansk Universitet in Odense, Denmark, I was assigned to the Center for American Studies and was much stimulated by its faculty, especially Helle Porsdam, Clara Juncker, David Nye, and Jan Nordby Gretlund. The students in my fall 1996 *kursus fag* seminar, with whom I read DeLillo, were wonderfully sharp and jogged my thinking at every meeting. Thanks, Jan, Stephen, Lone, Pernille, and Paul.

I appreciate the sage counsel of the readers for my articles (incorporated here in slightly different form) in *Contemporary Literature* and *Modern Fiction Studies*. I should also like to thank and half-seriously reproach the authors of the previous book-length studies of DeLillo: Thomas LeClair, Douglas Keesey, and Mark Osteen (I had the great privilege of reading Professor Osteen's book in manuscript). Their work, along with that of Frank Lentricchia, is so good as to discourage the academic community from doing with the DeLillo canon what was done with that of Pynchon and others, that is, create whole shelves of scholarly discussion. At the same time, however, I know that they will want the dialogue to continue.

Laura di Prete, my graduate assistant one semester, was a great help in tracking down secondary materials. Casey Clabough helped compile the bibliography. Kelly Innes helped with last-minute preparation of the manuscript. Justin Pittas-Giroux also helped, notably with some heroic photocopying. Barbara Pace, administrative assistant during the three years in which I served as my department's graduate director, took considerable pains to insure that a reluctant administrator had time for his research. Glen Scott Allen took the trouble to e-mail me his article on *Ratner's Star* at a time when my library did not subscribe to *Postmodern Culture* (an oversight since rectified). Jesse Kavadlo brought my attention to the DeLillo essays in the electronic journal *Undercurrent*. Richard Rorty was kind enough to answer a stranger's e-mailed query about a Heidegger reference. I also wish to thank Mr. DeLillo's agent, Lois Wallace, who arranged for me to receive an advance copy of *The Body Artist* months before its official publication. I had the good fortune to serve on the doctoral committee of Paul Price, whose 1995 dissertation on the artist figure in DeLillo helped me to see just how multivalent this author is. Paul's bibliography was especially valuable to the early stages of my project. I am happy not to be alone in saluting the work of Curt Gardner, whose Internet site on DeLillo is one of the very best of its kind. It is gratifying to see him recognized in scholarly citations and in reviews and articles in the popular press. Another first-rate website is that of the Don DeLillo Society, maintained by Philip W. Nel of Kansas State University.

One often reads touching tributes to long-suffering spouses and children left to their own devices during the long seasons of authorial travail. But as I look back over the period spent on this project it occurs to me that the work was frequently retarded because my children and parents and other relatives firmly insisted on my presence and participation in the daily business of family life. If ever I seemed impatient to return to my contemplation of the blinking cursor, I apologize, for I am fully aware that years hence one is unlikely to say: I wish I had spent more time at the office. Thanks, all, for slowing me down— I wouldn't for anything have missed those school pageants, those obligatory visits, those family activities. On a more serious note, I am deeply grateful for the love and support I have received from my daughter, Rachel, and my son, Chase.

Don DeLillo

Introduction

In his acute rendering of the bi-millennial moment, Don DeLillo ranks among the most important of contemporary novelists. But the trend away from books on single authors (a trend much discussed in the academic press) threatens even the most distinguished of living writers with premature obscurity—at least insofar as their reputations depend on acts of scholarly attention and commitment. If literature is to have any place in the increasingly utilitarian curriculum of the future, its academic custodians in the present must do a better job of articulating the unique importance of great works of the imagination. On the other hand, with the exception of certain lapidary *précieux,* the best contemporary writers embrace an encyclopedic range that confounds or precludes narrow-gauge analysis. Good DeLillo criticism, in any event, properly engages the whole landscape of postmodernism. It also engages the supreme humanities subject, the one that subsumes the specialized discourses of

1

science and mathematics as it ties together linguistics, literature, philosophy, history, anthropology, sociology, theology, and psychology. This subject, not emphasized in the otherwise admirable book-length studies of DeLillo by LeClair, Keesey, and Osteen, is language. The present book focuses on DeLillo's career-long exploration of language as cultural index, as "deepest being," as *numinosum.*

Throughout his twelve novels, DeLillo foregrounds language and the problems of language. He has an uncanny ear for the mannered, elliptical, non sequitur–ridden rhythms of vernacular conversation (the common response to "thank you" has somehow become "no problem"). He is an adept parodist of the specialized discourses that proliferate in contemporary society—in sport, business, politics, academe, medicine, entertainment, and journalism. The jargons of science, technology, and military deterrence offer abundant targets, too. But the author's interest in these discourses goes beyond simple parody, and it is the task of criticism to gauge the extra dimensions of DeLillo's thinking about language.

Though DeLillo strikes many readers as sui generis, his books are nonetheless highly representative of the most sensitive and innovative work being done in current American fiction. In a not altogether friendly review of the 1977 novel *Players,* John Updike admitted that

> Don DeLillo has, as they used to say of athletes, class. He is original, versatile, and, in his disdain of last year's emotional guarantees, fastidious. He brings to human phenomena the dispassionate mathematics and spatial subtleties of particle physics. Into our technology-riddled daily lives he reads the sinister ambiguities, the floating ugliness of America's recent history.[1]

In analyzing the oeuvre of a writer so gifted, one seeks fresh perspectives on contemporary literature. At the same time, one explores some of the basic aesthetic principles of the age. To be sure, DeLillo has contributed to the substantial, growing body of literature that explores the essential circularity of signification in all its forms. Since the publication of his first novel in 1971, he has taken his place among the postmodern masters, the writers who recognize, more or less instinctively, that language commonly represents only itself. The enigmatic quality of the DeLillo aesthetic suggests a recognition that language will always resist and betray attempts by the unsubtle to make it a transparent medium, a window on the world of things. Immured in language, one has, like Nabokov's Humbert Humbert, only words to play with—words that refer to other words and such reality as words may construct, but never to the world in its extralinguistic integrity. The named thing escapes.

Some postmodernists embrace this doctrine and specialize in the creation of separate, autonomous worlds wholly discontinuous with the familiar terra. This "ontological" emphasis, according to Brian McHale, is a major element in the postmodernist aesthetic.[2] A writer like John Hawkes is typical: he prides himself on making worlds, not reproducing or imitating them. Other practitioners—Nabokov, again, or Coover in *The Universal Baseball Association* or Kundera in *Immortality*—like to stage encounters, even contests, between their created worlds and the genuine article. In doing so they devise ontological puzzles, usually at the expense of traditional views of reality, and invite readers to admire the ease with which their factitious worlds achieve legitimacy alongside—and interact with—the preexistent world. The achievement of a rare art, the perfectly hermetic fictions of such writers, resistant to all but self-referential meanings, invite recognition of a seemingly infinite tolerance of the image and its ontological pretensions.

Two-dimensionality is the signature of the age. Americans live in an image culture, the artists of this age declare—not just a culture in which images proliferate, but a culture in which one recognizes no reality deeper than the image. Moreover, this or that icon of consumer lust or erotic transport or adolescent heroic fantasy is neither more nor less real than any other image the self entertains with regard to its true identity. At a local exercise studio, for example, the management has placed—in the lobby, off to the side, partly screened by a couple of robust aspidistras—a life-sized pasteboard cutout of Fabio. Bare-chested, clad in vaguely piratical leggings and boots, the figure repeatedly tricks peripheral vision, inviting the more direct gaze that discovers a faintly absurd but strangely familiar eidolon of romance masculinity. Beyond this recognition one descries, perhaps, a further joke: that Fabio exists *only* in this two-dimensional form. He defines and embodies a culture wholly wedded to the image, a culture that has long since discarded the assumption that signifieds exist behind or beneath signifiers. What, after all, does the pasteboard cutout "represent"? Only the flickering recollection of paperback book covers, margarine commercials, TV appearances: signifiers referring to other signifiers in an endless chain, an infinite regression.

A true postmodern, this Fabio. Like the canvases of Warhol and Lichtenstein, his image exemplifies a radical denial of the psychological, aesthetic, cultural, and graphic third dimension. The validity of this idea has become a matter of widespread if largely unconscious recognition. One knows, perhaps without being able to articulate the insight, that one cannot pierce the surfaces of contemporary life to encounter some deeper, truer reality. The only reality knowable is the one shaped by endlessly self-referential sign systems and by an art committed to replication, pastiche, and the commodified "mechanical reproduction" that Benjamin describes in his most famous essay. In short, the age of the simulacrum.

Baudrillard famously suggests that the image, which "*plays at being* an appearance" of some "basic reality," reigns supreme in the contemporary world. He describes the "successive phases" of the image as a four-step declension:

> it is the reflection of a basic reality
> it masks and perverts a basic reality
> it masks the *absence* of a basic reality
> it bears no relation to any reality whatever: it is its own pure simulacrum.[3]

These precepts seem almost to have been conceived with the fiction of Don DeLillo in mind. Certainly one recognizes in *White Noise* a kind of comedy of the simulacrum: the much-photographed barn, the nuns who are not *croyant,* the mosque that was once a "Moorish" movie theater, the band playing "live Muzak." In *Running Dog,* similarly, a Pakistani "might be Peter Sellers," and a TV personality is described as "all image. . . . He's a bunch of little electronic dots, that's all he is."[4] In *Great Jones Street* the narrator-protagonist jokes that he himself, his house in the mountains, and his manager are all "facsimiles." He and his girlfriend note with wry amusement how postcard photographers conspire to transform every "sleazy tourist trap" into "the canoeing grounds of the gods."[5]

Critics have not been slow to recognize and exploit the affinity between DeLillo and Baudrillard, but in doing so they have risked overstating DeLillo's involvement with—as opposed to criticism of—the image. John Johnston suggests that after a decade of writing "novels of language," DeLillo began to engage the primacy of the cinematic image: "Film now occupies a privileged place" in DeLillo's work, and "the image is the essential term in the relationship between the two media." Thus Johnston characterizes the emergent DeLillo vision as "post-cinematic." According to this view, "The world seems to have lost all substance and anchoring or reference points, except in relation to other images or what are conceived as images."[6] Johnston's analysis is acute, but in my view he has one crucial point backwards. DeLillo in no sense retreats from or becomes less engaged with language; rather, he recognizes and examines the way images themselves constitute a semiotic. DeLillo contemplates more and more of the sign systems—including the cinematic—that form branches of the language tree. Language subsumes image.

One or two critics have cautiously speculated about an element of conservatism in DeLillo. Paul Maltby, for example, notes neo-Romantic tendencies in the DeLillo of *The Names, White Noise,* and *Libra.*[7] But Tom LeClair more judiciously suggests that this author seems aware of competing novelistic paradigms, of successive postmodernisms on the one hand—and of fresh realisms on the other. Though his observation concerns only *The Names* directly, it suggests a critical perspective on all the novels: "DeLillo creates consistently enriching reciprocal relations between the transcultural observations of the New Realists and the semiotic skepticism of the metafictionists."[8] Glen Scott Allen, by the same token, sees the author as unwilling to surrender romantic and modernist constructions of the self. Perhaps, contrary to received opinion, DeLillo's work "represents a rejection of the postmodern subject (as figured in the works of critics like Benvéniste, Jameson, and Baudrillard to name only a few) as something nearly inseparable from the semiotic 'signal soup.'" Perhaps, too, the author construes "the theoretically obsolete individual as the only viable site of resistance to the ubiquitous terror of postmodern life."[9]

But this is too broad. From David Bell and Gary Harkness to Bill Gray and Nick Shay, the resistance proves inconsequential, unlikely to issue in any reversal of the postmodern condition. If there is a resister, it is DeLillo himself. If there is a site of resistance, it is language, the very medium that supposedly exemplifies the hopelessness of laying a foundation, making a stand. For however pervasive the cultural deference to simulacra, one would not argue that DeLillo is so true to his medium as to avoid affirming any reality or truth beneath the surfaces of contemporary life. One knows, after all, that a reality beyond image or word exists; indeed, the conviction is shared even by those philosophers and theorists who have most relentlessly called into question commonsense notions about sensory or linguistic representation of that reality. As will be seen in chapter 4, the author of *Ratner's Star* knows his eighteenth-century literature, and one imagines him reading Boswell and smiling at Dr. Johnson's elenctic kicking of the stone to dismiss Bishop Berkeley and the doctrine of subjective idealism.

Thus DeLillo does not defer to the poststructuralist view of language as a system of signifiers that refer only to other signifiers in infinite regression. DeLillo's texts in fact undermine this postmodernist gospel. Fully aware that language is maddeningly circular, maddeningly subversive of its own supposed referentiality, the author nonetheless affirms something numinous in its mysterious properties. He intimates, for example, that one can discern some larger significance in the naive constructions of those just learning to speak. Fascinated by the way children use language, DeLillo repeatedly suggests, in interviews, that even the babbling of infants contains meaning. Perhaps, to borrow a figure from *Americana,* the babbling infant simply bathes in "the river which is language without thought."[10]

In the hands of this resourceful literary artist language reveals itself as a system defiant of systems, a system whose complexity is at least as vast and inexhaustible as that of the world it constructs or attempts to represent. With or without thought, language flows, a river holy as the Ganges. Though post-Freudian psychoanalysts insist that the Symbolic Order estranges the subject from itself, DeLillo plays, like Rilke, with conceits of self-definition through some kind of cosmic verbal exchange:

Und wenn dich das Irdische vergass,
Zu der stillen Erde sag: ich rinne.
Zu dem raschen Wasser sprich: Ich bin.

As rendered by Thomas Pynchon, these lines from the twenty-ninth of Rilke's *Sonnets to Orpheus* represent a subjectivity realized in language:

And though Earthliness forget you,
To the stilled Earth say: I flow.
To the rushing water speak: I am.[11]

As it speaks, as it immerses itself in the riverine word, the "I" itself exists or flows. DeLillo, by the same token, imagines a symbiosis, a defining mutualism, of speaker and spoken. Language fosters subjectivity, which, however fluid, is another word for the sentience that makes us human. This study centers, then, on DeLillo's interrogations of language and on the fictive strategies by which the author contrives to make language yield up its secrets.

DeLillo himself has implicitly sanctioned a division of his career into at least two parts: "Some of the work I did in the 1970s was off-the-cuff, not powerfully motivated. I think I forced my way into a couple of books that weren't begging to be written, or maybe I was writing too fast." He identifies *The Names* (1982) as "the book that marks the beginning of a new dedication."[12] These hints have prompted the three-part organization of the present study. In the first part I group the more tentative early novels—*End Zone* (1972), *Great Jones Street* (1973), *Players* (1977), and *Running Dog* (1978). By no means inconsequential, these books show DeLillo trying out his ideas (and natural curiosity) about language. But I have not sought to discover in them more than is there. My discussions attempt to reflect their somewhat tentative and even athetic features. On the other hand, these books allow one to get comfortable with a laconic and sometimes disorienting style. By looking closely at them one is the better prepared to enter the more complex and subtle fictions to come.

One resists calling the novels of part 1 "apprentice" work, because they are contemporaneous with two masterpieces: *Americana*, DeLillo's first novel (1971), and *Ratner's Star* (1976). One option here would have been to include these in my discussion of the other early novels, but I have decided to begin with DeLillo work that lends itself to more gradual revelations of this author's characteristic techniques and themes. From this critical groundwork I proceed, in part 2, to a consideration of the superb fictions—*White Noise* (1985), *Libra* (1988), and *Mao II* (1991)—that have simultaneously gained DeLillo a popular audience and established him as the kind of contemporary writer who gets serious attention from academe and the more important periodicals. In the last section, having (I hope) established DeLillo's range and complexity, I turn to the five fictions in which his achievement is greatest. These, interestingly, include novels from every part of his writing life: the aforementioned early fictions *Americana* and *Ratner's Star,* the mid-career work *The Names,* the millennium-capping *Underworld* (1997), and the minimalist *The Body Artist* (2001).

DeLillo and Theory

The responses to DeLillo's massive eleventh novel, *Underworld,* express over and over again the expectation that its author will enjoy the full measure of literary recognition. Already, that recognition has become international—there are a growing number of translations, and articles on his work regularly appear in French, German, Spanish, and Italian. In 1999 DeLillo became the first American to win the Jerusalem Prize, joining such luminaries as Borges, Isaiah Berlin, Mario Vargas Llosa, Milan Kundera, V. S. Naipaul, and Bertrand Russell. Here and abroad, discriminating readers have recognized a remarkable body of work in which a mind of great range and fertility engages the full variety of late-twentieth-century American civilization: the spiritual enervation, the residual paranoia, the obsession with sport and entertainment and celebrity. DeLillo has emerged as a contemporary novelist of major stature—a literary genius to be ranked with the likes of Vladimir Nabokov or, in his own generation, Thomas Pynchon.

Born within six months of each other, Pynchon and DeLillo are the mythic cousins of American postmodernism. One imagines their mothers, like Elizabeth and the Virgin Mary, spending time together before the two important births. For a long time it has seemed obvious which of the blessed pair was the postmodern Anointed, which merely John the Baptist; but as DeLillo remains steadily inventive and Pynchon steadily self-effacing, seeming to aspire to fade from the scene like one of his own characters, we may come to judge DeLillo as the one who most consistently transforms the water of routine storytelling into literary wine.

As the author of one of the first books on Pynchon, I am in a good position to assay the growing reputation of his contemporary. Where the modernists saw myth as some kind of universal, instinctive truth, a DeLillo or a Pynchon starts from a recognition of the essential factitiousness of myth. From their postmodern perspective, they understand that myth reflects only the order-hungry needs of the psyche. But unlike Pynchon, who devises fictive myths only to undermine them (the Rocket in *Gravity's Rainbow* is the great example), DeLillo more radically denies myth altogether, recognizing how alien it is—in its pretensions to psychological and anthropological depth—to a culture wedded to the superficies of the present, a culture that seems to repudiate history. DeLillo may well displace Pynchon as the postmodern Henry Adams. Born exactly one hundred years after Adams, DeLillo is committed, like the author of *The Education of Henry Adams,* to gauging "the track of the energy" that makes or transforms a civilization. He follows that energy into language itself, and he seems prepared, as Adams was, to pursue meaning out of one century (indeed, millennium) and into another. Whereas Adams, elegizing a lost cultural unity, contrasts the multifarious technologies of power in his own time to the force embodied and concentrated in prior ages—in Venus or the Virgin—a DeLillo (or a Pynchon) charts much swifter epistemic shifts, recognizing that changes formerly taking hundreds of years now take place from decade to decade.

It takes an artist of rare gifts to represent the contemporary world's complexity. As Charles Molesworth has observed, "No other contemporary novelist could be said to outstrip DeLillo in his ability to depict that larger social environment we blandly call everyday life. Brand names, current events, fads, the society of the spectacle, and the rampant consumerism that has become our most noticeable, if not our most important, contribution to history, are all plentifully and accurately recorded throughout DeLillo's work." [13] One of the most resourceful and acute chroniclers of his age, DeLillo seems intuitively to grasp how a new *épistémè* displaces its predecessor. In his brilliant and disturbing fictions, DeLillo registers the vertigo that ensues when familiar paradigms of knowing warp and shift. But insofar as the emergent *épistémè* proves inchoate, DeLillo's engagements with it remain enigmatic. From time to time, he teases his reader with intimations of some profound insight; indeed, the experience of reading this author resembles a dream in which one can never quite close with a cryptic meaning that seems to hover at the edge of consciousness, constantly threatening to slip over the horizon of the sentence, the page, the volume. Readers respond to the acuity with which DeLillo captures the spirit of a postmodern America highly resistant to being understood in the old ways, but they find his fictions strangely protean, slippery, difficult to arrest in stable postures of meaning. In short, they find DeLillo relatively easy to read but not so easy to sort out.

He avoids thematic directness. His style is relentlessly oblique, and even the best critics have found his vision hard to come to terms with. His characteristic concerns—terrorism, political murder, nuclear war, the nature of language, the fate of America—are perfectly plain, but he tends to write all around these subjects, almost like a moth wise enough to know the annihilating power of the flame that attracts it. Like Polonius, he seems to want by indirection to find directions out. Even in *Libra,* in which the subject (the Kennedy assassination) is squarely before author and reader, there is a studied indirection, an awareness that where certain complex issues are involved the direct gaze betrays. DeLillo is like the stargazer who knows the tiny blind spot at the center of the eye, knows that to see a star one must look to the side of it. Thus his sentences and his plots work on the level of what in *Americana* he calls those "Oriental aphorisms which seem to convey a shattering truth while remaining stubbornly elusive. One senses the meaning but cannot quite clutch it." [14]

One must honor DeLillo's instinct for indirectness by avoiding critical or theoretical schematicism—even when the schema illustrates the author's thematic catholicity. Critics have occasionally suggested that DeLillo takes up, seriatim, the major conditions or institutions or obsessions of contemporary American culture: advertising and television *(Americana),* sport *(End Zone),* mathematics and science *(Ratner's Star),* the popular music industry *(Great Jones Street),* urban terror *(Players),* the unholy relationships among business, government, journalism, espionage, and pornography *(Running Dog),* academe and eco-disaster *(White Noise),* language games, cults, and third-world tensions *(The Names),* conspiracy and the politics of assassination *(Libra),* millenarian passions *(Mao II),* waste and weaponry *(Underworld).* But however useful such rubrics may seem, they promise more system than DeLillo will sanction. In his interview with Anthony DeCurtis, he makes clear his impatience with schematic approaches to his work.[15]

As a postmodernist committed to representing the discontinuous contemporary moment, DeLillo is resistant to the seductive appeal of totalizing theories, comprehensive accounts of the phenomenal world and the human place in it. Indeed, one could argue that the first book on DeLillo, Tom LeClair's *In the Loop: Don DeLillo and the Systems Novel* (1987), succeeds precisely because it transcends its thesis; LeClair, that is, does not make the mistake of trying to put every DeLillo fiction into the conceptual straitjacket of systems theory, that "metascience" of human systems that function cybernetically. LeClair realizes that too doctrinaire an application of his thesis will afford little latitude to gauge the profoundly anarchic qualities that, as DeLillo reveals, constantly disrupt the feedback loop. By the same token, even more eclectic applications of theory require caution—for to overdo theoretical readings of a writer like DeLillo can be an exercise in the redundant and the pretentious. Theory always threatens to make merely less immediate the fictive praxis of a DeLillo, a Pynchon, an Ishmael Reed, or an Octavia Butler.

Noel King has sketched elements of the debate over postmodernism (i.e., "whether it is best thought of as a cultural logic or as a set of representational practices") and related them to DeLillo's *White Noise,* which he characterizes as "one of the sharpest meditations on the postmodern available, a meditation, moreover, which is delivered in such a way as to resist further analytical description or elaboration." Thus "any act of criticism" might "seem *misplaced* not so much for having 'misread' an authorial intention . . . as for seeming to be everywhere already anticipated, pre-empted, forced into an unsettling critical space between the welcomed and the redundant." [16] In short, King fears that theoretically informed criticism of DeLillo will seem always to be a gilding of the lily. One notes here a strange, postmodern variation on the old idea of criticism as parasite on the healthy body of original art. But instead of arguing that theory has something of its own to contribute to our understanding—or suggesting that we dispense with theory and simply read DeLillo—King urges us to divide our attention between DeLillo and the theoretical discourse that parallels him. To that end, he juxtaposes "quotations from the novel and quotations from the cultural criticism of writers such as Barthes, Eco, Virilio" because "the roles of novelist and cultural critic must be regarded as, at all times, interchangeable" (76). In his view, "We now inhabit a historical moment where . . . the binary opposition of the 'fictional' and the 'critical'" must give way before something he calls the "ficto-critical" (74).

But I resist the argument that artistic expression and critical discourse are somehow indistinguishable. However true technically, this assertion fails the test of experience. King errs to declare that theory has nothing to tell the DeLillo reader; he compounds error with self-contradiction when he insists on giving us some theory anyway—rather than falling respectfully silent. The point, of course, is that in rejecting premises such as King's, critics and theorists alike reject the grounds of their own silencing. They see a writer of such enormous subtlety as DeLillo benefiting from a good deal of analysis and explication. The critic, in short, remains convinced that analysis can benefit from theory judiciously chosen and applied. But every critical gesture must be undertaken with humility, with a recognition that the primary text—the occasion for criticism, after all—remains at least provisionally foundational. Only through the stimulus of art can criticism achieve insights worth the world's time and attention. This is not to say that theory for the sake of theory is objectionable—only that it occupies a branch of learning and pleasure one finds less interesting than art itself.

In any event, one must seek out truly cogent theory and consider the ways in which it brings the DeLillo text more sharply into focus. If, as he has re-marked publicly, DeLillo does not "think of language in a theoretical way," does not read much of what Anthony DeCurtis, interviewing him, refers to as "the theoretical work being done in philosophy and literary criticism these days,"[17] then his fictions paradoxically provide strong evidence that theory really is the codification of contemporary conditions of knowing, as it claims to be. When a Coetzee or an Abish or a Curtis White writes like this, he invites interviewers and readers to see connections between his fictions and various ideas gleaned from the large and growing body of linguistic, philosophical, political, and psychoanalytic writing whereby we have learned to see language and the world in new and sometimes disturbing ways. But one sometimes feels that certain of our most sophisticated ideas about language and representation are all artificial overlays of something better encountered in its "natural" *of course!* state—in the pages of writers innocent of theory but attuned, nonetheless, to the Zeitgeist. I cannot help thinking that the real test of such ideas is their suitability in glossing fictions such as DeLillo's.

Theorists can nonetheless offer useful vocabularies to the critic, and to read DeLillo without theory would be to reinvent wheel after wheel. Theory gives criticism its common terms, some of them jargon, to be sure, but all conducive to discursive economy and precision. One must, at least initially, test DeLillo's various fictions against elements of the postmodernist aesthetic defined by such theorists as Lacan, Derrida, and Baudrillard: the foreshortened view of history, the unmooring of subjectivity, radical discontinuity, replication and parody, awareness of the constructedness of all knowledge and all myths, resis-tance to closure, indifference to what Lyotard calls "the solace of good forms," and that "new kind of flatness or depthlessness," that "new kind of superfici-ality in the most literal sense" that Fredric Jameson characterizes as "the su-preme formal feature of all postmodernisms."[18] Beyond these—more impor-tantly—are the earlier philosophers and theorists of language. This, again, is DeLillo's great subject, and one can with considerable profit read his books against the insights afforded by a select group of language philosophers, espe-cially Wittgenstein, Heidegger, and Benjamin. *elements of po-mo* *this wording first of all*

At the same time, however, one must read DeLillo closely for his own theory of postmodern reality. That is, one admits the practitioner as theorist. By this means one may hope to avoid the occasional sense that postmodern theory somehow "licenses" the practice of imaginative postmodern artists. In fact, authorial praxis is the truest theoretical standard. To read the best postmodern writers is to encounter, in a peculiarly cogent form, the very insights theory seeks to formulate. To read DeLillo, by the same token, is to encounter radical thinking that—specifically vis-à-vis the conceptualization of language—

Why is this deluse of theory & analysis felt as necessary?

proves healthily resistant to certain of the more reductive elements in deconstruction and its theoretical congeners. DeLillo charts new territory for literary art in fictions that constantly probe language for evidence of an epistemological depth largely denied by poststructuralist theory.

DeLillo is, in a double sense, an exemplary postmodernist. That is, his work lends itself to definition by example: this, one can say, proffering *White Noise, The Names,* or *Ratner's Star,* is postmodernism. On the other hand, DeLillo is also exemplary in that he resists what can be a hegemonic tendency in postmodernist thought and practice. After all, however much one attempts to codify its practices, postmodernism is not an exclusive club that bars certain ideologies or practices. It is open, eclectic, anti-hierarchical, and nondoctrinal. Though I defer at times to the familiar, antifoundationalist model, I remain convinced that all postmodernisms remain valid. As a broad rubric, the postmodern need not be construed as inimical to the artistic strategies of those—women, minorities—who remain passionately committed to the idea of subject positions from which they might challenge logocentrism, patriarchy, and a host of exploitative economic hegemonies.

The difficulties posed by DeLillo have their mimetic rationale in the confusion of contemporary American culture. As an instrument measuring what it means to live in the American present, this author mirrors the strange fluidity and rootlessness of an age in which, with or without the pronouncements of Lacanian psychoanalysis, the individual's sense of identity or self suffers progressive attenuation. DeLillo observes and records the way the contemporary mind, its attention span diminished, has seemingly been modified by film, by music, and, overwhelmingly, by television. But to transcribe this social and psychological reality is not to endorse it. If DeLillo seems in his fictions to *become* the American reality he scrutinizes—to become, that is, hip, young, image-crazed, and morally ambiguous—it may be that he does so out of a desire that is homeopathic, a desire to inoculate (in the most literal sense) cultural production against the tyranny of the two-dimensional that threatens to devalue it. This struggle with depthlessness by a seeming surrender to the image bears a superficial resemblance to "going over to the object," the strategy urged by Baudrillard for combating or circumventing the "evil" of subjectivity. But where Baudrillard actually endorses the turn against the subject, DeLillo merely feigns "going over." Baudrillard's conceit is recognizably an allegory of political transformation; DeLillo's is the stratagem of a spy within the postmodernist citadel.

A character in *Great Jones Street,* a writer who tries his hand at pornography, discovers that his material manipulates him, denies his autonomy as artist. Another character reproaches this novel's protagonist, the rock star who had once articulated a principled resistance to the burgeoning insanity of late-twentieth-century life in America, with having gone over to the madness about which he had warned his listeners. Perhaps one can see rocker Bucky Wunderlick as a metaphor for any artist—including DeLillo himself—tempted to love the age, to love the horror that provides such abundant and rich material. Because postmodern artists often face accusations of moral nihilism, Bucky's doubts and hesitations are at least potentially edifying. His resolutions remain inchoate, but his fellow artists (including his creator) may be engaged in deconstructing their own most cherished myths of ontological independence. Like Nick Carraway, perhaps, they aspire in some way to stand once more at a sort of moral attention.

Part One   **"For me the crux of the whole matter is language"**

1   **Football and *Unsäglichkeit***   *End Zone*

"It takes centuries to invent the primitive," DeLillo remarks in *Americana* (227). This cryptic observation seems to imply that an idea of the primitive can emerge only at a certain level of sophistication within a culture. In *End Zone* (1972) the author telescopes this socio-cultural development by presenting, as metonym for the primitive, the game of football as played by the team of Logos College, a dubious little institution at the brutal southwestern periphery of American sport. Here DeLillo imagines football as something primal—the key, perhaps, to larger manifestations of the violence to which the human instinct for aggression drives its victims. He suggests that contemporary America—a country with abundant wealth and many of the trappings of civilization at its most refined—has arrived at a level of thermonuclear sophistication sufficient to "invent the primitive" with horrific literalness. Though the Cold War has ended since the publication of *End Zone*, the novel has lost none of its edge, for the proliferation of nuclear weapons continues to foster anxiety. How much longer before terrorists have them? Is it really comforting to see the nuclear means of ending history concentrated in cis-Atlantic hands? The moral quandaries of America's power remain, especially as American culture itself remains problematic or corrupt.

With his second novel DeLillo joins the sodality of post–World War II American novelists who, following the lead of Jack London, Hemingway, and Ring Lardner, have successfully made sport the stuff of literature. These include Bernard Malamud, author of *The Natural* (1952); Mark Harris, author of *Bang the Drum Slowly* (1956); Robert Coover, author of *The Universal Baseball Association* (1968); and Peter Gent, author of *North Dallas Forty* (1973). To this list one might add superior journalistic efforts by Mailer, Oates, and Plimpton (in *End Zone* the narrator twice mentions his father's attachment to "a framed photo of his favorite pro team, the Detroit Lions").[1] Though he would in time write about hockey *(Amazons)* and baseball *(Underworld),* DeLillo opted to begin with football. In doing so, he produced the first serious fiction about that sport (unless one counts Frederick Exley's 1968 novel *A Fan's Notes,* in which football actually figures rather obliquely). *End Zone* came out in 1972, the same year as Dan Jenkins's funny but lightweight *Semi-Tough.* Both novels explore the comedy of hormonal extravagance on and off the gridiron.

Garrison Keillor once described testosterone as a substance known to reverse the effect of education in males. Yet virtually every American university boasts its monument to this education-vitiating hormone in the form of gymnasia, natatoria, football stadia, and other settings for fiercely competitive athletics. Though doggedly attempting to preserve its amateur status, collegiate athletics seems perennially bent on some larger convergence with professional sport (that byword of American capitalism). American higher education, in any event, has traduced the classical precept *mens sana in corpore sano.* This maxim, inscribed over the lintels of structures housing physical education facilities, identifies the healthy body as the ideal home to the healthy mind. But in America the healthy mind and the healthy body seem to have gone their separate ways, notwithstanding the existence of more institutions of higher learning and more *mens sana* inscriptions per capita than any other country in history. "Academics *and* Athletics" proclaim the billboards erected by colleges eager to disguise their faltering commitment to the first element in this binary (none of my dictionaries, by the way, allows the intended meaning of "academics," an insulting neologism based on the other, semantically anterior and hence privileged term). Largely divorced from the intellectual pursuits of the healthiest minds, athletics in the American university has become an end in itself. Thus when DeLillo's Coach Creed says "The mind first and then the body" (200), he is articulating his formula for the perfect athlete—not affirming the ancient ideal of balance. His assistants, meanwhile, attempt to reduce thought to the simplest tantric vestige, a mantra designed to obviate the need for ratiocination on the field: "Hit somebody. Hit somebody. Hit somebody" (28).

But DeLillo is far too subtle a writer simply to pillory mindless athletics—or simply to expose the progressive anti-intellectualism of academe. Thus he takes an almost Shavian delight in subverting the familiar modern stereotype of the athlete with cement between the ears (readers of Thurber's "University Days" will recall the football player unable to name a mode of transportation). Though engaged in daily training and weekly games that can only be characterized as brutal, the athletes of *End Zone*—especially Gary Harkness, the narrator—seem to spend all their waking hours in one kind of cerebration or another. The author pays considerable attention, moreover, to their mannered conversation, replete with the gleanings of their off-field studies. It is a measure of just how common the athletic stereotype is (and of how far America has drifted from the classical ideal of the thinking athlete) that one finds this collocation of physical and mental culture risible.

For the ancients, the healthy mind promoted the good life by devoting itself to innovation in science, statecraft, metaphysics, mathematics, and the arts. The healthy body, no small part of the good life in itself, enabled the mind to do its job longer and more efficiently. When necessary, this body lent itself to military training to protect home and hearth against the barbarians who wanted their civilization ready-made. Not that one fought only barbarians. In the ancient world war was a way of life among even the most civilized. To read Thucydides' *Peloponnesian War* (or for that matter the Old Testament books of Joshua and Judges) is to be struck with just how seamless was the tapestry of raid and counter-raid, revolt and punitive expedition, war and counterwar. One of the most appealing footnotes to Greek antiquity, nonetheless, was the custom of suspending hostilities once every four years to hold a set of purely athletic contests: the games at Olympia. One might think that the games coincided infrequently with periods of war and that the Olympic truce was therefore exceptional. But inasmuch as there was always war, the truce was routine. This fact lends itself to a larger symbolism: just as the rule-ordered, civilized striving of athletic competition exists only in the interstices of larger and deadlier struggles, so is peace always an island amidst war.

The neoteric sports event, with halftime islanded amid passionate striving, also exemplifies this idea. Indeed, like the Olympic Games, football lends itself to moralization, and DeLillo ingeniously structures his novel like the game its characters play. Ironically, however, his one sustained description of a football game occupies the spatial equivalent of halftime, filling the single chapter of part 2, which is bracketed by the eighteen chapters of part 1 and the eleven chapters of part 3.[2] As halftime in football divides and comments on the chaotic striving of the game's two parts, so do the relatively aleatory activities of Gary Harkness and his teammates come fully into focus only in the game described in the novel's short middle section. At the same time, emphasizing the endless, gritty head-banging of daily practice, the author keeps in view the idea that for human beings repose is considerably less common than violent physical activity. Thus he denies that human beings are rational creatures who sometimes descend into violence. Rather, he suggests, human beings are violent creatures for whom only exhaustion brings peace.

In *End Zone,* then, DeLillo ponders the mix of clumsy education and fanatical devotion to sport that characterizes the American university. Knowing its absurdity in modern academe, he parodies the ideal of simultaneous mental and physical training. What was normative in the ancient world—the idea of athletic intellectuals—becomes the vehicle for a satire on American mores in the nuclear age. The novel's comedy, that is, is based on the incongruous marriage of brutal action and amusingly cerebral dialogue. DeLillo fills his story with intellectual football players, and as they alternate between violent physical activity and lucubration, he contrasts the two sides of the human reality, translating the mind-body question to the football field.

Sport, Violence, and Writing

End Zone's critics have generally accepted the caution, ostensibly from the author himself, against "commentators . . . willing to risk death by analogy in their public discussions of the resemblance between football and war" (111). I would like to argue, however, that this caution is no more to be accepted than the remarks in the novel's second paragraph about a narrational commitment to simplicity. In other words, though it may seem the stale thesis of pop sociology, I think the novel works best if the reader accepts, up to a point, the proposition that football and war might really have much in common. After all, DeLillo goes to considerable trouble to develop the parallels between the violence of war and the violence of football.

For a delight in football—shared, perhaps, by the author, the reader, and that "exemplary spectator" Alan Zapalac—is a delight in violence (however ordered, however sporting) in which maiming and even death can take place. This delight figures somewhere on the spectrum of human fascination with more obviously abhorrent forms of violence—the fascination, for example, with atrocities, serial murders, and the ghastlier battles of the Great War (we savor the casualty figures from Verdun or the Somme—even the horrors of Buchenwald and Auschwitz). At the end of DeLillo's novel, Harkness and Taft Robinson admit to each other their baffled obsession with holocaust, whether the wholesale murder of ethnic populations, replete with the torture and murder of children, or the as-yet-barely-sampled nuclear variety. Robinson characterizes "the thought of children being tortured and killed" as "the worst thing there is." Though he "can't bear it," he has "read maybe eight books on it so far" (240–41). Like Harkness and Robinson, we consume atrocity stories guiltily, with self-disgust. Like them, too, we play or watch football blithely, with only occasional twinges of doubt about the healthiness of our passion. DeLillo hints that the two enthusiasms complement each other, illustrating humanity's conflicted soul from two ends of a moral spectrum.

But perhaps instead of interrogating this element of the novel, we should probe its intertextual dimension. In other words, the real competition here may not be between rival football teams or nuclear powers—but simply between one writer, one "strong poet," as Harold Bloom would say, and the terrible father with whom he consciously or unconsciously struggles. In trying to understand or justify a writer's thematic donnée, one risks forgetting that literature properly occupies itself with stripping away the film of familiarity and making known or clichéd experience new and newly meaningful—even if (indeed, especially if) the "experience" under consideration is the work of one's literary predecessors.

Might DeLillo, in other words, be engaged in some kind of agon with the author who set the standard for literary treatment of sport and the world's violence? Hemingway famously saw in sport an analogue to life as lived in the twentieth century, and his works teem with references to sporting activities: fishing, hunting, boxing, horse-racing, tennis, skiing, swimming, football, bicycle-racing, baseball, and of course bullfighting. In its orderliness and balletic grace, sport isolates and makes tolerable the conditions of existence—it can even become, in its ritual purity, a secular equivalent to religion. Blood sports like hunting and bullfighting provide moments in which the universal violence is controlled, made to answer to the human need to see death and defeat as something other than signs that accident mocks all human desire for heroic, transcendent, sacrificial, or redemptive action.

DeLillo offers new insights into the curious mix of sport, violence, and the precariousness of human existence; ultimately, he differs from Hemingway in the rigor with which he scrutinizes the sports analogy. If, like Hemingway, he sees in sport elements of cosmic principle, he also explores the subject's peculiarity to America, for he writes in a time when the nation's obsession with sport, notably the violent sport of football, coexists with a growing anxiety about the ultimate disposition of nuclear arsenals here and around the world. Juxtaposing the American passion and the American terror, he hints at an affinity between the two that goes beyond the Hemingway vision. Moreover, he deconstructs the Hemingway character's avoidance of thought. Where Hemingway's characters can seem almost anti-intellectual in their insistence that thought can lead only to despair or madness, DeLillo's think almost obsessively.

One does, however, see in *End Zone* a thematic parallel to the correlation between sport and the Hemingway style. The writer is also a kind of athlete, and Hemingway's style exemplifies his sense that certain elements of economy and grace make writing and sport alike the means of discovering or embodying order and meaning. Hemingway's spare, stripped-down writing reflects a profound distrust of abstraction. In a celebrated passage of *A Farewell to Arms*, Frederic Henry expresses his abhorrence of the abstractions—words like "sacred," "glorious," "in vain"—that have been used to justify carnage: "There were many words that you could not stand to hear and finally only the names of places had dignity. Certain numbers were the same way and certain dates and these with the names of the places were all you could say and have them mean anything. Abstract words such as glory, honor, courage, or hallow were obscene beside the concrete names of villages, the numbers of roads, the names of rivers, the numbers of regiments and the dates" (185). When Gary Harkness begins "to make elemental lists" (89) or when Billy Mast recites "a simple listing of things" (142) from Rilke's ninth Duino elegy, they indulge the same desperate instinct for reduction that Hemingway's lieutenant embraces.

Of course few readers are likely to mistake *End Zone* for warmed-over Hemingway. The idiom and the spirit of these writers are altogether different. Though Hemingway and DeLillo both connect violence and war to sport, and though they agree on the grim conditions of human existence, DeLillo, after the decade of "black humor" (Heller, Pynchon, Vonnegut, Barth, Bruce Jay Friedman), turns naturally to a comedic treatment of grim realities that tends to make Hemingway's stark irony seem virtually Sophoclean. By the same token, alongside Hemingway's spareness, the DeLillo style can seem almost baroque. DeLillo, finally, exploits sport to ends radically different from those of Hemingway. It is not too great a generalization to say that Hemingway never once reflects that bullfighting might be *gratuitously* barbaric. For him, sport is nearly always redemptive (only the occasional Robert Cohn finds it otherwise), for it teaches one how to live gracefully with contingency. DeLillo, on the other hand, seems finally to recognize in sport's competitive side, its violence, and its qualities of spectacle something akin to an index to the bellicose predilections of humanity.

Thus DeLillo's athlete-protagonist is intrigued by the idea of nuclear war. During his brief stay at the University of Miami, he discovers a book on the subject that gives birth to a lifelong fascination. At Logos he is drawn, moth to flame, to his Air Force ROTC instructor, Major Staley, who discourses with encyclopedic range about nuclear capabilities and the logic of deterrence in the oddly poetic jargon in which such things are written about and discussed. Staley comes by his knowledge through a kind of apostolic succession, having presumably had his first lessons in the subject at the knee of his father, a member of the air crew that dropped the bomb on Nagasaki and, consequently, Logos College's most famous alumnus (one assumes that Staley Hall is named for him). Staley *fils* can talk with great authority and concreteness on the subject of nuclear strategy, which he lives, eats, and breathes. Yet he is by no means the kind of militarist monster we know from Kubrick's *Dr. Strangelove* or Heller's *Catch-22*. The very soul of decent humility, just an earnest instructor at a minor college, he reminds the reader that the custodians of nuclear weaponry have always been sober, decent, earnest individuals. The most commonplace fact about Staley, however, may be the most damning, for he lives in one of those places that DeLillo considers an emblem of American sterility: a motel (already, by DeLillo's second novel, one can recognize a crotchet). Moreover, he seems to have lied about a family and household en route from his last posting. His stay at the motel, supposedly a matter of days, stretches on indefinitely. Major Staley takes naturally to the vocabulary of war-gaming, even imagining, at one point, that nuclear exchanges would tend toward what he characterizes as "humane" restraint, the balance of a sporting contest: "You'd practically have a referee and a timekeeper" (82).

But of course the analogy must break down sooner or later. The analogy between football and war, like any other, must not be taken as comprehensive. Analogy is effective as illustration, but beyond a certain point it becomes fallacy. Both human activities involve aggression, both are violent. The seeds of one may lie in the other's rich loam. But finally one *is* played by rules and seldom results in death, the other only deceives itself with rules—and always results in death. In the nuclear age, the death is on the grandest scale ever. Thus in a late chapter Harkness and Major Staley war-game their way to Armageddon in twelve easy steps. In other words, the conceit of refereed violence misleads: the real thing does not allow for the resumption of "play" on the morrow, the first day of plague and nuclear winter.

Football and war supposedly differ in that one is simple, one complex. Certainly the novel begins with remarks about the simplicity of football players, and variations on the word *simple* recur at regular intervals:

> Let's keep things simple. Football players are simple folk. Whatever complexities, whatever dark politics of the human mind, the heart—these are noted only within the chalked borders of the playing field. At times strange visions ripple across that turf; madness leaks out. But wherever else he goes, the football player travels the straightest of lines. His thoughts are wholesomely commonplace, his actions uncomplicated by history, enigma, holocaust or dream. (4)

Highly ironic, all of this. DeLillo seems to understand what Henry Adams calls "the extreme complexity of extreme simplicity." The drama here will in fact concern the ways in which the world's complexity—racial integration, nuclear war—makes itself felt among "simple" young men playing a "simple" game. But in the idea of "actions uncomplicated by history" one begins to discern the elements of a football pastoral. In an isolated, non-urban landscape, ostensibly far from the centers of government and society, the characters engage simplified versions of the issues facing a culture at an historical crossroads. Like the swains of more conventional pastoral, Gary Harkness and his fellows grapple with questions of mortality and human nature—especially when a teammate dies in a car crash and when a coach, Tom Cook Clark, commits suicide. They embrace their exile and their simplicity, half glimpsing the affinity of their present calling with the violent simplemindedness that may yet eventuate in global conflagration. *End Zone* presents a pastoral allegory of atomic-age civilization in the thirty chapters it takes to describe a single August-to-December football season.

Language and the Untellable

In the course of his story, Harkness begins to pass up meat at meals, and by the end he declines to eat altogether. A series of remarks about exile and silence, meanwhile, hints further at the narrator's nascent sense of vocation: though he never says so directly, he aspires to be not a running back but a hunger artist, a Stephen Dedalus, a writer. His task—realized in the book we hold in our hands—is to connect language and culture in an artistic meditation on American attitudes to sport and nuclear war. Thus he reproduces the specialized jargon all around him and is drawn especially to the language of nuclear holocaust. Interestingly, he can render the actuality of nuclear conflict in either military jargon—"words and phrases like thermal hurricane, overkill, circular error probability, post-attack environment, stark deterrence, dose-rate contours, kill-ratio, spasm war" (21)—or plain English: "Horrible diseases, fires raging in the inner cities, crop failures, genetic chaos, temperatures soaring and dropping, panic, looting, suicides, scorched bodies, arms torn off, millions of dead" (240). Only an artist can change verbal clothes so easily.

DeLillo, the artist behind the artist in an age of progressive spiritual desiccation, takes as his subject the way language mediates between American sterility and the world's complexity. In language DeLillo locates the register or index of that sterility and the energy that might reverse it. Thus the author punctuates the action on and off the field with samples of the specialized discourse to which the athletes are exposed in those portions of their lives not devoted to football. John Jessup, the tight end, studies "monolithic integrated circuitry" (25). Raymond Toon, reserve tackle on defense, declaims the arcana of economics: "'Time-adjusted rate of return,' he said. 'Redundant asset method. Capital budgeting. Probable stream of earnings. Independently negotiated credit balances. Consolidation. Tax anticipation notes'" (23). The place-kicker, Bing Jackmin, opines that "reality is constantly being interrupted" (28); he devises a theory of "psychomythical" atavism that ranges from sentient footballs to football players as latter-day gladiators (36, 209). Jimmy Fife, on the disabled list, spouts mathematical jargon: "'Balance,' Fife said. 'The equality of effective values with respect to the applied number of reduced symbolic quantities on each side of an equation, excluding combined derivatives'" (207). Anatole Bloomberg, offensive left tackle, founds his "notion of probability on a given number in a given pattern expressing the likelihood of the occurrence of a sequentially ordered set of events, such as the ratio of the number of coordinate elements that would produce the set of events to the total number of elements considered possible" (50–51).

DeLillo seems to engage here certain ideas articulated by George Steiner in the essays collected in *Language and Silence,* which came out in 1967, five years before *End Zone.* Steiner makes the point that the progressive barbarization of language in the social sciences betrays their attempt to reach for a mathematical authority that is actually beyond language—or in any event expressible only in the newly invented, specialized, and evolving symbologies of true science. Translating Steiner's fulminations into comic exempla, the author of *End Zone* seems almost to delight in what he mimics, whether it is Raymond Toon practicing his sportscasting or Harkness and Billy Mast spontaneously shifting at one point into the language of pilots and astronauts:

"What is your thermal passive mode control?"
"Vector five and locking." (148)

Nevertheless, the jargons that turn up periodically in DeLillo's story illustrate a brutalization of language analogous to the physical brutality of football.

Though DeLillo presents all of the characters here as verbal grotesques or caricatures, he allows some to seem deeper than others as their observations about language take on a certain genuine gravity. In addition to the narrator, Gary Harkness, these characters include Anatole Bloomberg and reserve defensive back Billy Mast. Harkness obsesses over questions he has not fully learned how to formulate. Bloomberg, a kind of oracular schlemiel, meditates on ethnic identity, history, the fear of death, and metaphysics generally. Billy Mast's special educational focus may be the most important of all. He is taking a course in the "untellable," in which the students train themselves to recite in languages they do not know (there may be a future for Billy in Jack Gladney's educational enterprise at the College on the Hill in *White Noise*). Billy memorizes Rilke's ninth Duino elegy, which contains hints of *End Zone*'s larger themes, notably the tension between what language can express and *lauter Unsägliches* ("wholly untellable things").

Rilke, one of the century's greatest poets, grappled with the limitations of language, tormented by powerful experience that defied expression in words. But in "The Ninth Elegy" he affirms the artist's sacred duty, ultimately, to the tellable, not the untellable:

> Bringt doch der Wanderer auch vom Hange des Bergrands
> nicht eine Hand voll Erde ins Tal, die Allen unsägliche, sondern
> ein erworbenes Wort, reines, den gelben und blaun
> Enzian.[3]

> [The wanderer on the mountain slopes does not bring a handful of earth to the valley, untellable earth, but only the pure word that blooms like a gentian on those upland meadows.]

To tell with the pure word, says Rilke, is to tell *things*—house, bridge, fountain, gate, jug, olive tree, window—and thereby to praise not the untellable but the known, ephemeral world. "*Hier* ist des *Säglichen* Zeit, *hier* seine Heimat" [*Here* is the time for the *tellable, here* its homeland]. We thereby achieve an "*invisible* inner resurrection" (*unsichtbar / in uns erstehn*)—not the physical immortality for which we yearn but the redemption of all that we have experienced. DeLillo may have had this elegy in mind when he remarked in an interview, "Rilke said we had to rename the world. Renaming suggests an innocence and a rebirth." [4]

Rilke finished the *Duino Elegies* in 1922, the year after Wittgenstein published the *Tractatus Logico-Philosophicus*. Wittgenstein was part of the philosophical movement, dating back to Kant, that engages in the criticism or "critique" (to use the Kantian word) of philosophical subject matter and discourse. This effort anticipates and complements the movement to critique language, which proves capable of expressing only its own tautologies. The world, says Wittgenstein, consists of "facts" that language only seems to represent. In fact, bound to language as the instrument of conceptualization, one cannot know or philosophize about vast tracts of reality. The *Tractatus* concludes with a famous statement, the negative complement to Rilke's affirmation: "Whereof we cannot speak, thereof we must be silent."

Wittgenstein famously published only the *Tractatus* during his lifetime, but he spent his last thirty years demolishing his original thesis and devising a new, designedly unsystematic one, published posthumously as *Philosophical Investigations*. Harkness, as it happens, describes his own philosophical musings as "investigative projects" that tend somehow, inevitably, to diminish their subject matter, revealing themselves as "parodies of hunger or grief or exile" (65). Hungry for enlightenment, in other words, he ends up merely hungry. Instead of some meaningful political exile, he embraces an inner exile, "the state of being separated from whatever is left of the center of one's own history" (31). In his confused exile and hunger, he drifts toward a final paralysis, an absolute alienation.

In Wittgenstein, early or late, one encounters someone who investigates "the nature of propositions" and the limitations of language. Though named only in the closing chapter, Wittgenstein is a presence throughout Gary Harkness's story. This philosopher, who demonstrates the built-in fallacy of confident naming, appropriately figures as something of a ghost-presence in the story of a college named for the Word, the indwelling principle of articulate reason in Western philosophy and theology. Indeed, institutions of higher learning came into existence in the service and pursuit of that ideal of knowledge the *Logos* supposedly represents. Yet the late founder of Logos College, a man who "believed in reason" (7), was mute. There is an ironic contradiction of premises in this detail, a hint from the author that one can fail the Word and perhaps be failed by it. The story's narrator, who conscientiously builds his vocabulary, adding a word a day, recurs often to the phenomenon of the word that, repeated frequently enough, becomes meaningless: "Words can escape their meanings" (17); "words could lose their meaning" (54). He remains troubled, moreover, by silence. The enigmatic Taft Robinson, on the other hand, becomes at the end a connoisseur of silences: "The kind of silence that follows the playing of the radio is never the same as the silence that precedes it. I use the radio in different ways. It becomes almost a spiritual exercise. Silence, words, silence, silence, silence" (240). Robinson is the character who moves beyond language here, the character who embraces Wittgenstein's special brand of mysticism—which is the recognition of the realities beyond language that silence harbors.

Harkness wonders about a piece of tape on the wall of Robinson's Spartan room. In a minor epiphany, he recognizes in this scrap of tape the sign of an abortive wish to hang a poster. The unhung poster, the narrator concludes, could only have borne the visages of Ludwig Wittgenstein and his circle: "Two parts to that man's work. What is written. What is not written. The man himself seemed to favor second part. Perhaps Taft was a student of that part" (233).[5] Like the author of this novel, Robinson rightly opts to make Wittgenstein an absence rather than a presence and thereby to salute that philosopher's insights into language and the reality beyond representation in language.

The narrator describes Robinson, whose name glances at an historic integration of the sports world, as his own narrative's shadow presence, its "invisible man" who "no more than haunts this book" (3). At the periphery of the team and of the nation, Robinson also exists at the periphery of the narrative. His dark glasses and shaved head mystify his teammates. His views remain obscure, even when, at the end, he engages for the first time in a genuine conversation with his teammate, Gary Harkness. The point is that Robinson is invisible to language itself—an example of precisely the reality that language, at least as socially determined in this country and this century, cannot adequately represent. One must struggle to bring to consciousness the extent to which reality is served by, for example, the language of unreflective racism that limits the guard, Cecil Rector, to the perception that "Coloreds can run and leap but they can't concentrate" (40–41). Though "it remains the author's permanent duty to unbox the lexicon for all eyes to see" (90), DeLillo takes relatively little interest here in the problem of racism per se. What engages his attention is the way racism exemplifies his Wittgensteinian thesis regarding language and its limitations.

The reader of End Zone, then, must look beneath the story's frequently antic surface to see the seriousness of its attention to questions of great importance, questions that frustrate logic. Chief among these questions, of course, is the logic of nuclear deterrence, which boasts its own hideous variation on Unsäglichkeit, untellability. "There's no way to express thirty million dead. No words. So certain men are recruited to reinvent the language" (85). The reference is to Major Staley and the other conceptualizers of nuclear deterrence, but it invites the reader to see DeLillo, too, as a person reinventing the language to give a more truthful account of the contingencies that politicians and cold-warriors, mouthing military and social science abstractions, never even approach.

Gary's disinclination to eat, along with his exilic proclivities, his tropism for the desert, partakes of the imagery of asceticism in DeLillo's setting and in the proclivities of his characters. Even Emmett Creed, the head football coach at Logos College, has a picture of St. Teresa of Ávila on his wall. Harkness, however, is DeLillo's exemplary ascetic. He ruins one chance after another to distinguish himself at the major football colleges through an inchoate instinct for reduction, simplification, and exile. In retreating to the godforsaken landscape of Rooster, Texas, he obeys the imperative of ascetics in every age: go to the desert, simplify, purify, prepare for the end: "Each day . . . I spent some time in meditation. . . . Simplicity, repetition, solitude, starkness, discipline upon discipline. . . . The small fanatical monk who clung to my liver would thrive on such ascetic scraps. And then there was geography. We were in the middle of the middle of nowhere, that terrain so flat and bare, suggestive of the end of recorded time, a splendid sense of remoteness firing my soul" (30). Here he half-consciously seeks ritual purification, even progressing through vegetarianism to an absolute, death-wish fast from which he can only be rescued by nutrition delivered in the "plastic tubes" that provide the novel's portentous closing image. Indeed, the reader at last recognizes the cruel pun in DeLillo's title—the same pun that figures in an early Barth title: *The End of the Road.* DeLillo, with his plastic tubes, may be recalling the chilling last word in Barth's novel: "Terminal." Each writer glances, in closing, at an eschatology of the whimper.

Harkness, it seems, has been trying to commit suicide, enacting a death wish that may be culture-wide. Hence his attraction to a woman who wears a mushroom cloud appliquéd on the front of her dress. Hence, too, the intensity of the anagnorisis when, walking across the desert from a visit to Major Staley in his motel, he comes upon a pile of excrement, waste surrounded by waste. Compelled to "terrified" attention, he experiences an unpleasant insight, for he recognizes in "simple shit . . . the one thing that did not betray its definition" (88). Signifier marries signified at last, in a reductive connection that will structure a cult's obsession in DeLillo's later novel, *The Names.* More prosaically, Harkness recognizes, too, an emblem of death:

> There was the graven art of a curse in that sight. It was overwhelming, a terminal act, nullity in the very word, shit, as of dogs squatting near partly eaten bodies, rot repeating itself; defecation, as of old women in nursing homes fouling their beds; feces, as of specimen, sample, analysis, diagnosis, bleak assessment of disease in the bowels; dung, as of dry straw erupting with microscopic eggs; excrement, as of final matter voided, the chemical stink of self discontinued; offal, as of butchered animals' intestines slick with shit and blood; shit everywhere, shit in life cycle, shit as earth as food as shit, wise men sitting impassively in shit, armies retreating in that stench, shit as history, holy men praying to shit, scientists tasting it, volumes to be compiled on

color and texture and scent, shit's infinite treachery, everywhere this whisper of in-existence. (88–89)

Whether it arrives for the individual or for the species, death must give the final, absolute lie to the spiritual pretensions with which human beings disguise the "destiny" of collapsing sphincters. Small wonder that in recent years, in Cormac McCarthy's *Blood Meridian,* for example, or in films like Wertmuller's *Seven Beauties* or Arthur Penn's *Missouri Breaks,* death in a jakes has become almost a convention.

This vision of unredeemed mortality continually troubles the century, figuring, classically, in literary images of the wasteland. DeLillo's version of this trope is so understated as to suggest the attenuation—characteristically postmodern—of myth itself. One sees DeLillo's originality by comparing his wasteland to that of, say, Bernard Malamud. The author of *The Natural* is at pains to replicate the myth fully and uncritically in his baseball story: the natural of the title is the Perceval figure, a holy fool who promises to revive the fortunes of the New York Knights and their Amfortas-like manager, "Pop" Fisher. DeLillo, by contrast, allows the reader to descry the lineaments of this myth only as a kind of modernist pentimento beneath the surface of his postmodernist canvas. The desert setting evokes the wasteland itself clearly enough, but one can barely recognize in this story's natural, Taft Robinson, the trappings of the holy innocent who alone can restore the reputation of the head coach and Fisher King, Emmet Creed (the name, ironically, means "ant faith"). Only gradually does one recognize the mythic identity of Creed, survivor of a disgrace that leaves him morally and physically debilitated. Jocularly said to have been born in a manger and more seriously credited with an ability to bring "order out of chaos" (10), he is the impotent god-king of this wasteland, another two-dimensional T. J. Ekleberg looking down on the mortal struggle. His health, like that of the archetype, seems directly related to the condition of his kingdom—or at least to the progress of the football season. By mid-season, he walks with "a slight limp" (96); toward the end he is confined to a wheelchair (204).

The desert in which Logos College is located, then, is at once the wasteland, the ground of the ascetics' spiritual purification, and an earnest of the end— not the "promised end" but the absurd self-annihilation of a species whose ingenuity with weapons outpaces its moral maturity. "Blast area. Fire area. Body-burn area" (90), Harkness thinks as he wanders into the desert near campus to meditate on apocalypse, to indulge his fascination with nuclear holocaust in a kind of parody of Ignatius of Loyola's spiritual exercises (which frequently involve attempts to visualize the graphic aspects of mortality). On one such expedition into the barren wastes, where he has bared his "saintly feet" (as for treading on holy ground), Harkness comes upon "a single round stone, painted black"—a shocking anomaly in an otherwise undifferentiated landscape (42–43). He has wandered, as it were, into Wallace Stevens's "Anecdote of the Jar," in which wilderness takes on order as it relates to a single artificial object to which it can be oriented. But the full orientation remains inchoate when Harkness first notices the stone, then banishes it from his mind to get on with his meditation on the deaths of millions. Much later in the story, he learns that the stone-painter, "metaphorist of the desert" (43), is none other than his roommate, Bloomberg. Upon learning that his "mother had been shot to death by a lunatic," Bloomberg had not gone home for the funeral. Instead, he explains, "I went into the desert with a paintbrush and a can of black paint. Among all those flat stones I found a single round one. I painted it black. It's my mother's burial marker" (188). Bloomberg suffers the same bereavement as Camus's Meursault in his North African wasteland. His response is roughly on the same level: a single stone painted black, an infinitesimal speck in a desert of stones. This much he grieves, in a gesture that parodies Lewis Carroll's cheerful bookmarking of experience: "I shall mark this day with a white stone."

Beyond its intended symbolism, this black stone hints disturbingly at the insignificance of the single death vis-à-vis the numberless deaths of plague, war, and nuclear holocaust: one pebble differentiated from an infinitude of pebbles, *e pluribus unum.* Traversing the desert on yet another occasion, Harkness reflects on all the "men embedded in the ground, all killed, billions, flesh cauterized into the earth, bits of bone and hair and nails, man-planet" (89). Ostensibly a mild subversion of Wordsworth ("A Slumber Did My Spirit Seal") and William Cullen Bryant ("Thanatopsis"), this observation actually functions proleptically to characterize the inevitable thermonuclear blending of flesh with the elements. As Glen Selvy reflects in *Running Dog,* "Landscape is truth."[6]

DeLillo seems to invite a connection between the stone that Bloomberg paints black and Taft Robinson's "black stone . . . in old Mecca" (241). Associated with that primal desert dweller, Abraham, and housed for centuries in the *Kaaba* that Harkness had earlier noticed in a dictionary (Owen Brademas will speculate on it in *The Names*), this Muslim holy object also functions like Stevens's jar. It is the universal omphalos—the thing lost to post-religious humanity. Like Abraham—or for that matter his son Ishmael (ancestor of the Arabs)—Harkness, Bloomberg, and Robinson are "outcasts or exiles" (4), subsisting at the periphery of a world that has long since lost its center. Indeed, from the description of "three players converging on a safetyman" (22) to racist speculation about the ability of "coloreds" to "concentrate," DeLillo fills his novel with the imagery of centering and decentering. Like many other contemporary fictions, *End Zone* laments the center that, in the postmodern world, has lost even the minimal cohesion last glimpsed by Yeats. Badgered by a coach with a vision of team spirit, Harkness remarks, "It was a good concept, oneness, but I suggested that, to me at least, it could not be truly attractive unless it meant oneness with God or the universe or some equally redoubtable superphenomenon" (19).

In *End Zone,* then, DeLillo brings together language, silence, football, nuclear war, and the writer's need to transcend the anxiety of influence. He contrasts orgies of physical action on the gridiron with the pathological asceticism of his narrator-protagonist. In the healthy body and unhealthy mind of Gary Harkness, he locates unsettling answers to the most profound questions of our day. From Rilke to Wittgenstein, he arranges for Harkness to brush up against the disturbing, iconoclastic insights of the geniuses who, in their different ways, sought ways to encounter the "untellable." In allusions to Wittgenstein, he invokes a trans-linguistic reality that mocks the shortcomings of language; at the same time, in allusions to Rilke, he contemplates the redemptive mystery of the word so pure as to make numinous the thing it names.

2   **Pharmaceutical Philomela**   *Great Jones Street*

The desert, saints and martyrs, asceticism—all recurrent conceits in DeLillo. In *Great Jones Street* (1973), disaffected rock star Bucky Wunderlick, half-suicidal like Gary Harkness, retreats from a corrupt world into the wastes of the Lower East Side. "Great Jones Street, Bond Street, the Bowery. These places are deserts," says his sometime companion Opel Hampson.[1] Here, as in those half-comic Renaissance paintings of assorted demons tormenting St. Anthony in the wilderness, Bucky attempts to fend off an endless stream of tempters, including Globke, Hanes, Azarian, Watney, Skippy, Bohack, Dr. Pepper, the funseekers Opel invites to his birthday party, and reporters from ABC and the Running Dog News Service.

Exhausted by fame, excess, and the rigors of touring, Bucky goes into seclusion when he can no longer resist the gravitational pull of suicide—the classic exit for people in his line of work. In his withdrawal, his passivity, and his immobility, he becomes a picture of anomie, largely indifferent to his surroundings and incapable of responding to the overtures of those who project onto fame such as his a host of appetites and obsessions. Chief among those who badger Bucky are the members of Happy Valley, "a rural group that came to the city to find peace and contentment" (36). Unlike its presumed namesake, the Edenic place from which Rasselas and his companions set forth, this Happy Valley is a cultlike, violent outfit supposedly committed to restoring privacy in American life. Taking Bucky's withdrawal from the public sphere as a kind of sacramental, even messianic gesture, emissaries from Happy Valley ironically become the most determined violators of their hero's own privacy.

When Bohack, the commune's unsavory front man, urges Bucky to commit suicide, the scene invites recognition of its literary and mythic antitypes. One thinks, perhaps, of those tableaux—in Spenser, in Marlowe—in which a diabolical tempter gives dramatic immediacy to the abstraction "despair" by offering the hero rope, knife, poison, firearm, and other instruments of self-elimination. The Marlovian parallel is especially suggestive, for Bucky is a postmodern Faust. Indeed, like Mann's Adrian Leverkuhn, he is a musician whose gifts seem to involve a chthonian bargain with the decadence of his society. Like Mann's composer, that is, Bucky has committed himself to a career and a life in which the most powerful artistic expression proves somehow complicit with a vast societal disease—a canker or imposthume that, outwardly invisible, rages unchecked in the nation's vitals. Though he recognizes the disease, Bucky remains unsure whether to resist or embrace it.

Spending what seems very much like forty days and forty nights in his urban desert, Bucky also resembles Jesus in the wilderness, climactically tempted by the satanic Bohack to cast himself down from a sixth-floor pinnacle. Indeed, Bucky's story constantly gestures toward a restaging of the passion of Christ as tawdry rock tragicomedy. Temptation resisted, Bucky proceeds to a Golgotha that takes the form of Longboy's injecting him with the experimental drug that robs him of language. He becomes, as Lancelot Andrewes says, the Word without a word. Bucky's Magdalen, the pathetic Skippy, joins him in his subsequent harrowing of the Bowery. In his last words to the reader he savors the rumor that he has become patron saint to derelicts, for he recognizes an affinity with publicans and sinners. Throughout the narrative, finally, he wrestles with the problem of whether (and how) to return to public life and resume making music and touring. The question of this "second coming" (67), however, remains problematic.

Whatever apocalypse looms may strike the reader—not to mention Bucky himself—as under-energized. The narrator is too spiritually fatigued to do more than fantasize vaguely about the fire station that, over and over, attracts his attention as he gazes out his grimy window. Bucky must in any event decide whether to return as some kind of musical deliverer or in the role his girlfriend suggests may be closer to his true calling—that of "antichrist" (88). Prior to his flight from fame and excess, on his *"Pee-Pee-Maw-Maw"* album, he had sung of the beast's being loose (118–19). "But who's the beast?" Opel asks rhetorically (87). If Bucky does not strive to defeat the beast, she implies, he must become the beast.

Twisted Siblings

Bucky's apocalyptic vision, such as it is, differs from that of an earlier period precisely as the postmodern differs from the modern. On the one hand Yeats, embracing a mythic idea of history, imagines the rough beast slouching out of the desert toward Bethlehem; on the other hand Bucky, unconsciously committed to and subsumed by a cool, postmodern aesthetic, strives to imagine apocalypse against no historical horizon at all. Unfolding in a febrile present, his narrative invokes knowledge of the past only in the brief, ridiculous appearance of Dr. Pepper, the drug assayer, as a "Professor of Latent History." DeLillo may intend an instructive contrast here between modernist high culture and postmodernist popular culture. Though gestures like making a rock musician one's protagonist are commonly taken as expressive of postmodernism's repudiation of high cultural (often specifically modernist) elitism, I do not think DeLillo wants his readers to accept Bucky Wunderlick and his profession uncritically. Bucky is in fact something of a cipher, and readers may need to monitor their own susceptibility to the temptation that overcomes the many characters who project personal convictions or obsessions onto the charismatic and suddenly sphinxlike superstar. The reader enamored of popular music will perhaps see in Bucky a heroic figure; the reader who considers rock insipid will project a possibly imaginary authorial contempt onto Bucky. The reader or critic, in short, must decide whether to view Bucky's agon as anything more than what Terence Rafferty, in another context, once called "the spiritual crisis of a shallow man."

Shallow or not, he is rich, famous, and troubled spiritually. The convergence of these attributes is peculiarly American, as Max Weber argues in *The Protestant Work Ethic and the Rise of Capitalism*—a source, perhaps, for one of Bucky's song titles, "Protestant Work Ethic Blues." Here the lyricist imagines the white-collar worker "waiting for the strength to take that existential leap" (111), though he leaves ambiguous whether he means the leap to death to which he himself is tempted or the "existential" leap of faith. Bucky's allusiveness, one suspects, is unconscious and accidental, but in the echoes of Weber and Kierkegaard one hears another, less confused artist perpending—in part through allusions like these—the forces of materialism and spirituality that exist in unholy symbiosis in America.

Profoundly corrupt, heavily implicated in the instrumentalities of capital and power, rock functions in *Great Jones Street* as the falsely spiritualized servant of materialist culture. Mark Osteen, who takes up and turns to new account Oriard's idea that DeLillo is engaged in a search for Walden Pond, notes how warped the "Thoreauvian economies" must become "in the light of the late capitalist economy of commodity consumption."[2] Similarly Anthony DeCurtis emphasizes the inescapable universality of the consumer ethos: "What DeLillo depicts in *Great Jones Street* is a society in which there are no meaningful alternatives, in which everyone and everything is bound in the cash nexus and the exchange of commodities, outside of which there stands nothing. Everything is consumed, or it consumes itself: murder or suicide, exploitation or self-destruction."[3] Thus Bucky himself, would-be anarch, has helped to create Transparanoia, a "spreading inkblot of holding companies, trusts, acquisitions and cabals" (138) that has mushroomed out of control (the corporate portfolio, he discovers, includes even the shabby tenement in which he has taken refuge). By the same token, because rock's anarchic energies stoke rather than resist the totalitarian tendencies of "underground" power, Bucky's art does not serve the Dionysian dream its devotees think they embrace. DeLillo ultimately characterizes America as the land where business rapacity and mass desire, its twisted sister, engage in what Pynchon would call endless, convoluted incest. By turns violator and violated, Bucky is this America's amphibium, the middle ground of contending forces. Even his lodgings on Great Jones Street suggest a spatial metaphor: blocked cerebration above (the desperate artist Fenig), inarticulate unconscious below (the almost subhuman Micklewhite boy).

One errs, then, to see DeLillo's protagonist as engaged in the heroic struggle of the romantic artist. Bucky Wunderlick's lyrics, after all, range from the puerile to the asinine, and his self-wrestling remains largely inconsequential. One can easily read his story not as the meaningful agon of an artist but as the sulking of a parody-Achilles of the entertainment world in his Lower East Side tent. Distrustful of Bucky's musical métier, DeLillo exploits it as ideal vehicle for certain perceptions about contemporary America, where rock concerts un-dam, channel, and warp into hysteria a host of powerful if inchoate passions. Rock's appeal, DeLillo intimates, lies in its ability to echo and amplify tidal, anarchic pulse-rhythms, to bring to a boil the hormonal salmagundi in young veins. Wholly committed to depthlessness, wholly wedded to an ontology of the present, wholly indifferent to history, rock embodies the most puerile tendencies in American society. In the land of perpetual youth, rock fuels an unceasing celebration of adolescent innocence, adolescent idealism, adolescent superficiality, adolescent energy, adolescent confusion, and adolescent appetites.

As the only artists of their time with anything like a bully pulpit, popular musicians can shoulder, if they so choose, considerable social responsibility (hence the earnest anti-drug, pro-education statements that rap stars—to the peril of their aesthetic—are occasionally inveigled into making). In other words, when not given merely to participating in the disorder of the times, popular music and musicians can occasionally impart some direction to the unruly appetites of the masses. These options eventually present themselves to a Bucky who finds himself increasingly resistant to the archetypal expectation that he commit suicide or at least perish under ambiguous circumstances in some foreign city. He recognizes that he can become the mirror and willing agent of the darkest forces abroad in the land—or he can attempt artistically to counter the moral chaos of America in the late Vietnam years.

Bucky's companion Opel Hampson articulates for him a precept that may provide moral guidance. "Evil," she says, "is movement toward void" (88). Repeated (150, 237), this becomes a kind of mantra—all he has to hang on to as, on the one hand, the world conspires to lure him back to public life and, on the other, he strives to define his own desire. As his withdrawal continues, Bucky seems to recruit. "I had centered myself, learning of the existence of an interior motion, a shift in levels from isolation to solitude to wordlessness to immobility" (85–86). He begins to plan a return whose shape remains vague. He will need new material, and he will need to go on tour again.

But the lure of a negative decision remains powerful. With Opel he refers—twice—to the temptation to undertake an unwholesome, nihilistic "passage from suicide to murder" (86), a course more evil, they agree, than dealing drugs. Bucky's desire, finally, may be nothing more than to become fully complicit in American evil:

To stencil myself in its meager design. . . . I might yield to the seductions of void, taking a generation with me into blank climates. . . . I'd have to hand myself over to the structures that defined the time. . . . Become obese with power and self-loathing. . . . It was an evil thing to consider, allying myself with the barest parts of mass awareness, land policed by the king's linguists, by technicians in death-system control, corporate disease consultants, profiteers of the fetus industry. (67–68)

But what—besides death—is this void, and how does one embrace it? When, later, he remarks, "I've ass-licked around the edges of some mean conceits" (244), he means that he has indulged the monstrous temptation simply "to love the age" in all its designless, appetite-driven confusion. To stencil oneself in the age's meager design is to become the marker for aimlessness, a superficial labeling of the superficial. Thus to become an intrinsic part of the age is to surrender to a void at once metaphysical and ethical.

The reader may find puzzling the question of just how, concretely, he might yield to that void. Certainly he can become merely a mirror, not a protester or moral critic—"become the least of what I was." He can represent the "dull . . . horror" of American reality as "even duller and more horrible" (87). Opel calls this "to go back out as a Las Vegas version of what you were," by which, presumably, she means to connive at the prostitution to the tawdry, the superficial, and the cheaply sensational that is the peculiar hell of entertainment in Las Vegas. Bucky will risk becoming "the other thing," says Opel—the dull horror his act was originally intended to mock. Indeed, she observes, "You embraced the insanity you were telling us about. So maybe it's a natural evolution. You were too much in love with the horror going on because it formed your sound for you and you were fascinated by it as subject matter" (88).

Another capitulation to evil, Bucky feels, would be release of the tapes he had made during an earlier visit to his mountain house. He speaks of the mountain tapes (which Opel retrieves and puts into his hands as a birthday present) as his companion's challenge to him to be as evil as he has said he may want to be. Bucky's sense that release of the tapes would constitute a moral retreat stems from more, I think, than a reluctance to see Globke and his machine commodify his private musical ramblings. The mountain tapes may in his mind represent a failure to strive for fresh creation. "I didn't even have to create new material. That was part of the point of it all" (149). Little more than musical doodling (and unperformable), the tapes represent a temptation to dodge the challenge that alone holds redemption for the artist.

Paradoxically, though the temptation to exploit the mountain tapes is artistically a dead end, the sentiments they express reveal the singer groping toward a cherished conceit of DeLillo's, one that would flower in *The Names,* in which the son of James Axton struggles to find words adequate to the spiritual mystery of speaking in tongues. Bucky speaks of his "babble" on the mountain tapes, which he further characterizes as "genuinely infantile" (148). "Baba / Baba / Baba" run the lyrics. Yet "I was born with all languages in my mouth / . . . Undreamed grammars float in my spittle" (204, 205). Just here DeLillo signals what will be a career-long meditation on the idea of language as it exists in the "unimprinted" minds of the very young. As Lancelot Andrewes observes in a famous passage, the literal meaning of the word *infant* is "without speech," and DeLillo, like Andrewes (and T. S. Eliot), savors the paradox of some infinitely supple, even numinous linguistic possibility that dwells in the mouths of the wordless.

The Loom of Philomela

The mountain tapes spend most of the narrative in a package identical to the one that contains the strange new drug that Happy Valley has stolen from a government research facility. Each of these commodities involves some kind of annihilation of verbal sense, destruction of the word. DeLillo's plot turns on passions frustrated by the withdrawal, the falling silent, of a rock idol—and on the other, related passions stoked by the appearance of the new drug. As various interests vie to possess the drug and to get the rock star back to making music and money, DeLillo assays the American need for euphoria, whether from controlled substance or from Dionysian abandonment in music. He recognizes in drugs and rock, that is, related commodities now romanticized as rebellion, now dismissed as the twin vehicles of profit and mindless escape from responsibility and "existential" pain.

In that it destroys the cortical capacity for language, the drug brings a curious form of escape. Its takers (who come to include an unwilling Bucky Wunderlick) do not simply fall silent—they completely lose touch with the word. Like the Micklewhite boy, they can manage only "chronic dribbling." As Watney explains, "The drug attacks a particular region in the left hemisphere of the brain. That's the verbal hemisphere, it seems. Where the words are kept" (228). Thus the novel climaxes with Bucky's pharmaceutical exile from language. He makes—understandably—little attempt to render such unthinkable experience, for as Wittgenstein says, "philosophical problems arise when language goes on holiday."[4] Perhaps, though, we are expected to make the ironic connection between the "articulate" rock star and the wordless one, the one who at the beginning opts for what he takes to be a meaningful silence, and the one at the end who has silence thrust upon him.

Bucky must determine his responsibilities, if any, to his "closest followers." Even at the beginning he understands that language holds the key to remaking himself and perhaps his culture. "Either I'd return with a new language for them to speak or they'd seek a divine silence attendant to my own" (3). Both alternatives are seriously imagined. In his first encounter with Skippy, the emissary from Happy Valley, she makes what will prove an ironic remark: "I'm nonverbal just like you" (17). One descries a similar irony in the Micklewhite boy's representing for Bucky "the beauty and horror of wordless things" (52). The ironic foreshadowing of Bucky's fate extends even to objects: "A telephone that's disconnected," says Bucky, "has made a descent to total dumbness, and so becomes beautiful" (31). Bucky anticipates in these remarks his own descent into a wordlessness—an approximation, perhaps, of Kristeva's Chora or Lacan's Imaginary—in which he discovers a strange beauty. Indeed, at the end, as the drug wears off and speech returns, he is surprisingly wistful, pining for some "permanent withdrawal to that unimprinted level where all sound is silken and nothing erodes in the mad weather of language" (264–65). This literally ineffable regression ought perhaps to be thought of not as a pre-linguistic state but as one in which the relation between language and things is wholly without friction.

Whatever that might mean. Though one cannot, ipso facto, express such an experience in words, it may approximate the anagnorisis of classical tragedy. One of the climactic ironies of *Oedipus Rex* occurs when the protagonist, having at last "seen," blinds himself. In much the same way, Philomela, so rudely forced, becomes truly articulate only when the barbarous king cuts out her tongue. At her loom, she transcends the theft of speech and becomes the type of the artist who transforms mute suffering into a higher form of communication. Thus DeLillo, in another "land policed by the king's linguists" (68), imagines fresh variations on the Philomela archetype. Some of these are more hideous than others. The cutting of Azarian's throat, for example, is a taking of speech that admits no redress; but Bucky, the novel's pharmaceutical Philomela, experiences a loss of language beyond that of tonguelessness. Perhaps his art, in future, will like DeLillo's strive toward conceptions of language in which one discerns a kind of mystical linguistics.

In his clumsy attempts to settle on a course of action or inaction preferable to or more honest than suicide, and torn between capitulation to the darkest forces of American life and some scarcely imaginable alternative, Bucky goes through a dark night of the soul. Self-murder, he comes to realize, is not a viable option. Part of his decision may be owing to his older, British counterpart Watney, who denounces suicide in some of the straightest talk in the book. Watney argues that it would be meaningless:

> One's death must be equal to one's power. The OD or assassination . . . means little unless it reverberates to the sound of power. The powerful man who achieves a gorgeous death automatically becomes a national hero and saint of all churches. No power, the thing falls flat. Bucky, you have no power. You have the illusion of power. . . . Nothing truly moves to your sound. Nothing is shaken or bent. You're a bloody artist you are. . . . The true underground is the place where power flows. . . . The presidents and prime ministers are the ones who make the underground deals and speak the true underground idiom. The corporations. The military. The banks. This is the underground network. (231–32)

"You're a bloody artist you are" is one of the most enigmatic and suggestive lines in a book that, even for DeLillo, seems to harbor a passionate distrust of directness. Though the unsympathetic Hanes makes the point, DeLillo seems to subscribe to the pronouncement that "life itself is sheer ambiguity. If a person doesn't see that, he's either an asshole or a fascist" (132). Watney can be understood to be saying that Bucky is not much of an artist—or, more suggestively, that Bucky is *only* an artist. The grand gestures of mere artists, he implies, carry no weight in a culture in which the real power remains untapped, unshaped, and unchanneled by art.

Nowhere is this seen more clearly than in the desperately under-inspired Ed Fenig, Bucky's upstairs neighbor. Fenig is the writer-craftsman in an ungracious age, completely marginalized, a "harmless drudge" indeed.[5] As, to some degree, DeLillo's own self-parody, Fenig is the literary artist in late-twentieth-century America—further gone, even, than the "unpaid, uncelebrated" writer whom Pound, in "Hugh Selwyn Mauberley," calls "the stylist" ("He exercises his talents / And the soil meets his distress"). Fenig anticipates *Mao II*'s Bill Gray and his bitter recognition that the literary artist can no longer "alter the inner life of the culture."[6]

Unable to lift his sights to something great, Fenig looks for precisely the kind of sensational gesture or language or techne that confers fame on rock stars. He even tries to create an altogether new and daring genre, "pornographic children's literature" (49), only to recoil, eventually, from the reptiles he discovers breeding in his own mind. "Every pornographic work," he declares, "brings us closer to fascism" (139, 224). His fulminations on this score may strike the reader as oddly gratuitous, for the attempt to confer intellectual or political cogency on the sentiments of Mrs. Grundy tends always to sound curiously strained. But DeLillo's point has little to do with pornography per se. Rather, the author asserts (as he does in *Americana*) that an affinity exists between the politics of totalitarianism and the absence—so characteristic of pornography—of nuance and ambiguity. Pornography, he implies, violates the rule articulated by Henry James and known to every real artist: true art is always indirect.

As a justification for his own ambiguity, a great deal of the DeLillo aesthetic inheres in this precept and in its corollary—that the absence of ambiguity constitutes a peculiarly dangerous, an especially abhorrent discursive or mentational mode. In other words, a more powerful, less clichéd idea finds its indirect expression in Fenig's diatribe against pornography, which "puts people on the level of things" (223). That is pornography which manipulates the artist, rather than affording the artist the latitude to manipulate or shape. "I failed at pornography," observes Fenig, "because it put me in a position where I the writer was being manipulated by what I wrote" (223). These remarks echo Bucky Wunderlick's similar pronouncement on his own immobility: "The artist sits still, finally, because the materials he deals with begin to shape his life, instead of being shaped, and in stillness he seeks a form of self-defense" (126). In an age in which a widespread societal sickness shapes the only art that can be conceived and executed, the artist can only withdraw or, in various movements toward the void, produce a pornography of the unsubtle and unnuanced—to wit, rock music, and much of what passes for literature.

Where, exactly, is the artist Don DeLillo here? Shaped or shaping? No doubt there is a certain rueful recognition of his own impotence in a world little interested in or deferential to writers like himself. Authorial death of this literal sort has for one reason or another coincided in our culture with the death or collapse of other ideas of authority. No one can resist the terrifying, anarchic fluidity. No one—least of all the literary artist—remains to provide direction for a world constantly striving to enlarge the chaos seen on the nightly news: the resurgence of ancient blood feuds in the Balkans, the endless fratricide of Africa both east and west, the copious ordinance (much of it nuclear) stockpiled everywhere against the final buckling of civilized restraint.

Whatever Bucky Wunderlick's eventual notions regarding his power to influence the spiritual health of the republic, DeLillo himself can have few illusions about the ability of a mere "bloody artist" to stave off disaster. But perhaps he looks toward a day when, the lust for blood and for popular entertainments having alike consumed their most passionate exemplars, the world will again be ready to listen to, to honor, and even to take guidance from such artists as may continue to exercise the moral imagination. Perhaps DeLillo signals something remotely redemptive when, in the last paragraph, he mentions—not for the first time—the "painters and sculptors" moving into Great Jones Street (264, cf. 239). On the other hand—since ambiguity reigns here—these immigrants may signal only the beginnings of Soho gentrification, the encroachment of a corrupt civilization upon the once-pure desert wastes to which DeLillo's ascetics perennially gravitate.

3   **Mortal Stakes** *Players*

Like *Ratner's Star, Players* (1977) begins with air travel. In his introductory
chapter, a proem or (more accurately) prolusion, the author presents seven
unnamed persons—"four men, three women"[1]—who desultorily watch an in-
flight movie from the piano lounge of a jumbo jet. Not wearing headsets, sere-
naded by the piano, they momentarily become the audience at a much older
form of cinematic screening. They enter a kind of cultural time-warp in which
low-tech entertainment coexists with high-tech transportation.

    The picture one gets of these anonymous travelers, like the long shots of
golfers and their playing field in the film, is "a lesson in the intimacy of distance" (6). Introduced anonymously, the travelers resemble the abstract alphabetical marks—characters—that constitute writing. Entering the prologue,
one momentarily regresses to an analphabetic state, puzzling over "characters"
that, like those of writing in an unknown language, are "legible" but not

yet "readable." Indeed, this prologue classically illustrates what Barthes calls the *scriptible* text, the text in which meaning remains enigmatic, suspended, unclear.

After reading the novel, however, one can go back and recognize in the prologue a dumbshow that introduces the "players" of the drama[2] presently to unfold: the heterosexual couple are Lyle and Pammy Wynant, the homosexual couple Ethan and Jack; the stewardess is Rosemary, the woman drinking ginger ale, Marina. In the movie spooling behind them one sees other "players" (film actors, players of golf) systematically murdered by terrorists—themselves "players" in the esoteric sense that most interests Lyle and perhaps DeLillo himself. The man who supplies an ironic musical accompaniment to the film is the slippery double or triple agent J. Kinnear, player of the piano, player in the personal drama of Lyle Wynant, and player on the stage of international terrorism.

In one of the more suggestive passages here the narrator muses obscurely over cinematic representations of past and present, seeking, perhaps, to go beyond the simple irony achieved when old-fashioned nickelodeon music accompanies a contemporary, Godardesque depiction of suburban terror:

> We're prompted to remember something here, although this act of recall may be more mythic than subjective, a spool of Biograph dreams. It flows through us. Upright frames in a thousand nickelodeons. Heart-throbbing romance and knockabout comedy and nerve-racking suspense. History this weightless has an easy time of it, we learn, contending with the burdens of the present day. (9)

"The spool of Biograph dreams" is the "something" one is "prompted to remember." In that it floats grammatically, however, the phrase communicates very much as does the mythic "recall" of music one has not heard in its original setting. Though not old enough to have actually attended a nickelodeon and heard the naive music, readers know its sound and the stock situations it accompanies (romance, comedy, suspense—all figure, in sardonically twisted form, in the narrative to come). This music and the images it once accompanied are part of a seemingly inconsequential cultural past. In the observation that this "weightless" history "has an easy time of it . . . contending with the burdens of the present day," the narrator suggests more than the disparity of effect when puerile music can be made to serve ironic ends, made to mock and subvert anything as dead-serious as terrorism. Among the most terrible of contemporary "burdens," terrorism is itself to be understood as implicated in the history of cinematic images, the history of simulacra. After all, the terrorism before us just now exists only in a film, and perhaps we are to reflect that terrorism can hardly be said to have existed before the media that terrorists exploit and depend on.[3]

In interviews the author describes his opening chapter as "the novel in miniature."[4] One of DeLillo's more explicit metafictional gestures, this prologue exemplifies the special kind of *mise en abîme* described by Linda Hutcheon as a "mode of reflexion," in which a text replicates itself as in a small mirror.[5] Lucien Dâllenbach calls such a *mise en abîme* "transcendental" when the mirror text reflects the aesthetic theory or "code" of the larger, matrix text.[6] Encoded for indeterminacy, the *Players* prologue signals that the story introduced will be similarly abstract and fluid, similarly resistant to one's desire to understand it in terms of traditional motive, action, and character. Because DeLillo presents his characters as literally "up in the air"—before their service in any plot he may devise—readers who try to relate the "action" of the prologue to the main body of the novel are frustrated. They must learn the rules, the code.

Intertexts

Lyle and Pammy, DeLillo's main characters, joylessly pursue their livelihoods at two of the great workplaces of late-twentieth-century America: the Stock Exchange and the World Trade Center. They also attempt to introduce a bizarre element of play into their work. Pammy, who works in "grief management," commits adultery with the nominally gay companion of a colleague. When this abortive affair leads to a suicide, grief becomes more than a professional concern. Lyle, a trader, playfully involves himself in a terrorist plot to blow up the Exchange. Here, too, play and work prove immiscible.

DeLillo told Tom LeClair that his interest in play centers on sports and games, grounded in or ordered by rules. Repeatedly in his fictions

> people whose lives are not clearly shaped or marked off may feel a deep need for rules of some kind. People leading lives of almost total freedom and possibility may secretly crave rules and boundaries, some kind of control in their lives. Most games are carefully structured. They satisfy a sense of order and they even have an element of dignity about them. . . . Games provide a frame in which we can try to be perfect, [a frame in which] we can look for perfect moments or perfect structures. In my fiction I think this search sometimes turns out to be a cruel delusion.[7]

So it is here. Lyle and Pammy are aimless victims of the contemporary urban anomie—each tries, ironically, to defeat ennui by escaping into forms of play that ultimately prove even less centered or purposeful than their present lives. For Lyle, whom DeLillo describes in an interview as an "intelligent, high-strung, spiritually undernourished person,"[8] this means attempting to connect with what is always imagined as some vast conspiracy of espionage and terror. His playing of all interests against each other seems absurd until one realizes that he seeks to understand the big picture, to learn the rules, to be a "player."

One can further illustrate Lyle and Pammy's plight (a word etymologically related, as will be seen, to *play*) by briefly considering the problematic treatment of work and its nominal opposite in what may seem a couple of unlikely analogues, Frost's "Two Tramps in Mud Time" and Joyce's "Counterparts." Like the DeLillo novel, these works explore the work-play binary, but at the same time they offer instructive contrasts in the degree of their reflexivity and in their thematic means and ends, notably with regard to politics. (The Yeats poem "Adam's Curse" also comes to mind, but it fails really to complicate its descriptions of work with a vision of play.)

I juxtapose "Two Tramps in Mud Time" and *Players* not because of their differing answers to the question "can one's work be play?" but because of the divergence of their respective political subtexts. The speaker of the Frost poem, a man pleasurably absorbed in the work of splitting firewood, understands in the ingratiating remarks of a passing tramp an implicit claim: "He wanted to take my job for pay."[9] The poet admits that he

> had no right to play
> With what was another man's work for gain

—but he nonetheless asserts the sanctity of any task in which work and play coalesce:

> Only where love and need are one,
> And the work is play for mortal stakes,
> Is the deed ever really done
> For Heaven and the future's sakes.

Writing during the Depression, the conservative Frost risks a seeming callousness to the plight of those without work to construct one of his many paradigms of poetry writing. Like "The Silken Tent" or "Birches" or "For Once, Then, Something," "Two Tramps in Mud Time" is about its own medium and the playlike absorption poets bring to their laborious "making." It is *poetry,* finally, that he characterizes as "play for mortal stakes," play with a moral dimension ("Heaven") as ultimate coordinate. DeLillo, on the other hand, imagines a profoundly disaffected worker who brings a murderous form of play into the workplace. Writing at a time of burgeoning terrorist activity and even anticipating the day when the World Trade Center would itself be-

come a terrorist target, the author contemplates terrorism divorced from political conviction, terrorism as "radical" play. Thus Lyle speaks ideologically
only to joke. Characterizing "the capitalist system and the power structure and
the pattern of repression" as "themselves a struggle," he captiously describes
the archetypal agon of left against right as "the struggle against the struggle"
(34). The real horror of Lyle has to do with his acting without political animus.
More or less gratuitously, he "turns," enlists under the banner of anarchy-as-
diversion.

"Counterparts" offers a yet more extensive set of intertextual congruences.
Indeed, DeLillo has commented publicly on his interest in Joyce. In the LeClair
interview he defends his reclusiveness as a version of the Joycean "silence, exile,
and cunning," and he seems to have learned a trick or two from the Irish
master. Though he mentions only *Ulysses* as an influence, DeLillo can hardly
be innocent of the stories in *Dubliners*. Like Joyce in "Counterparts," he slyly
offers an encyclopedic meditation on the meanings of his one-word title.
Moreover, each author structures his tale in A-B-A form, beginning and ending with a coldly objective view of the characters. In contradistinction to the
main body of the story, names do not figure in the opening and close.

In the scenes that begin and end "Counterparts" the narrator refers to the
brutal main character only as "the man." These scenes take place at work and
at home, respectively. They frame a central sequence in which the author refers
to his character by name: Farrington. Joyce suggests that only as a pub-crawling
drunk, only while inebriated, does Farrington have an identity. In the two
spheres in which he ought to have his real being, he is an anonymous cog,
"counterpart" to all the other nameless cogs in the urban-industrial system.

Joyce contributes here to what might be called the literature of exemplifica-
tion, writing in which an author undertakes to play—now selectively, now
exhaustively—with or on some common term. Often this exercise takes the
form of simple definition, as in Thomas Hood's "November" or Marianne
Moore's "Poetry." Sometimes—as in Hardy's "Hap" or Stevie Smith's
"Pretty"—one unpacks the multiple, often paradoxical meanings of a single,
resonant word. Thus the author of "Counterparts" undertakes to incorporate
every variation on the word—it can mean matching, complementary, or contrasting sets—that is his title. At his job, for example, Farrington copies out
duplicates or "counterparts" of legal documents. By the same token, Farrington is at once like and opposed to his domineering boss. They are counterparts
as employer and employee, as Dubliner and Ulsterman, as bullies. When
drunk, Farrington abuses his wife; she abuses him when he is sober—they,
too, are counterparts. Their son Tom is, as victim, another of the counterparts,

and Joyce's final, objective references to him as "the boy" are chilling in their implications.

DeLillo uses the same techniques, but to less thematically straightforward ends. The novel begins with a prologue, "The Movie," and ends with another titled chapter ("The Motel") that is at once conclusion—it is more integrated with the novel's main action than the prologue—and epilogue. No character names figure in either. At the end the sleeping woman (Rosemary) and the watching man (Lyle) wait, like Vladimir and Estragon, for the next call from J. Kinnear, the Godot whose agency may confer another moment of purpose on their otherwise aimless lives. They wait in a place of consummate sterility, the motel room DeLillo once called "a peculiar form of nowhere."[10] To go from one motel to another, the character who will be revealed as Lyle remarks in the novel's opening paragraph, would be "self-realizing" (3). Given the constant sterility of motels in DeLillo, this remark suggests just what the Lylean self might realize: its own emptiness.

Like Joyce, too, DeLillo arranges for his reader to discover extraordinary semantic and thematic riches in the single, commonplace word that, as title, seems a promise of larger meanings. This title draws attention most specifically to "those who play": actors, musicians, participants in a sport, and (in a kind of streetwise lexicon) "those in the know, those who matter socially, professionally, politically." But these meanings hardly exhaust the "play" of DeLillo's title. One has only to browse a dictionary or two (in the present instance, a *Webster's Collegiate* and an *American Heritage*) to discover that DeLillo has created a lexical minefield in which a host of submerged meanings threaten, as it were, to explode, flinging semantic shrapnel in all directions. From the *American Heritage Dictionary* one learns of the West Germanic (and Old English) word *plegan,* meaning "pledge for, stake, risk, exercise oneself." One of the words ascending from this root is the Old English *pliht,* meaning "danger, peril: plight." Another scion, *play,* has acquired quite a number of meanings. Besides "to amuse or divert oneself," it can refer to the musical and dramatic activities previously noted. It can also mean "gamble"; "trifle"; "to move or function freely, esp. within prescribed limits"; "to engage in or as if in a game"; "exploit, manipulate"; "wreak," e.g., "play havoc"; "to keep (a hooked fish) in action"; "to take part in or assent to some activity" ("play along with"); "to act so as to prove advantageous to another," e.g., "play into the hands of"; and "to pretend to engage in" (as children play house).

All of these describe Lyle or Pammy—sometimes both.

The same goes for the equally suggestive combinative forms: "play both ends against the middle," "play by ear," "play politics," "play possum," "play second fiddle," "play ball" (in the sense of "cooperate"), "play the game" ("to act

according to a code or set of standards"), and "play around" ("to have pro-
miscuous or illicit sexual relations"). Last—and most suggestive of all when
one contemplates the ultimate sterility of the two central characters—"play
with oneself."

Language

One can imagine, too, an extra-lexicographical meaning to DeLillo's title.
"Players," that is, may also suggest "signifiers," the phonemes and "atomic
'words'" (38) that are the Lincoln Logs or Legos of language. These signifiers,
one says, are "in play"—as if language were in fact a childhood activity or
game. Thus the great philosopher of propositions, Wittgenstein, suggests in his
term "language games" the affinity or correlation between the economies of
speech and play. "Players" immerse themselves in "games" and their rules;
they enter the game economy precisely as the infant, learning language, enters
the Symbolic Order. The infant is a player and knows itself only through the
estranging medium of the "game" that is language. This game, like any other,
is self-contained, it operates according to rules, and it invites the misperception
of a relationship between itself and a reality external to itself. Words, one assumes, represent things; games, by the same token, must represent the larger,
more serious arenas of human competition. Both, however, are self-referring,
bound by *différance.*

In his fifth novel DeLillo plays language games of greater and lesser complexity. But he alone (unless one counts the subtle J. Kinnear) plays them with
any understanding of their workings or rules. His character Lyle lapses into
mystical passivity when trying to fathom the sign systems—the language
games—of television, marriage, adultery, finance, and terrorism. On the Stock
Exchange and among the terrorists he senses but cannot parse the grammars
of power, the mysterious shiftings-about of "secret currents": capital, weapons, political loyalties and motivations. A Rosicrucian of the contemporary
world, he moons over "waves, systems, invisibility, power" (157).

The author takes a particular interest in language games at their most spare.
Even linguistic investigations that remain unrealized or vestigial contribute to
the larger project of parsing minimalist economies of signification. As DeLillo
told LeClair,

> The original idea for *Players* was based on what could be called the intimacy of lan-
> guage. What people who live together really sound like. Pammy and Lyle were to
> address each other in the private language they'd constructed over years of living
> together. Unfinished sentences, childlike babbling, animal noises, foreign accents,

ethnic dialects, mimicry, all of that. It's as though language is something we wear. The more we know someone, the easier it is to undress, to become childlike. But the idea got sidetracked, and only fragments survive in the finished book.[11]

Childlike babbling. Animal noises. At one point in the novel the narrator observes that the names "Pammy and Lyle" resemble those "of chimps learning language" (138). Here again DeLillo is drawn to an idea of language in some inchoate form. The conversation of married people, he suggests, has something of the same economy as the babbling of infants. In its minimalism it offers clues to larger meanings behind the fact of language.

"Sidetracked" or not, the exploration of marital discourse contributes to a project everywhere visible: language reduced. Lyle's thoughts, for example, are "unwordable rubble" (22). Pammy fears "stupor and mutism" (67). The narrator characterizes the "aimlessness of their evenings" as "a retreat from . . . language" (57). Pammy encounters a pervert whose "way of speaking" consists of public masturbation (25). Her father, too, is "a man who preferred gestures to speech" (55). With Jack and Ethan she plays with pseudo-primitive constructions, as for fetching wood: "'Fire come,' she said. 'Make big for heat the body'" (136). In a movie that she watches, a man's son, "either unable to speak or refusing to," lapses into a "reduced sensibility" (205). Lyle, watching television, takes little interest in content and switches channels obsessively, seeking "fresh image-burns" in which "random moments of content" become "pleasing territorial abstractions" (16). He watches without sound—just as, in the beginning, he and his fellow travelers view the in-flight film without benefit of headsets. The ironic nickelodeon music of the prologue modulates, in the main narrative, to a circumambient tonal irony. On one occasion, like Rob Softly in *Ratner's Star*, Lyle even "puts words in quotes," rendering strangely unstable certain clichéd terms associated with lovemaking: "perform," "satisfy," "service" (35).

With the skeletal languages of irony, gesture, aphasia, and connubial codes as background, the author plays an edifying game of deceptive referentiality— or so I interpret this text's abundant motivic symmetries and elaborate counterpointing of detail. For example, DeLillo structures the novel in two equal parts, each with ten numbered chapters and a paratext (prologue or epilogue) in which the characters are nameless. The two viewpoint characters, Pammy and Lyle, balance each other, and they take separate routes into contrasting cul-de-sacs. Various phrases, gestures, and situations, when not complementary, are mysteriously replicated. Thus the novel begins at first dark, ends at first light. Early in the story Pammy encounters a pervert in an automobile (25); later Lyle encounters one (161). On two separate occasions Lyle is accosted by a crazy woman (45, 110–11). When he "turns," Lyle becomes "a second George" and, like the first one, sleeps with Marina (109). Kinnear and the first Burks seem both to be products of Jesuit education. The narrator mentions Lyle's "eyeballs rolling" in the prologue (6); when, at the end, Pammy stops at a delicatessen, an eye-rolling counterman waits on her (206). Before his suicide, Jack clasps his hands behind his neck; later Pammy does the same thing. Ethan Segal imagines an old age (202–3) almost identical with that of Pammy's father (55). The narrator speaks in the first-person plural in the prologue and epilogue, and the last sentence in the book, "We know nothing else about him" (212), repeats one of the first: "We know nothing else about her" (4).

These parallels and interconnections, largely unnoticed by the characters, mock the reader's desire for the kind of meaning that normally emerges in pattern. Rather, they model the mechanics of language, the concatenation of complementary signifiers. The one-to-one correspondences here "represent" that which supposedly obtains between the thing and its sign. Here one sees only shadows and images mirroring each other, a play of simulacra in which there is no privileged plane of reality, no secondary or subordinate plane that is mere representation. The text frustrates expectation that one of its registers will be substance, the other signification. Thus a stunning correlation such as that between the domestic situation McKechnie describes to Lyle and the plot of the shallow movie Pammy sees on her return from Maine hints at a significant collapse of the distinction between "real life" and its simulacrum. That is, the notion that one register here is real, one two-dimensional, breaks down when the reader remembers that McKechnie and his family (not to mention Lyle and Pammy) are themselves unreal, themselves fictional characters, mere images. Similarly, the murder on the floor of the Stock Exchange that Lyle witnesses is not more real than the terrorist attack on the golfers in the movie described in the prologue.

Not that there is always more than one register. The narrator, looking through Pammy's eyes, takes the white aftlock that is Jack Laws's most distinctive feature as "the mark, the label, the stamp, the sign, the emblem of something mysterious" (19). Yet it is without meaning: the signifier as free radical, not integrated in any symbolic order. Presently Jack stumbles into the same limbo. Desperately unsure of his sexual identity, he experiences the radical disconnection that leads to his ghastly suicide. It is also significant that self-immolation, the supreme icon of principled resistance scant years before, now takes place in a context devoid of political relevance. Here, too, the sign has come unmoored.

Like the narrator/protagonist of *End Zone,* Pammy knows that words sometimes detach themselves from their meanings, "subsisting in her mind as language units that had mysteriously evaded the responsibilities of content." In the reader's last view of Pammy she finds herself momentarily unable to understand the word *transients* on a "flophouse marquee" (207). Its meaning and its meaninglessness are both significant. A reminder of mortality and contingency, the word denotes the brief, the ephemeral, the short-lived—all that will trouble DeLillo's later Lyle and Pammy, the Jack and Babette of *White Noise*. The word also hints at the very semantic lapse Pammy now experiences. Signifiers, too, are transient ("not settled, established, or permanent"), and occasionally, as now, they present themselves to the mind in baffling semantic disconnection. This episode of aphasia—part of the emotional aftermath of Jack Laws's suicide—serves briefly to foreground the arbitrariness of the sign, its unreliability as index to objective reality.

It also represents the understated culmination of a theme explored throughout the narrative: dislocation of consciousness. As noted previously, both Pammy and her husband suffer from that affectless condition known to existential psychology as anomie. Both psychological and social, this condition represents the breakdown of the most commonplace standards of civilization. Thus the narrator, mentioning Pammy's work in "grief management," takes the trouble to explain the first term as if "intense mental suffering, deep remorse, extreme anguish, acute sorrow and the like" had become wholly unfamiliar or attenuated (18).

Etymologically, anomie means "without law," without an ethical center. The troubled human psyche summons its mirror state in the social environment, which becomes similarly unanchored. As the superego shrivels, the usual sanctions—against adultery, against the planting of bombs in public buildings—become inoperative. The resultant ethos is not one of license—not some contemporary urban Feast of Fools, in which one violates various rules with a feeling of emancipation—but rather one of unmotivated, apathetic drift. Perhaps at first there is an element of transgressive gratification or some idea of goading jaded senses into shock or excitement, but presently one simply embraces antisocial acts gratuitously.

Though the idea of "grief management" seems parodic, Pammy retains some capacity to feel. Indeed, DeLillo remarked to LeClair that he imagined her as the more "humane" of his two central characters.[12] After Jack's self-immolation, which she may have unwittingly prompted, she does experience an emotional aftermath—and she is unlike Lyle in that she seems actually capable of emotion. It is surely significant that, always bored with flying, she insists on taking the bus back from Maine after Jack's suicide. Having introduced her in the lounge of a 747, the author has brought her down to earth in more senses than one. No longer above it all, Pammy is no longer a player immune to the dirty or frightening business of living.

One recurs to the strange parallel between the movie Pammy watches (204–5) and the situation outlined by McKechnie—his wife seems to have some dread disease, his son descends into a kind of catatonia, his brother is a gambler in trouble with the mob. The reader notes, first, that Lyle does not react to the real-life version of the story, though it is nominally, at least, a friend who is suffering its details. Pammy, on the other hand, responds to the same story in its cheap cinematic form and its "bogus sentiments" with powerful emotion (206). It channels the feelings she brings with her from Maine and Jack's horrible death. Yet the reader does not conclude that Pammy is saved because she can feel, Lyle damned because he cannot. In the first instance, only something completely artificial seems capable of causing Pammy to feel, and this strikes one as an indictment, an empathic distortion. There may be a spectrum defined by these two characters, but it is a narrow one. As John W. Aldridge has remarked, "They have never possessed, and do not come to possess, the redeeming powers of compassion and will." [13] Thus Pammy's relatively greater humanity is not sufficient to lend purpose to her life, and she remains profoundly troubled: "I don't think I can stand the idea of tomorrow" (42). In going off to Maine and in the under-motivated fling with Jack, she seeks to defeat the creeping, deadening everydayness that has engulfed everyone in her world, but her gestures toward the kind of Rilkean "change" that Ethan speaks of (43–44) prove abortive.

She and her husband are "complex"—a word that figures repeatedly. The first Burks calls Kinnear "a complex individual" (128), for example, and Lyle and Pammy repeatedly wonder (he on two occasions, she on three) if they have "become too complex" (14, 17, 58, 70–71, 169). The term seems straightforward enough. These characters—capable between them of flirtation with terrorism and at least three adulterous relationships—seem unimpeachably "complex." Yet the word feels deceptive when people like Lyle and Pammy, people largely incapable of introspection, apply it to themselves. Vaguely self-congratulatory, it discloses an etymological irony: the root of "complex" is the Latin *complexus*, "twisted."

There is a logic here, but the reader experiences considerable difficulty trying to gauge the character of Lyle's volition and the extent of his percipience. Does he seek some vivifying sense of danger? Does he involve himself with Rosemary, Marina, J. Kinnear, and their shadowy colleagues out of a vague desire to engage the phantoms that are contemporary reality? In another vision of political terror—that of Conrad, for example—one might come to certain conclusions regarding terrorists and their sympathizers: that they are political fools, pawns of ruthless and subtle manipulation—or that their actions illustrate the moral bankruptcy of a given state or society. It is even possible (as in Michael Ondaatje's *In the Skin of a Lion*) to applaud the act of commitment and resistance carried out by the terrorist, in whom one may recognize a node of conviction in an otherwise corrupt world.

DeLillo ingeniously arranges for Lyle's involvement with terrorists not to fall into any such familiar categories. If Lyle is a fool—if he has isolated himself in a position surrounded by what Kinnear calls "pure void" (179) or let himself in for the mechanized sodomy hinted at in Rosemary's dildo[14]—this is not the whole or even the main story. Lyle acts as one who instinctively understands that contemporary reality is a play of images and shadows—and nothing else. This is the point of his near-obsessive viewing of television, which offers training in the different reality of images and the language they structure—a reality composed of shadows and challenged less and less, these days, by substance. The true "terror" of DeLillo's vision in *Players* has to do with the perfect logic of Lyle's perceptions and acts. In a kind of Foucauldian sense he is not a monster—he is someone acting on the logic of experience. In the novel's final irony Lyle becomes precisely the "player" he sets out to be: a person who, capable of living with fear, likewise lives without conviction, without commitment, without substance.

4　The Naive and Sentimental Reader　*Running Dog*

Like *Players,* with its elaborate variations on the multiple meanings of "play,"
Running Dog (1978) features its own key word, which appears at least eight
times. As DeLillo unpacks the various meanings of the word *code,* his story
modulates thematically from plane to plane. A code is a more or less sophisticated language, a system of symbolic equivalents to speech or writing. A code
is also a codex: a book of laws. Indeed, the Lacanian "Law of the Father" is
articulated throughout the code of the Symbolic Order. *Running Dog* concerns
the encryption of experience and ideology in this great code (language) and in
such subsumed or subsidiary systems as the droll *"linguistic subfamily of German"*[1] that Chaplin speaks in *The Great Dictator;* or the "code of behavior"
that has always been enjoined on soldiers and spies; or the secret codes on
which intelligence operatives rely to exclude enemies, competitors, the unini-
tiated generally. "Espionage" itself, according to the journalist Moll Robbins,

"is a language" (111). "I believe in codes," declares Glen Selvy, the novel's protagonist, when he and Moll encounter a drunk who speaks of "the code of
Harry's Tropical Bar" (33). Selvy will learn, however, that codes are arbitrary,
not foundational.

The fate of "belief" becomes, in fact, central to DeLillo's story. "When the
priests stop believing, what does it mean?" wonders Grace Delany (218), Moll's
superior at the muckraking periodical *Running Dog* (the nuns in *White Noise*
will provide one kind of answer). "I don't believe. I used to believe, but now I
don't," admits Arthur Lomax (217), the mid-level spymaster who "runs" Selvy
(the title of the novel also refers to its central character). Lomax ruefully points
out to Earl Mudger, his boss, that Selvy "believes." Whatever his failings, he
"believes in the life" of being an agent (141). In the end, "The only ones who
believe in what they're doing" (220) are this same Selvy, who dies meaning-
lessly, and the Mafia family that possesses itself of the novel's McGuffin: two
reels of Hitler's jejune theatrics.

The pursuers of this ostensibly pornographic film turn out to be, to a man
(one excludes Moll Robbins), connoisseurs or entrepreneurs of the obscene:
Lightborne, Senator Percival, Earl Mudger, Richie Armbrister, Talerico, and
the families. The promise of the prurient image is effective shorthand for a
world of desire—in both the common and Lacanian senses of the word. In
often startling ways *Running Dog* anatomizes pornography as multiple, layered, and complex: fascism, power, hypocrisy, brutality—all are pornogra-
phies, studies in obscenity (and, one kind of expectation dashed, there *is* obscenity in the idea of Hitler's impersonating Charlie Chaplin in Eva Braun's
home movie). One constructs the obscene or pornographic out of the desire
to experience and be aroused by the enjoined, the forbidden, the taboo. The
ultimate proscription, however, concerns the mother's body, which every human being guiltily yearns for (to repose on that bosom, to reenter that womb).
This means, in Lacanian terms, that the Imaginary is eroticized, and one can
learn in the Symbolic Order to configure all desire as ultimately pornographic.

The sexual thematics here (including both ostensibly sensational pornography and a quite rich psychoanalytic subtext) represents a further development of DeLillo's sustained meditation on language and its attributes. Though
sex figures less prominently in Lacan's system than it does in Freud's, one
knows from the musings of Edna Lown in *Ratner's Star* that DeLillo takes an
interest in the idea that all language has what Moll, in *Running Dog*, calls
"sexual sources and coordinates" (111). In earliest infancy there is a relationship
between language—immersion in the Symbolic Order as major component of
the Oedipal Phase—and psychosexual development, whether one speaks of
Freud's phallic ambition and castration anxiety or of Lacan's Law and Nom du

Père. These and other, more philosophical economies come into play when DeLillo's protagonist, Glen Selvy, returns to Marathon Mines, the place of his figurative birth, early training, and entry into the Symbolic Order. Here, at the end, he undergoes a bizarre Oedipal punishment in circumstances that seem to mock sacrificial pretension.

In one of the more arresting passages in the book (an anticipation of *The Names* and its central conceit) Earl Mudger crafts one of his many knives while musing on language, the "names of things" (119), wherein the father-custodian of the Symbolic Order invests his authority. En route to Marathon Mines, Selvy buys a "bolo" or Philippine machete "for the name," which he ironically characterizes as "romantic" (191). The connection between weaponry and names receives further attention in some thoughts—evidently Mudger's—regarding language in wartime. Because language can be an instrument of clarity and discrimination such as might complicate persuading young men to lay down their lives, the fathers who sent the sons to Vietnam waged "a war based on hybrid gibberish" (208). The elaborate nomenclature of weaponry, on the other hand, became "the soldier's counterjargon to death" (209), something concrete in the "realms of ambiguity" (208).

The Legacy of Vietnam

In *Running Dog,* with its search for the supposedly pornographic film of Hitler, DeLillo anticipates precisely the kind of hysteria that would be unleashed by publication, in the following decade, of the Hitler diaries. Unlike the diaries, the film proves authentic, though its obscenity takes an unexpected form: totemic evil presents itself as pentimento beneath a familiar figure of innocence. This cathected "object of ultimate desirability and ultimate dread," as DeLillo calls it in an interview,[2] offers an insight long familiar to psychoanalysis: what one most desires can prove strangely congruent with what one most fears.

But the atmosphere of this novel derives less from Hitler's war than from that other conflict waged from the fifties into the early seventies—a war that divided the American people and proved unwinnable (except, perhaps, at the prohibitive price of a much vaster engagement with China or the Soviet Union). DeLillo has tentatively characterized *Running Dog* as "a response to the war in Vietnam," an attempt to deal with its legacy of moral confusion, a gauging of "how the war affected the way people worked out their own strategies, how individuals conducted their own lives. . . . All the paranoia, manipulation, violence, all the sleazy desires are a form of fallout from the Vietnam experience."[3] When the Vietnam war came to its chaotic end on the roof of the American embassy in Saigon, it left no moral victors—even the war resisters had been forced into such ethically dubious positions and destructive, civilization-impairing gestures as broadcasting from Hanoi and blowing up ROTC facilities. Those who went to the war and survived it, meanwhile, returned to a fuller understanding of just why their sacrifices had never been valued. Physically disabled or whole, they struggled, often, with various forms of emotional disability.

Indeed, even before the war ended, the confused, disaffected, sometimes murderous Vietnam vet became a fixture of American fiction and cinema. David Morrell's 1972 novel, *First Blood* (which spawned the *Rambo* films), concerns an ex-POW who goes on a rampage, deploying the many counterinsurgency techniques his government taught him to use in a faraway country. The two main characters in Robert Stone's *Dog Soldiers* (1974) allow wartime drug trafficking to destroy their postwar lives. In Thomas Harris's first thriller, *Black Sunday* (1975), another ex-POW attempts to murder eighty thousand spectators (including the president) at the Super Bowl. In Bobbie Ann Mason's *In Country* (1985), a dead soldier's daughter and brother (himself a Vietnam survivor) try to deal with their grief in a variety of ways, including a visit to the Vietnam War Memorial.

These fictions develop a similar premise: Vietnam made the home country sick. Metaphorically, the tormented, violent vet functions as the agent of a disease alternately imagined as organic or psychological. In the organic version the angry veteran embodies a kind of virus the nation thoughtlessly contracted. Vietnam loosed a contagion in the American bloodstream that, waxing and waning like malaria or raging like Ebola, has caused and continues to cause irremediable damage to the social host. In the psychological version the troubled veteran becomes an emblem of all that America refuses to face. Though never a great mystery, what Americans saw and did in Vietnam had to be repressed as the kind of reality human beings cannot bear very much of. Home from Vietnam, then, the American veteran returns as the repressed in the nation's unconscious and presently makes unignorable an ugly, post-Vietnam neurosis. Tim O'Brien's *In the Lake of the Woods* (1994), for example, one of the most impressive Vietnam-inspired novels of recent years, concerns memories of My Lai that cannot be kept at bay indefinitely. But whether one favors the metaphor of repression or of viral infection, the upshot is the same: there are violent, angry men with a host of military skills among us, consciously or unconsciously exacting their revenge on a home front guilty of complacency, hypocrisy, profiteering—in short, every species of bad faith.

More insidious yet, the many forms of hypocrisy in American society find themselves strangely mirrored in the cynical, embittered, twisted minds of these emotionally damaged veterans. Perhaps counterintuitive, this mutuality is something other and more insidious than the oft-iterated argument that an unexamined, fascistic evil in American institutions exposed itself in the war it prosecuted in Vietnam. Only the occasional fiction of this period manages fully to gauge the idea that the corruption fostered by the war extended as a matter of course to the doves as well as the hawks. In this regard *Running Dog* ranks alongside O'Brien's *The Things They Carried* (1990) as a masterful study of the vexed relations between Vietnam and what the grunts called "the world."

DeLillo ingeniously avoids the formal error of Vietnam fictions that center on a troubled veteran. Viruses and neuroses, after all, require incubation—until full-blown they manifest themselves only in minor symptoms. A character who embodies the sickness should appear at the periphery of the action—in disguise perhaps, but in any event only gradually recognizable as a human pathogen. Thus in *Running Dog* the carrier of plague is not, as in other Vietnam fictions, the central character. Glen Selvy, significantly, did not serve in Vietnam (as will be seen, he retains an innocence that makes him the pawn of those who have learned the war's dark lessons). It is the relatively secondary Earl Mudger who returns from Southeast Asia infected with the virus that can bring a whole population to its moral knees—Earl Mudger, whose disaffection stems not from having been traumatized but from having savored too much the strange mix, in-country, of terror and godlike power.

Through Mudger, in fact, the author of *Running Dog* brilliantly reconceptualizes—a year before Coppola's *Apocalypse Now*—the drama of Kurtz and the heart of darkness. Conrad, one recalls, does not in the end imagine the atavistic evil he probes as quarantined in some colonial outpost—it exists, rather, within the breast of even the most civilized human beings. Thus DeLillo invites his readers to imagine Kurtz as having survived and returned to civilization after the unspeakable indulgences of his time at the Inner Station. Where Conrad emphasizes the in-country horror and merely inveighs against the "whited sepulchers" in Europe, DeLillo sets his entire fable within the culture to which the American Kurtz returns. Setting up shop here, Mudger develops local versions of the darkness he has embraced in the jungles of Asia.

Mudger worked for the CIA-sponsored Air America in Laos and Vietnam, trafficked in weapons and drugs, directed counter-insurgency operations, and "set up provincial interrogation centers, where Vietcong suspects were tortured." Enamored of the power and the absence of accountability,

> he became something of a legend in Vietnam. Apparently he established a feudal barony complete with loyal ARVN soldiers (loyal to him, not the government) as well as pimps, black marketeers, shoeshine boys, war refugees, bar girls, deserters, pickpockets and others. It was suspected to be a drug operation with a thriving sideline

in black-market piasters. As head, Mudger dispensed land, money, food and other favors. (84)

A Kurtz act translated to these shores, this circus shrinks to microbe size, gaining in deadliness even as it dwindles in scale. Mudger brings home with him selected retainers (the ARVN rangers) and a version of the savage mistress, a Saigon bar girl. With Lomax as harlequin, he soon parts company with PAC/ ORD, the legitimate arm of U.S. intelligence, and becomes again a law unto himself, flexing his muscles among the stateside civilians.

In *Running Dog*, then, one encounters an American culture still troubled by the war in Southeast Asia, still counting the casualties among combatants and noncombatants alike. Although DeLillo scrutinizes more than one of the myths spawned by the war, revealing in the process more than one of the stark, unlovely truths they mask, he insists on discriminating among the cultural fictions enjoying widespread currency. Thus the recognitions here are not predictable and not all negative. The author resists, for example, the popular conviction regarding conspiratorial power in high places. In paranoia, in fact, DeLillo discovers a sheep in wolf's clothing.

Although Senator Percival's estranged wife obsesses over the Warren Report (71, 199), although Moll speaks of "the age of conspiracy," with "links inside links" (111), and although there is a nice handling of progressive complication, as more and more characters turn out to be in bed with each other (literally and figuratively), the reader should not conclude that DeLillo embraces a paranoid vision or endorses conspiratorial views of the contemporary world. Committed to what Patrick O'Donnell calls a "demystification of the romance of secrecy,"[4] the author of *Running Dog* separates himself from any kind of straightforward indulgence in conspiracy obsession—the widespread paranoia that made the post-sixties decade so hospitable to endless speculation about the grassy knoll and the second gunman, not to mention films—*The Parallax View* (1974), *Three Days of the Condor* (1975)—arguing with varying degrees of subtlety that one or more tremendous conspiracies lay behind the proliferating assassinations and catastrophes. In an interview with Adam Begley, DeLillo observes: "Certainly there's an element of paranoia in my work . . . although not nearly so much as some people think." A remark on the same occasion regarding the temporal setting of *Great Jones Street* applies as well to *Running Dog*: "Those were the days when . . . the most paranoid sort of fear was indistinguishable from common sense. I think I tried to get at the slickness connected with the word *paranoia*. It was becoming a kind of commodity. It used to mean one thing and after a while it began to mean everything. It became something you bought into."[5]

Running Dog does not, then, promote that oddly comforting fiction of mighty forces arrayed against merit and virtue. Not for DeLillo that vision of ultimate string-pullers. Rather, he gauges the general corruption of those who have somehow escaped accountability. The forces at play are *not* linked. Whatever his credentials in "Systems," whatever his standing as a Morlock among the Eloi, Mudger is *not* in the loop. A rogue, operating outside the regular intelligence establishment, he has already begun, like the similarly monomaniacal Brock Vond in Pynchon's *Vineland,* to lose crucial support. His chauffeur quits, apparently to return to PAC/ORD, and he orders the only trained intelligence agent available to him "adjusted."

This agent, Glen Selvy, undergoes debunking of a different kind, for among DeLillo's satiric targets here are the conventions of the literary romance Americans so love. As the hero of a thriller that implodes, collapsing into its own clichés, Selvy is exposed as a kind of parodic Marlboro man, an American primitive, a Puritan, even, who cannot be persuaded to differentiate erotica from "smut" (28, 29, 56) or to recognize when "the life" (141) has lost all semblance of legitimacy. Lomax, Selvy's handler, tries in vain to make his man take a more sophisticated view of things. "Pure of heart" (113), avoiding commitments to women, and homing on the wilderness where he learned his ascetic calling, Selvy is a latter-day Natty Bumppo or Huck Finn. Though he fits D. H. Lawrence's famous description of the "essential American soul" as "hard, isolate, stoic, and a killer,"[6] Selvy enacts the eclipse of the archetype. Cartographically, his movement westward is also a movement downward, and his death suggests the post-Vietnam fate of one kind of American innocence.

Selvy's designation in the argot of intelligence hints at a curious relationship with the person perusing DeLillo's novel. As a "reader" (28, 54, 94, 156), Selvy fails to master certain levels of meaning in his text, or—since "he was reading Senator Percival" (28)—perhaps he simply neglects some important intertexts, paratexts, and subtexts. Eventually he becomes less deserving of LeCarré's "naive and sentimental" epithet, but his virtual suicide or connivance at his own death suggests a comprehensive and disabling disillusionment. Readers in the traditional sense—readers of *Running Dog,* that is—may find themselves in danger of similar shortsightedness. DeLillo's readers must not, like Selvy, indulge a tendency toward naive faith in the larger significance, coherence, and integrity of the system—or fiction—in which they find themselves. Though he may despise Earl Mudger, the guileful author of *Running Dog* shares with him a dislike of predictability and a predilection for new enterprises. Indeed, as Selvy discovers himself the gratuitous victim of or meaningless sacrifice to interests largely indifferent to his inconsequential purity, so do readers find a yawning void in the space they thought comfortably occupied by a highly predictable genre of popular storytelling. They discover that the spuriousness of the novel's grail (the Hitler film) mocks their expectations of escapist diversion. By the same token, DeLillo gives his readers a hero familiar to them from countless thrillers, then mercilessly allows him to be defeated by humorless forces of political and personal rapacity.

Themselves naive and sentimental, perhaps, readers eventually recognize the parodic and *noir* features of this ostensible thriller. Their enlightenment takes the form of recognizing the hybridity of the fiction they have just read—recognizing, that is, the need to see beyond the lone agent (island of integrity in a world of corrupt interests), the bewildering layers of political control, the sporadic survival of dirty business from World War II, Korea, and Vietnam, and the other trappings of the spy thriller. Patrick O'Donnell remarks that *Running Dog* "refutes its own generic identity and referentiality."[7] John Frow, comparing DeLillo's novel with four different Ludlum thrillers, observes that "the labyrinthine plotting, the complex primary and secondary doublings, the persistent tension between ambiguity and revelation . . . offer a material which can be worked against the grain of the genre."[8] *Running Dog,* then, proves to be something other than a thriller, its hero more than the familiar operative of Ludlum, Deighton, Forsyth, and Trevanian. This novel in fact modulates into and out of various genre conventions, in the manner of Robbe-Grillet and Calvino (notably in *If on a Winter's Night a Traveler*). When Nadine says, "This is turning into a Western" (186), one smiles at the lateness of the attempt to orient the action to some familiar category of fiction, whether escapist or, as Earl Mudger casually surmises, "epic" (209).

This last lies behind the more or less comic proliferation of quests and questers. Moll, for example, undertakes the kind of journalistic quest Woodward and Bernstein made famous: she seeks evidence of a senator's secret corruption—seeks the "smoking gun" that has its pop art representation in the neon objet d'art on her wall. Her quest complements other quests—those of Lightborne, Mudger, Percival, Richie Armbrister, and the families for the mysterious film from Hitler's Berlin bunker; of Cao and Van for Glen Selvy; and of Selvy himself for some kind of oblivion, whether through sex, heavy drinking, driving with his eyes closed, or the Zen-like purity of purpose he seems to find in facing his death in the desert amid "the sense of topography as an ethical schematic," where "landscape is truth" (229).

At the culmination of the central, structuring quest, as she awaits the screening of the film from Hitler's bunker, Moll reflects on the psychology of grail-hunting:

Moll was suspicious of quests. At the bottom of most long and obsessive searches, in her view, was some vital deficiency on the part of the individual in pursuit, a meagerness of spirit. . . . Even more depressing than the nature of a given quest was the likely result. Whether people searched for an object of some kind, or inner occasion, or answer, or state of being, it was almost always disappointing. People came up against themselves in the end. Nothing but themselves. (224)

Commenting most obviously on those who want the film, Moll also indicts her own investigative reporting and the collective journalistic enterprise behind it, especially the periodical *Running Dog*. Among those who "came up against themselves in the end," as one presently sees, was Adolf Hitler, whose quest for world domination ended—DeLillo imagines—in a few absurd moments as clown during the final assault on his Berlin bunker.

But what of the self Hitler came up against? To raise the question in a story of such overdetermined "questing" is to recognize the extent to which DeLillo turns out to be examining identity in terms remarkably similar to those of Lacanian psychoanalysis, predicated on the theory of an ego fundamentally divided or split and thus subject, as Ellie Ragland-Sullivan observes, to an "insatiable Desire *[manque-à-être]*, which destines humans to be questing, lacking creatures." This ego, Ragland-Sullivan adds, "can only experience itself in relation to external images and to the gaze of others."[9] Thus it is that, in *Running Dog*, a pair of twinned and mythic courters of the public gaze (Chaplin the actor, Hitler the demagogue) play a cinematic game of identity with each other, taking turns at a *"burlesque, an impersonation"* (61). When Moll Robbins, having accompanied Glen Selvy to *The Great Dictator*, declares that she will always, thereafter, associate him with Chaplin, she hints at a much vaster potential for sharing identities. When Lightborne—himself a Chaplin, with his walking stick and flapping shoe—observes that "people like to dress up" (244), one may recall that the novel has taken considerable interest in sartorial impersonation of one kind or another. It opens, after all, with the death of Christoph Ludecke, dressed as a woman. "These days, what is it? Everybody's in disguise," observes a police sergeant. "All this dressing up" (8). With this remark, slyly lumping his plainclothes colleagues with the murdered transvestite, the sergeant anticipates the rule at Nadine's "Nude Story-Telling" establishment: "If you keep your clothes on, it means you're a cop" (122).[10] Similarly, Moll jokes with Selvy about "Apparel Personality Exchange," a "movement" in which people will "wear each other's clothes" (39). Another transvestite, she dons his underwear after lovemaking.

Though DeLillo stops short of saying that gender is constructed, he allows recognition that no aspect of identity is essential. Thus reel one of the long-sought film ends with a profoundly disquieting image: Chaplin's *"sweet, epicene, guilty little smile"* (236) on the face of Hitler. It is the smile of ambiguous identity, any-gendered and replete with knowledge of the infinite fluidity of the self. Portraying the Chaplin who, in *The Great Dictator,* has portrayed *Der Führer* twice over (for the great comic portrays both Hitler himself and the little barber who, as the plot unfolds, impersonates Hitler), Hitler subverts and reverses the original satire, characterizing identity as a hall of mirrors, a simulacrum's simulacrum. *"Dead, but still with us, still with us but dead"* (as Barthelme says of his own monolithic Dead Father),[11] this most terrible of fathers reaches out from the grave with a disturbing message regarding the inessential self, the illusory ground of all desire.

Memory and Playback

DeLillo's ascetics seem always to struggle with a death wish, and Selvy joins Gary Harkness and Bucky Wunderlick in a gesture of morbid withdrawal, postmodern parody of the hermit's retreat to a spiritual purification in the desert. In the closing pages Selvy experiences what the narrator repeatedly characterizes as filmlike "memory" or "playback" (222, 229, 239), and what is evoked would seem to be more than the protagonist's having been in southwest Texas before—more, even, than a return to the "praying and fasting" with which Selvy half-facetiously claims to have occupied himself during the Vietnam years (112). Freud, in *Beyond the Pleasure Principle,* identifies repetition as the signature of the death drive, and Selvy's powerful sense of repetition at Marathon Mines at the end (like the doubled tableau in which, head lowered, arms over knees, he crouches by a window [113, 192]) reifies what was always implicit in his choice of profession, his affinity with the desert, the closing of his eyes while driving (151, 157), and the curious fatalism with which he drives that straight line from New York to southwest Texas (straight lines in DeLillo are always anti-vital). "He'd come all the way down the straight white line," the narrator remarks, evidently with reference to the highway, that traditional image of the course of a life (192). Perhaps, too, one thinks of the white line that figures in cocaine-sniffing. For Selvy, death will be a high.

The repetition motif, foregrounded in Selvy's return to Marathon Mines, can also be read in post-Freudian terms. For Lacan, repetition contributes to ego-building, and in a sense the memory and playback that Selvy half-consciously reviews are the acts of *prior* repetition carried out at Marathon Mines during the figurative infancy of his training, part of the laborious construction of the ego. But the identity thus constructed must remain always a fiction, wedded to the illusory mirror-self that infantile consciousness tragically takes to be foundational. At the center of the story yet himself uncentered, Selvy is the hollow, post-Freudian subject, the self as simulacrum. His passing occasions little actual distress on the reader's part.[12]

In that they denote natural and technological versions of repetition, and in that they are themselves repeated, the words *memory* and *playback* hint at the numerous philosophical, psychological, and religious meanings one can read into Selvy's story and fate. "Memory," for example, is a reproduction or simulacrum of some prior event or experience. As such, it partakes of the Symbolic economy, and our relationship to experience through memory is parallel to our relationship to reality through language. The real, like the event on which memory is based, is irrecoverable. Remembering takes place within the endless exile of signification. The iterations of "memory" and "playback" gesture, too, toward the anamnesis or "reminiscence" that Plato, according to Lacan, "places at the centre of his entire theory of knowledge";[13] toward the Kantian idea that original experience seems inextricable from its processing and reproduction by the senses; and toward doctrines of repetition in Nietzsche and Kierkegaard as well as Freud and Lacan.

Many of these doctrines have their uncanny or postmodern instantiation in film and videotape, media in which "playback" is virtually illimitable. Infinitely repeatable as well as ontologically privileged, film and videotape realize Nietzsche's doctrine of eternal recurrence: "This life, as thou livest it at present, and hast lived it, thou must live it once more, and also innumerable times."[14] But Nietzsche's precept is not metaphysics—it is an existential litmus test. Either one is crushed by the prospect of such recurrence, or one learns, in contemplating it, to reorder radically one's thinking about life as it is lived. If Selvy were capable of such a recognition, it would transfigure his death and the actions leading up to it. Affirming his embrace of the infinite playback, he would become a version of the Overman. In *Ecce Homo* Nietzsche characterizes the doctrine of eternal recurrence as the "highest formula of Yea-saying to life that can ever be attained,"[15] but even Zarathustra cannot finally accept the doctrine's corollary: "Eternally he returneth, the man of whom thou art weary, the small man."[16] If the actions of a Selvy or a Chaplin recur through some kind of cinematic eternity, so, too, do those of Hitler. Indeed, *Running Dog* depends for much of its effect on the expectation that certain unheroic events in the bunker will, having been filmed, prove infinitely repeatable.

Karmic recurrence also figures here. Thus *Running Dog* ends with a piece of Zen illogic as the sacerdotal Levi Blackwater contemplates Tibetan obsequies for the headless Selvy. "He knew for certain how you started. You started by plucking a few strands of hair from the top of the dead man's head" (246). His proposing to pluck hairs from a head no longer available is the equivalent of a *koan,* one of those little logical impasses that, in Zen Buddhism, are enjoined upon the disciple who would circumvent the snares of logic and language. Perhaps, then, invited to discard familiar categories of experience and spiritually retrograde common sense, DeLillo's reader takes a small step toward a different moral or philosophical economy.

In the end Selvy at once opts out of and submits to the system that has made him. In the desert he is unsupported by and has no allegiance to any external set of values. He has only his own gut sense of integrity, his willingness to die defiantly, however empty such defiance must prove. If Selvy's death seems also to be a kind of Buddhist exercise, a simplification, a reaching for purity, the talk of dying as "an art in the East," as something "heroic, a spiritual victory" (233), only makes more bitterly futile Selvy's perishing. Levi makes clear that Selvy deceives himself if he expects to move toward Enlightenment: his death will not be that of a soul freed from the repetition or eternal recurrence of the karmic wheel. "You think you're about to arrive at some final truth. Truth is a disappointment. You'll only be disappointed" (233). In these assertions, post-structuralist as well as Buddhist, Levi speaks for the author, who similarly refuses to affirm any final significance to Selvy's gesture.

The story of Glen Selvy concerns, among other things, the discovery that an ideology or creed or code, long taken for granted, is an empty vessel. But his fate represents more than a quasi-Marxist parable of false consciousness. Selvy recognizes that those who trained him "want perfect specimens, physically and otherwise. It's less resonant if you're flawed." His training has been the "ritual preparation" of a scapegoat: "All this time he'd been preparing to die . . . to be killed by your own side and with no hard feelings" (183). An unspared Isaac, Selvy goes to a death sanctioned by neither religious nor political principle. Nor is it supported by an idea of the patriotic (even the narrow ideology of Western capitalism). Victim of an Abraham with a pathological devotion to instruments of sacrifice, this Isaac dies gratuitously.

In its meditation on the post-Vietnam ethos, *Running Dog* looks closely at the vexed relations between the father and those who might challenge his supremacy. In this novel one notes, in fact, a proliferation of fathers, from the "advertising immortal" (39) who sired Moll to Nadine's ineffectual parent— once "pretty close to being an all-out bastard" (154). Often the fathers exude incestuous menace. The father who employs Nadine, the mobster Talerico, obliges her abjectly to narrate "Flaming Panties," an incestuous story she finds disturbing (126). Moll, on the other hand, must fend off the advances of two successive fathers: the unscrupulous Earl Mudger and the lecherous sexagenarian Senator Percival, who ends up married to a twenty-year-old. When Mudger asks about her current sex partner, she remarks, "That's what my father used to ask me," and Mudger responds: "Was he jealous?" (169). The exchange makes sense only as it figures in the text's larger engagement with or thematization of incest. Moll's boss, Grace Delaney, is less resourceful in resisting exploitation by the fathers, and she is sexually blackmailed by Lomax. The name he and Mudger give her—"Flat-Chested Bitch" (138, 220)—suggests that, even though older than her seducer, she is another daughter-*puella,* another victim of symbolic incest. The last—or first—of these victims may have been Geli Raubal, the niece with whom Hitler, according to Lightborne, is said to have had an incestuous relationship. Indeed, the more terrible the father, the more certain the incestuous appetites.

Mudger looms in the story as arch-father. His wife, Tran Le, whom he describes as "a gook" (91), is more than thirty years his junior. That he makes knives and has a large collection of them suggests his unconscious guilt at violation of the incest taboo, for in dream and fantasy the multiplication of phallic symbols represents a warding-off of castration. At the same time, of course, the collection represents a symbolic—ultimately literal—discouragement of Oedipal ambition among younger men, notably the Glen Selvy who possesses, in Moll, a woman Mudger desires. When Lomax enumerates the reasons for Selvy's becoming a "subject," he suggests that the agent has, among other things, compromised the operation against Percival by facilitating Moll's discovery of the senator's secret gallery: "Motive, obvious, sex, clearly" (107). But one suspects that Selvy's alleged transgressions merely provide pretexts for an "adjustment" dictated by Mudger's sexual jealousy.

Labeled a renegade son, Selvy cannot win at the psychosexual game. Normally, as a part of his tradecraft one would think objectionable to the fathers, he sleeps only with married women. Yet it is precisely when he becomes involved with unmarried women (first Moll, then Nadine)—when, that is, he seems in effect to renounce Oedipal desires in the classic, Freudian scheme of maturation—that he runs afoul of Mudger. Mudger's fury is caused, in part, by his thinking that both Selvy and Moll have penetrated Senator Percival's secret gallery, his cornucopia of erotic delights. Approached through a hidden passage like a birth canal, this gallery is a symbolic womb, violated by "children" who gratify the guiltiest, most universal, most forbidden wish.

Selvy's story culminates in another return to the womb—the desert around Marathon Mines where, for all practical purposes, he came into being (except for Levi's valedictory musings on the father who was a military officer, the mother who was neurasthenic, Selvy seems in fact the romantic cliché Moll briefly reflects on—the man without a past). Here, Orestes-like, he confronts Cao and Van, his Furies, and suffers the symbolic castration ordered by Mudger, manufacturer and keeper of the phallic knives. Himself equipped with only a single, inadequate blade, Selvy loses the fight with the Vietnamese rangers and is beheaded by Earl's brother-in-law, Van, a surrogate father.

In the rich montage of the novel's conclusion, this dénouement is intercut with the anticlimactic screening of the Hitler film. The two sequences complement each other at the fantasy level as primal scene and Oedipal punishment. A play within a play or other embedded performance, says Norman Holland, tends to be a symbolic rendering of the primal scene,[17] and here the reader, who has already witnessed two such ekphrastic performances (Nadine narrating her story, Moll and Selvy watching *The Great Dictator*), is promised the most terrible father in the West *actually doing it.* But what Moll and Lightborne eventually see is not the *literal* primal scene for which they and the reader have been prepared. Rather, they encounter something supremely disappointing, at least in the realm of pornographic expectation.

Perhaps, though, they learn or relearn one of the profound lessons of post-Freudian psychoanalysis. Lacan, after all, shows us in numerous ways that the "primal" is inaccessible. We can see only the signifiers of that from which we are ultimately barred by the very mechanisms of representation. That the film contains only Hitler dressed up as Charlie Chaplin (a weak parody of Chaplin's own prior charade in *The Great Dictator*) drives home the Lacanian premise— we seek in vain after originals infinitely removed or deferred along the signifying chain. It is the same with perceptions of identity, the original self, because "the *moi,*" as Ragland-Sullivan explains, "is a dialectical project of becoming, a suspension, a set of signifying potentials, which never ceases to displace Desire along an endless chain in the incomplete story of identity."[18] According to Lacan, it is desire that drives us—desire to know ourselves, desire to return to the pure *jouissance* of pre-Symbolic life. But our understanding of these precepts must, in DeLillo, accommodate desire for the supremely erotic or pornographic image, desire for a more conventionally orgasmic *jouissance*— even though, as old roués know, every such image presently palls, and one can never close the gap that frames and generates desire.

Part Two **"Before everything, there's language"**

5   *Timor Mortis Conturbat Me*   *White Noise*

White Noise has generated more critical attention than any other DeLillo novel (unless one considers the journalistic reception of *Underworld*). The author's most engaging and accessible work, *White Noise* appears on many syllabi, and it has already joined *Dubliners, A Portrait of the Artist As a Young Man,* and *Sons and Lovers* in the small but elegant collection of casebooks published by Viking/ Penguin. As Mark Osteen points out in the introduction to *"White Noise": Text and Criticism,* responses to this novel—those of John Frow, John Duvall, Leonard Wilcox, and, to some extent, Osteen himself—have variously engaged the author's critique of image culture and consumer capitalism as fostered by televisual simulacra. In interesting contrast to these culturalist analyses have been the tentative (or not so tentative) arguments—advanced by such critics as Paul Maltby, Lou F. Caton, and Joseph Dewey—regarding what are represented as the novel's "neo-Romantic" or sublime or religious elements. At the same time, nearly all discussions of the book—including the present one, as will be seen—involve some continuation of Tom LeClair's project of gauging its postmodern or "systems" reflexivity, as well as consideration of DeLillo's desire to conceptualize language in terms other than those implicit in his own deft mimicry of cliché, jargon, and media-speak.[1]

Cornel Bonca has argued cogently against interpretations that stress the primacy of image culture and the absconding signified. Bonca characterizes "DeLillo's attitude toward the world of his novel" as "generous-spirited; it is not so much that he is uncritical toward a mass consumer society as that he has attempted to complicate the stiff categories of ideological or cultural critique. The novel does not 'celebrate' the white noise of advertising and mass media—of course not. But it realizes that it is in that noise that our terrors and longings can be read." DeLillo, he says, "appears to see language as a massive human strategy to cope with mortality."[2]

If there is a problem with Bonca's reasoning it may be that he too readily allows the category "white noise" to subsume language—not just the oppressive or sterile language of the marketplace (which one concedes readily enough) but *all* language, defined as a kind of reflexive, intra-species buzzing that "emerges from a definable though mysterious source—the human terror of death."[3] This view strikes one as illiberal, and Bonca's conclusion sorts poorly with one's sense that when language descends into white noise it becomes language betrayed, deflected from its proper end. DeLillo sees language as the great model of discrimination and difference—the embodiment of a complex system of communication that is unique to humans. Thus language remains for this artist a major concern and almost, at times, the supreme criterion of human value. In *White Noise* it subsumes every metaphorical economy—whether one speaks of "the natural language of the culture," "the language of economic class," "the natural language of the species," or "the language of waves and particles, or how the dead speak to the living."[4] The metaphor extends to language imbricated, as German is said to be, in "deathly power" (31) and to "the other-worldly babble of the American family" (101). Stretched, it extends to the imagining of death as a purely sonic phenomenon, final collapse of the differentiation that characterizes language:

> "What if death is nothing but sound?"
> "Electrical noise."
> "You hear it forever. Sound all around. How awful."
> "Uniform, white." (198)

Nor must one forget the constant example of DeLillo's own performative prose, which from sentence to sentence resists the summons to homogeneity, the blandishments of blandness. The prose gives the lie to every reductive thing one can say about language.

Still, Bonca obliges recognition of a painful truth: in the present novel, emphasizing language traduced, DeLillo finds less latitude for what Arthur M. Saltzman calls a "vision of the abiding, empowering mystery of language."[5] Like Saltzman or Nicoletta Pireddu I am not convinced by the argument that Jack Gladney experiences real "transcendence" when he hears Steffie murmuring "*Toyota Celica*" in her sleep (155).[6] The transcendence is merely what Freud disparaged as "oceanic"—as it is when, shooting Willie Mink, Jack declares: "I saw beyond words" (312). The same reticence figures throughout the narrative: at no point is the reader invited to find redemptive the mysteries of German, say, or the babbling of infants. The one infant here, Wilder, may be protected by his innocence, but that innocence does not seem rooted, as Joseph Dewey argues, in his embryonic relation to language.[7] Nor does Arnold Weinstein have it quite right when, commenting on "Wilder's marathon crying jag," he observes: "DeLillo reveres that ultimate opaque language . . . prior to all codes and grammars."[8] This is true enough about DeLillo in a general way, but I do not think the point is really illustrated by Wilder's inarticulate misery. The fact is that language emerges from sonic disorder and can return whence it came. To the extent that it approaches the condition of white noise, language fails to impede what Horst Ruthrof calls "the decline of concept formation."[9] Less abstractly, it participates in an economy of death, a poetics of *timor mortis*.

Although critics have addressed the theme of death in this novel, they have not, I think, paid sufficient mind to its realization in purely sonic terms. DeLillo develops a vision of progressive or incremental breakdown of aural discrimination—a vision that transcends its initially metaphorical status. This aural vision (if one may be allowed the oxymoron) can be profitably juxtaposed to and illuminated by a sound-oriented theory of multiplicity advanced by Michel Serres. Though not translated until 1995, Serres's *Genesis* (1982) derives from the same decade as *White Noise* (1985). As usual I do not argue any actual awareness of this book on DeLillo's part—only the affinity of two lyrical, metaphysically ambitious performances. But before discussing these matters— Serres's cosmology of sound, the foregrounding, in *White Noise*, of aural and linguistic elements expressive of *timor mortis*—I propose to introduce this most deft of DeLillo's novels by quoting at length, in the manner of Erich Auerbach, from one of its central passages. By invoking the author of *Mimesis*, incidentally, I mean to suggest that the postmodern crisis of representation, with which DeLillo is commonly thought to be involved, must be recognized as a late chapter or postscript to that history and theory of the mimetic imperative to which Auerbach made so signal a contribution. For all our poststructuralist or Lyotardian handwringing over the allegedly unrepresentable, we continue to struggle with representation and its discontents.

In his description of the Gladney garbage, the author invites the reader to encounter what lies beneath the colorful surfaces of American consumption:

> No one was around. I walked across the kitchen, opened the compactor drawer and looked inside the trash bag. An oozing cube of semi-mangled cans, clothes hangers, animal bones and other refuse. The bottles were broken, the cartons flat. Product colors were undiminished in brightness and intensity. Fats, juices and heavy sludges seeped through layers of pressed vegetable matter. I felt like an archaeologist about to sift through a finding of tool fragments and assorted cave trash. . . .
>
> I unfolded the bag cuffs, released the latch and lifted out the bag. The full stench hit me with shocking force. Was this ours? Did it belong to us? Had we created it? I took the bag out to the garage and emptied it. The compressed bulk sat there like an ironic modern sculpture, massive, squat, mocking. I jabbed at it with the butt end of a rake and then spread the material over the concrete floor. I picked through it item by item, mass by shapeless mass, wondering why I felt guilty, a violator of privacy, uncovering intimate and perhaps shameful secrets. It was hard not to be distracted by some of the things they'd chosen to submit to the Juggernaut appliance. But why did I feel like a household spy? Is garbage so private? Does it glow at the core with personal heat, with signs of one's deepest nature, clues to secret yearnings, humiliating flaws? What habits, fetishes, addictions, inclinations? What solitary acts, behavioral ruts? I found crayon drawings of a figure with full breasts and male genitals. There was a long piece of twine that contained a series of knots and loops. It seemed at first a random construction. Looking more closely I thought I detected a complex relationship between the size of the loops, the degree of the knots (single or double) and the intervals between knots with loops and freestanding knots. Some kind of occult geometry or symbolic festoon of obsessions. I found a banana skin with a tampon inside. Was this the dark underside of consumer consciousness? I came across a horrible clotted mass of hair, soap, ear swabs, crushed roaches, flip-top rings, sterile pads smeared with pus and bacon fat, strands of frayed dental floss, fragments of ballpoint refills, toothpicks still displaying bits of impaled food. There was a pair of shredded undershorts with lipstick markings, perhaps a memento of the Grayview Motel. (258–59)

In that this passage at once recapitulates and anticipates DeLillo's other work, one discovers in it a kind of grammar of the author's motifs, a language that operates by the constantly varied deployment of recombinant elements: words, images, mythemes, characteristic locutions and structures. There is more here, in other words, than such artful rhetorical flourishes as paratactic chiasmus ("What habits, fetishes, addictions, inclinations?"), parallelism

("What solitary acts, behavioral ruts?"), and the catalog ("hair, soap, ear swabs, crushed roaches," etc.). Like the famous page of *Finnegans Wake* in which Joyce puns on the title of each story in *Dubliners,* this passage invites recognition of numerous DeLillo paratexts, from the general—the characteristic verbless sentences, the anatomizing of "consumer consciousness," the obligatory motel reference—to the specific: that "ironic modern sculpture," for example, calls to mind the pieces like "carefully crafted afterbirth" in the studio of Sullivan, the artist friend of David Bell in *Americana,* [10] not to mention the treatment of cast-off B-52s as *objets trouvés* in *Underworld,* another book about adultery and waste (including nuclear waste, which really does "glow at the core"). The archaeological image here has its congeners in *Great Jones Street, The Names,* and *Ratner's Star* (a book, by the way, that foregrounds "obsessions" and "occult geometry"—including the geometry of occultation itself). Similarly, Jack Gladney's involvement with garbage reminds one of the neighbor, in *Americana,* who leaves his excess trash outside David Bell's door—or of Lee Oswald's midnight forays with the household trash in *Libra* (where Win Everett, noting the "tendency of plots to move toward death," [11] echoes the narrator of *White Noise,* who declares: "All plots tend to move deathward" [26]). The knotted twine here also links Gladney to Oswald, and one recalls Gary Harkness's self-characterization, in *End Zone,* as "a piece of string that does not wish to be knotted" (13). Jack's attempts to "read" the knots resemble those of Nicholas Branch, *Libra*'s fictional CIA historian. Like Oswald, whose effects included similar bits of knotted string (the Warren Commission's attention to such detail fascinates DeLillo), Jack Gladney will prove capable of highly calculated violence. As pharmaceutical grail, moreover, the Dylar that Jack seeks resembles the mystery drug developed by the government and stolen by Happy Valley in *Great Jones Street.* It has another counterpart, of course, in the mystery tapes of that novel, not to mention the Hitler film of *Running Dog,* the baseball of *Underworld,* the code that will explain the supposedly extraterrestrial message in *Ratner's Star,* or the rationale behind the cult in *The Names.*

Characterizing garbage as household ordure, the author re-stages, finally, the encounter of *End Zone*'s Gary Harkness with that pile of feces in the desert surrounding Logos College. Harkness recognizes an emblem of the mortality that so exercises Jack Gladney: "final matter voided, the chemical stink of self discontinued." [12] How ironic, then, Babette's concealing of her Dylar tablets in the bathroom—or Jack's searching for them in the contents of that technological cloaca, the trash compactor. Each undertakes a desperate act of deconstruction, attempting to construe or hoping to discover an aporia—Dylar—in the place of excremental death, the dominion of final absence. Unlike Gary Harkness, who recognizes in "simple shit . . . the one thing that did not betray its definition,"[13] Jack actively mythologizes his own stool sample, imagining that "technicians" will examine this "daub of the most solemn waste of all . . . with the mingled deference, awe and dread we have come to associate with exotic religions of the world" (275). In excrement, that is, one sees an earnest of the mortality that spawns religion. Yet ultimately Jack quails before the message of waste: he and his family generate it and will presently join it.

DeLillo's description of the Gladney trash exhibits a power that derives from what one might call its fecalization of consumer culture. Murray Jay Siskind, entering the supermarket from which much of the Gladney trash comes, remarks that "everything is concealed in symbolism, hidden by veils of mystery and layers of cultural material" (37). But where does one find the symbolic referents, and what is here at the "core"? Only more signs, signifiers endlessly deferring their signifieds. If one strips away a bright yellow signifier, the banana skin, for example, one finds only another piece of consumer trash—itself a deceptive signifier. Inside the male sign, the deconstructing female sign, a tampon, functioning phallically. No center, no presence, no sense. Underneath all the surfaces of contemporary life, there is only this infinite withdrawal of presence and meaning. The images illustrate both the vacuousness of our culture and the terrifying void endlessly rehearsed by contemporary linguistic epistemology.

Looking for Dylar, Jack finds only the detritus of lives lived and exhausted on the way to death. Like Yossarian with the disemboweled Snowden in *Catch-22*, he discovers the proximity of living, breathing body to garbage. In some sense Jack finds himself in the waste that he and his family "submit to the Juggernaut appliance." DeLillo compares the trash compactor to the great wheeled vehicle under which devotees of the Hindu deity Jagannath (avatar of Krishna, avatar of Vishnu, "Lord of the World") were once thought to fling themselves. But a Juggernaut is at once a "massive inexorable force that advances irresistibly, crushing whatever is in its path" *(Webster's New Collegiate Dictionary)*, and that which "draws blind and destructive devotion, or to which people are ruthlessly sacrificed, such as a belief or institution" *(American Heritage)*. As will become clearer in *Underworld*, the true Juggernaut is the trash itself, as well as the economic system and the cultural imperatives that generate it.

Who Shall Deliver Me?

In a grim catalog of the classes of people death will not spare, the medieval poet William Dunbar includes intellectuals: "He spairis," Dunbar notes, "Na clerk for his intelligence" (lines 33–34).[14] *White Noise* concerns an academic (as the twentieth century styles its clerks) who wears a "medieval robe" (9) and grapples with the fear of death—his own and that of his wife. In effect, Jack Gladney echoes Dunbar's refrain—"Timor mortis conturbat me"—and Saint Paul's rhetorical question: "Who shall deliver me from the body of this death?" (Rom. 6.24). The Dunbar poem concludes with an exhortation congenial to an age of faith:

> Sen for the deid remeid is none,
> Best is that we for dede dispone. (lines 97–98)

Unfortunately, the world seems to have lost all clues regarding ways to "dispone"—to arrange, that is—for death.

Hardly an exemplar of the life of the mind, Jack is a caricature of the contemporary intellectual. His home base, College-on-the-Hill, is an institution of higher learning at which the educators focus on popular culture or on science and technology, and no one studies a past older than half a century. The reader encounters full professors who, as Murray notes, read nothing but cereal boxes. Murray himself lectures on Elvis and car crashes. Jack chairs the Department of Hitler Studies, which he founded, and one imagines that this program, focusing on a period going back five whole decades, is widely perceived to be profoundly historical.[15]

Yet Jack, however tainted by the shallowness of his milieu, is something of a thinker and so comes to "what we eventually confront if we think long enough and hard enough," as DeLillo remarks in an interview.[16] What we eventually confront is death, a subject that DeLillo incorporates in ways that modulate from the direct and explicit to the subtle and nuanced. In the most seemingly inconsequential locutions, in fact, DeLillo gestures toward his terrible theme. In the transports of self-realization through shopping, for example, Jack remarks, "Brightness settled around me" (84), unconsciously echoing a famous line from Thomas Nashe's poem "In Time of Pestilence":

> Brightness falls from the air;
> Queens have died young and fair;
> Dust hath closed Helen's eye,
> I am sick, I must die.
> Lord, have mercy on us.[17]

Set in a new time of pestilence, *White Noise* concerns a latter-day plague, a mental and spiritual wasting, the affliction of a godless age, an age disarmed of virtually all spiritual weapons in the struggle with mortality.

DeLillo has confirmed that one of the influences on *White Noise* was *The Denial of Death,* the 1973 book whose author, Ernest Becker, not only discusses a culture-wide failure to come to terms with death (since we no longer have the spiritual wherewithal to keep it at bay) but also argues that our dread is the powerful motivating force within modern culture.[18] Thus one of the titles DeLillo considered for his novel was "The American Book of the Dead," for death is the novel's subject and theme, and its characters discuss the Egyptian Book of the Dead, the Tibetan Book of the Dead, and the Mexican Day of the Dead. They are also exposed to a veritable cloud of death, the Airborne Toxic Event, whose treatment in the media, DeLillo observes, "resembled a national promotion for death, a multimillion-dollar campaign backed by radio spots, heavy print and billboard, TV saturation" (158).

White Noise, then, is about the fear of death in a world that offers more and more insidious ways to die—and fewer and fewer structures conducive to the acceptance of death. Such structures traditionally figure in religion, but the twentieth century manages little in the way of spiritual vision. Although the Gladneys observe Christmas after a fashion (on a trip to the mall, Jack invites the children to go ahead and pick out their presents), although Babette describes herself (in the Kierkegaardian formula of religious despair) as "sick unto death" (263), and although Tibetan and Hindu practices are briefly glanced at, the Gladneys never even consider the possibility of religious comfort. In the Gladney environment one phrase hovers unvoiced amid the triadic advertising references that punctuate the narrative: "The Airport Marriott, the Downtown Travelodge, the Sheraton Inn and Conference Center" (15); "Dacron, Orlon, Lycra Spandex" (52); "MasterCard, Visa, American Express" (100); "Krylon, Rust-Oleum, Red Devil" (159), "Leaded, unleaded, super unleaded" (199), and so forth. Whether these phrases emerge from a speaker somewhere or simply figure as the Brownian motion of Jack's mind, the vitality of all the familiar, highly advertised trade names makes all the more poignant the desuetude of that once-ultimate trinity, the three-personed God.

Though it offers nothing for *timor mortis,* the world offers an abundance of systems and structures that promise to confound mortality and deliver fulfillment. These structures are the products of a culture dominated by advertising, dubious politics, suspicions of conspiracy, and accelerating developments in technology and science, which become more terrifying as, addicted, the world discovers the trade-off between, on the one hand, environmental havoc and, on the other, convenience and mastery over our environment and our everyday lives. Mark Conroy observes that "throughout the novel, DeLillo charts a recursive movement whereby the large, impersonal forces of technology first produce death-dealing consequences and then offer themselves as palliatives to the fear of death they have aroused."[19] Technology, then, "the daily seeping falsehearted death" (22), delivers more and more temptations to squander our terrestrial birthright. "This is the whole point of technology," says the delphic Murray. "It creates an appetite for immortality on the one hand. It threatens universal extinction on the other. Technology is lust removed from nature" (285). In the *Paris Review* interview, DeLillo notes "a certain equation" in *White Noise* between technology and fear: "As technology advances in complexity and scope, fear becomes more primitive." [20] One recognizes an idea also articulated by Mailer's Stephen Rojack:

> To the savage, dread was the natural result of any invasion of the supernatural: if man wished to steal the secrets of the gods, it was only to be supposed that the gods would defend themselves and destroy whichever man came too close. By this logic, civilization is the successful if imperfect theft of some cluster of these secrets, and the price we have paid is to accelerate our private sense of some enormous if not quite definable disaster which awaits us.[21]

Rojack's "not inconsiderable thesis that magic, dread, and the perception of death were the roots of motivation"[22] may similarly lie behind Murray's declaration: "I want to immerse myself in American magic and dread" (19).

American dream. *American* magic and dread. Like Mailer, DeLillo insists on the Americanness of his subject, specifically the "American forces and energies" that "belong to our time."[23] But he is by no means unaware that these energies have an historical context, and in the name of the institution that employs Jack, College-on-the-Hill, DeLillo echoes a figure with particular American associations. Important to American history and literature, Christ's phrase about public virtue—it is like the light not hidden under a bushel or the city on a hill (Matt. 5.14)—was invoked by such American originals as Peter Bulkeley and the John Winthrop who, in his 1630 sermon on board the *Arbella*, used it to describe the shining example that America would become:

> For wee must Consider that wee shall be as a Citty vpon a Hill, the eies of all people are vppon vs; soe that if wee shall deale falsely with our god in this worke wee haue vndertaken, and soe cause him to withdrawe his present help from vs, wee shall be made a story and a by-word through the world.[24]

American culture, says DeLillo, remains on its hill, but God's countenance has been withdrawn—or perhaps simply petrified by the gorgon face of secularism and superstition.

At College-on-the-Hill, in any event, the "American magic and dread" have moved one particular faculty member to seek spiritual refuge in a bizarre way. Founding the Department of Hitler Studies, Jack attempts to "mithridatize" (to borrow a term from Michel Serres) his anxiety about death. As Murray tells Jack, Hitler and the Nazis made of death a vast enterprise and so might seem paradoxically to offer shelter from the individual's immediate mortality (287). As the physician introduces discreet quanta of some weakened pathogen into the body to stimulate its immune system, so will Jack, in a professional embrace of the chief death merchant of his age, promote his own resistance to *timor mortis*. But Jack's attempt at philosophical inoculation fails conspicuously to armor the mental immune system.

Nor is this the only failure of the homeopathic premise. Jack's exposure to the Airborne Toxic Event, a literal inoculation with death, might be expected to stimulate his body's defenses, but physicians detect no such benign effect. The mechanics of inoculation go awry, Jack is obscurely infected, his fear comes more fully into the open, the anxiety metastasizes. (One notes in passing that DeLillo leaves to his reader the working-out of the disaster's acronym and its symbolism: in Greek mythology ATE is the goddess of discord, sister of Fear, Panic, Terror, and Trembling).

But as an E. M. Forster character remarks, "Death destroys a man: the idea of Death saves him." [25] Among other things it drives humanity to art, as artists from Keats to Malraux to John Gardner have asseverated. Whitman, too, testifies to the artistic capital to be found in the contemplation of death. In "Out of the Cradle Endlessly Rocking," for example, Whitman describes his calling to poetry as grounded in moments of intense empathy with the mournful song of a bereaved bird. In a single word, spoken out of the vasty deep, Whitman discovers the heart of the poetic mystery, and it summons him to moral growth, adulthood—and art:

> the sea,
> Delaying not, hurrying not,
> Whisper'd me through the night, and very plainly before daybreak,
> Lisp'd to me the low and delicious word death,
> And again death, death, death, death,
> Hissing melodious, neither like the bird nor like my arous'd child's heart,
> But edging near as privately for me rustling at my feet,
> Creeping thence steadily up to my ears and laving me softly all over,
> Death, death, death, death, death. [26]

Hitler, says Jack, enthralled crowds with words emanating from something like Whitman's sea; Hitler's "language," that is, "came from some vastness beyond the world" (72). When Jack tells his students about what drew the crowds to Hitler, he passes on, with similar "whisper'd" intensity, the insight of Whitman: "Let me whisper the terrible word, from the Old English, from the Old German, from the Old Norse. *Death*" (73).

In contradistinction to the Hitler who made of death the centerpiece of his legacy—or the Jack and Babette who are simply overwhelmed by the stark fact of mortality, a Whitman or a DeLillo makes of death the occasion of his art. Each embraces, with the Wallace Stevens of "Sunday Morning," the precept that "death is the mother of beauty." Indeed, Whitman's epiphany about death is juxtaposed to an image of the rocking cradle, for death's strange sibling is birth. Thus the poet characterizes "the word up from the waves" as "the key"—the key in which he sings and the key to "all songs." DeLillo, on the other hand, exposes this affirmation to the greater ambiguity of his age. Winnie Richards presents Jack with a version of the Stevensian idea: "I think it's a mistake to lose one's sense of death, even one's fear of death. Isn't death the boundary we need? Doesn't it give a precious texture to life, a sense of definition?" (228). But Jack himself, in a later conversation with Murray emphatically demolishes her argument: "What good is a preciousness based on fear and anxiety?" (284).

The book ends, nonetheless, on a note of something other than despair—or so argues Ellen Pifer in a reading of the mysterious sequence in which Wilder peddles his tricycle across a busy highway. One of the most acute readers of this episode, Pifer sees it as focusing on and emphasizing the "communal effort" to deliver the child from calamity.[27] But insofar as every such DeLillo set piece is replete with ambiguity (as Pifer also notes) one need not view this one as wholly positive. Wilder escapes motorists symbolically associated with the swarming, baleful dead: "There is an expressway beyond the backyard now," Jack observes at the beginning of his narrative, and it impinges as "a remote and steady murmur around our sleep, as of dead souls babbling at the edge of a dream" (4). One can read Wilder's transit, then, as a metaphor for the precarious and doomed passage of the living among the dead, whose great congress they must eventually join. "In *White Noise*," observes Paula Bryant, "everyone is under ambiguous death sentence, as we are in life itself."[28] Wilder's deliverance is temporary.

His adventure, ostensibly a picture of childhood insouciance in the face of death, is really the ironically negative index of just how far into the dread those fully initiated into *timor mortis*—Wilder's parents, for example—have strayed. The Gladneys, senior, are immersed in dread and neurosis. Others, older than they and in need of Babette's classes in walking and eating or her readings from the tabloids, are even more pathetic. But Wilder's older siblings seem to be at home with randomness, contingency, technology, quantum mechanics, relativity, waves, particles, radiation, chaos, and the routineness of disaster. If the Gladney children, even as they gain in consciousness and sophistication, seem unconsciously convinced of their own immortality, Wilder remains, as infant, the true standard of insouciance. Like the mongrel Jack imagines outside the tent of Attila the Hun (100), Wilder "doesn't know he's going to die." Murray, who makes this point, suggests that simple ignorance of death confers enchantment on Wilder's childhood (one recognizes, again, an echo of Whitman, who dates the end of his own childhood from the understanding of mortality that came to him as mournful birdsong). In noting Wilder's "exemption from harm" (289), Murray overstates the literal benefit of nescience, but he hints at the old folk conviction that some providence looks out for children and fools. Like little Wallstreet Snopes walking untouched amid the melee of spotted horses in Faulkner's *The Hamlet,* Wilder survives immersion in a stream of potential violence, the stream of traffic that contributes its own white noise to the Gladney environment.[29]

Murray characterizes Wilder in his innocence as "a cloud of unknowing" (290), a figure that originates as the title of a treatise by an anonymous fourteenth-century English mystic (Eliot invokes this work in "Little Gidding," and the troubled Nick Shay, in *Underworld,* finds himself musing on it, too). The treatise offers counsel on how to come closer to God (wholly other and unknowable by normal sensory means) through contemplation and mystical discipline. Rhetorically, the figure of the cloud exhibits an obscurity befitting what it describes: the "darkness" between God and the soul. "When you first begin" the life of mystical contemplation, says the author, "you find only darkness, and as it were a cloud of unknowing. . . . Do what you will, this darkness and this cloud remain between you and God, and stop you . . . from seeing him in the clear light of rational understanding." And this, of course, is the point: the human intellect is inadequate to the apprehension of God. Thus "if you are to feel him or to see him in this life, it must always be in this cloud, in this darkness."[30]

Babette wishes desperately that Wilder might stay his present age forever. Jack recognizes in him something immensely appealing, an earnest of something he cannot quite put a name to. "You want to get close to him, touch him, look at him, breathe him in," Murray notes (289–90). Whether one calls it the infinite or simply exemption from the fear of death, Wilder is the cloud through which Jack and Babette intuit something for which they experience— to use the word favored by the author of *The Cloud of Unknowing*—a tremendous "longing." The calamity they fear is Wilder's growing up, surrendering the ignorance of mortality that is a form of immortality and losing touch with whatever intimations of transcendence small children enjoy. They know to their sorrow that Wilder will inevitably become heir to their own adult anxiety, their sickness unto death, and their inability even to imagine a "cloud" other than the toxic one that pursues them—or the cloudlike "nebulous mass" detectable in Jack's body (280).

Before the Butterfly Wing

Michel Serres's theory of multiplicity speaks to DeLillo's novel at a number of points, for the death Jack fears is the relapse into the unfocussed random within which, in the beginning, consciousness coalesces. "We start our lives in chaos, in babble," Murray tells him. "As we surge up into the world, we try to devise a shape, a plan" (291). Imagining genesis, Serres, too, invokes a primal chaos and emergent order: "In the beginning," he writes, "is the echo," a fluctuation in the multiple, "the very first seeding upon the cloud or the white noise." [31] This *Urstoff* is a cloud of unknowing, too, for it marks the boundary of consciousness and the discrimination it enables. Moreover, like the medieval mystic, Serres strives to embrace and celebrate the primal chaos out of which differentiation emerges and into which it relapses.

Though fond of the word *fractal,* Serres is only obliquely engaged with chaos theory (which actually concerns especially subtle forms of order). Serres undertakes to rescue the idea of chaos from its imprisonment in the equivocal lexicon favored by theorists of butterfly wings and fractal geometry. In his own estimation, he undertakes to define "a new object for philosophy" (2), to wit, the true formlessness that provides the background to all that the human mind conceptualizes or rationalizes. For this matrix, this ground of multiplicity, he favors aural figurations, shifting between two terms—in French, *bruit* and *noise,* which his translators render as the same word with and without italics: "noise" and "*noise*" (the first referring to actual sonic disorder, the second to other, more generalized forms of chaos or discord). Serres undertakes a freeform meditation on what he characterizes as the "background noise" of existence: "the ground of our perception" (7), the "permanent . . . ground of the world, the backdrop of the universe, the background of being, maybe" (62). This white noise is at once literal sound and, metaphorically, the tumble of chaotic, thalassic matter that overwhelms the human mind, obliges it to isolate and conceptualize some momentarily salient element.

Serres would say that white noise, the great tide of multiplicity, threatens to overwhelm the "concepts" by which Jack Gladney keeps his terror of mortality at bay. "The noise, gray deep and breeze that breathes, the noise, the surge, is a multiplicity of which we do not know the sum. We do not know how to integrate it in a sound, a sense, a harmony, we do not have a concept for it" (67). By the generic term "concept" Serres means any rationalistic construct that comforts us by affording a handle with which to heft the package of multiplicity. The concept is always, fundamentally, a betrayal of that terrible, "un-differentiated" reality (34). "A concept is a multiple reduced to the unitary" (108). Repeatedly, Serres characterizes it as rearing up out of the primeval chaos like a pyramid—a monumental tomb.

> What terrifies is not the meaning of the noise—the thing spoken, forspoken—but the increasing multiplicity that says it. Fear comes from the swarming, the tide, the dread multiplies like flies, knowledge through concepts regiments this nauseous herd under the pure generality of the one. The concept is reassuring at first, it represses the press of the crowd. Rationality was born of this terror.
>
> Rationality buries empiricism alive. (66–67)

Yet Serres is not so naive as to imagine that the multiple might remain our sustained focus: "We must think on the side of the thinkable. . . . We must tack toward science, toward the same, toward the one and stability, but . . . we must then be ready to think the unthinkable . . . We must then change our tack, toward the pure multiple, we are continually tacking back and forth, the method being a fractal meander, to one side for safety, to the other for freedom" (114). Like Kant, who "tries to reconcile Democritus and Newton, the knowledge of chaos with the order of the diamond" (137), Serres "propose[s] the hypothesis . . . that the universe vibrates between the one and the other" (130).

Among other things, Serres notes how power misrepresents itself vis-à-vis the primal chaos. "It would seem that power has the role and function of making people believe that both concept and reason, closure and domination exist, where there is only ever pure multiplicity without any unity" (126). Such an assertion complements Murray's suggestion that Jack, founder of Hitler Studies, is drawn to the world's most notorious totalitarian because he could marshal so much of the world's death-dealing, thereby perhaps drawing its sting for those who, no longer actually oppressed by fascism, go in dread of the mortal relapse into the state of non-differentiation, the death that is another name for chaos. Jack is postmodern, educated humanity, wanting to see the great pyramid, reason, but less and less able to deny the ultimate supremacy of the undifferentiated multiple, the foul matrix one surrenders to—reenters— at death.

DeLillo represents the foul matrix that threatens Jack as the proliferation, this side of the grave, of white noise, the "panasonic" mixture of undifferentiated frequencies one hears between stations or at either end of the radio dial (241). As Arnold Weinstein observes, "'Panasonic' was an earlier working title for this novel, and DeLillo has actually embodied this sense of an all-pervasive sound scheme, strangely analogous to what Melville was after visually in his meditation on the whiteness of the whale: a scaled picture of tiny space occupied by humans in the larger spectrum of noise and image made audible or visible or imaginable by the text's semiotic strategy."[32] A kind of chaos, an absence of meaningful differentiation, the sonic equivalent of entropy and heat death, white noise is what Bucky Wunderlick, in *Great Jones Street*, calls "music of a dead universe."[33] It figures in the hum and buzz of contemporary life, in malls, supermarkets, and other public places, and especially in the constant sound of the appliances that proliferate all around us: refrigerator, microwave, washing machine, dryer, dishwasher, stereo, radio, and, of course, supreme in its ubiquity, the television.

Hence the disembodied voices that make their way into the story:

Meanwhile here is a quick and attractive lemon garnish suitable for any sea food. (178)

A California think-tank says the next world war may be fought over salt. (226)

In the four-hundred-thousand-dollar Nabisco Dinah Shore. (239)

And so forth. These phrases, like the "trilog lists" Patti White calls "a sort of narrative toxin,"[34] are white noise in the brain. Though employed with considerable economy, this touch implies that the Gladneys and their fellow Americans are perpetually surrounded by a fatiguing glut of noise and advertising and information. This aural clutter threatens to shape the human mind in its own image.

Indeed, this is precisely what happens to Jack's nemesis, Willie Mink, whose speech, colonized by phrases and bits from the media, functions as a *stretto* recapitulation of the more spaced tags from TV and advertising that have figured previously in Jack's narrative. He is, as N. Katherine Hayles observes, "information personified."[35] When Jack walks in on him, however, Willie Mink is watching TV without the sound, surrounded by faint white noise. Like the actor who plays the TV in *The Day Room*, he provides his own sound, for he has reached the point at which audible words pose a bizarre threat. His mind scrambled by Dylar addiction, Willie Mink suffers from another of DeLillo's endlessly imaginative (and suggestive) language states. He cannot differentiate words from what they describe. If Dylar worked, of course, he would be, like the character in the Peter Weir film *Fearless,* completely exempt from *timor mortis.* But Jack has only to speak words denoting mortal danger—"hail of bullets," "fusillade" (311)—to reduce Willie to abject, floor-crawling terror.

This imagined condition parodies the referentiality that has become so problematic for postmodernist thinkers. Willie's affliction comically exemplifies the poststructuralist assertion that language shapes reality, rather than merely labeling it. Language has, among other properties, the uncanny ability to say the thing which is not, to participate in the constructing of hypothetical realities that are sometimes ontologically potent, sometimes merely verbal, and sometimes both. "The Germans are gone," one learns, from the "section in Iron City called Germantown" (301). Presently, however, one encounters a group of German nuns who do in fact live and work there.

The nuns ostensibly signify, for a secular world, the possibility of belief. One recalls that Bucky Wunderlick, in *Great Jones Street*, wants a nun when his girlfriend Opel dies: "perhaps of German descent, someone who believed in the sacredness of dying and the veneration of the dead."[36] But the nuns of *White Noise* are not believers. In a "world . . . full of abandoned meanings" (184), they exist to provide a teasing intimation of an ultimate, a transcendental signified that, on examination, dissolves into just another mirror trick. "DeLillo gives us another perfect postmodern moment," observes Paul Cantor: the nun as "simulacrum of religious faith."[37] One notes, that is, a fresh turn on the familiar modernist crisis of belief. In the modernist paradigm, various spiritual props having given way, the individual finds faith impossible. But in Jack Gladney's experience with the nuns DeLillo deconstructs the very *representation* of belief. The author toys with a naive equation: we believe that the nuns believe. The nuns are the signifiers of a divine signified. But in fact the nuns believe only that we must believe they believe: a circularity, which is the circularity, the infinite deferral, of language itself.

In this scene the story comes full circle, as it were, from the visit Jack and Murray make at the outset to "the most photographed barn in America." The barn itself is preceded by "signs" for the barn: "We counted five signs before we reached the site." But "once you've seen the signs about the barn, it becomes impossible to see the barn" (12). Even though they understand the mechanism that precludes seeing, they cannot see the barn. Nor can the reader. "Significantly," remarks David Nye, "the passage . . . scarcely describes the barn itself, but deals with the organization of collective attention, specifying neither its color nor its architectural style."[38] In other words, DeLillo is self-conscious enough to signal to his readers that, like the other visitors to this site, they must not expect to *see* the barn. Readers experience the barn only through linguistic signs—which are not different from other signs supposedly expressive of reality.

Engaged in an act of "tourism," visitors to the most photographed barn in America experience it in the same way that the hypothetical "sightseer" of Walker Percy's essay "The Loss of the Creature" experiences the Grand Canyon:

"Instead of looking at it," says Percy, "he photographs it." Both Percy and DeLillo emphasize the traffic in postcards, slides, and pictures, the "taking pictures of taking pictures" (DeLillo 13). "What was the barn like before it was photographed?" Murray wonders. "We can't answer . . . because we've read the signs, seen the people snapping the pictures" (13). Percy asks much the same question about the Grand Canyon:

> Why is it almost impossible to gaze directly at the Grand Canyon under these circumstances and see it for what it is—as one picks up a strange object from one's back yard and gazes directly at it? It is almost impossible because the Grand Canyon, the thing as it is, has been appropriated by the symbolic complex which has already been formed in the sightseer's mind. Seeing the canyon under approved circumstances is seeing the symbolic complex head on. The thing is no longer the thing as it confronted the Spaniard; it is rather that which has already been formulated—by picture postcard, geography book, tourist folders, and the words *Grand Canyon*. [39]

In that final phrase Percy identifies words, too, as part of the "symbolic complex," and though he lays ultimate emphasis on direct, essentialist, "creaturely" perception (that is, on experience not "packaged" by expectation), he is very much aware of post-Saussurean linguistics, where presence is precisely that which language can never capture or contain.

Like Percy, the author of *White Noise* draws attention to the way a touristic simulacrum renders an actual vista invisible, perhaps irrecoverable. Bertrand Gervais, noting that the most photographed barn in America figures in the most discussed passage in DeLillo, makes a witty observation about the similarity between touristic and critical response: at both levels the reproduction of an image begins to preclude one's seeing the thing itself. "The barn, already a symbol in the text, since its appearance in the novel is previously media-fied [*médiatisée*] by its situation and its interpretation, becomes doubly so by readings that make it yet more emblematic of language, of knowing." He characterizes the barn as "à la fois élément d'une fiction, argument d'une critique et application d'une théorie." [40]

But even without the fortuitous development of one passage into a locus classicus that can no longer be experienced directly (so shaped are perceptions by the clicking of critical shutters), the sequence with the barn introduces a text replete with parodies of the signifying chain and its chimerical first links: one sees them in the variations on SIMUVAC exercises, in the "tall old Moorish movie theater, now . . . a mosque" (89), in the band playing "live Muzak" (84), in the unsettling observation that "something lurked inside the truth" (8), and in the *déjà vu* phenomenon, in which one intuits a present sensation's phantom predecessor: "Is it possible to have a false perception of an illusion? Is there a true *déjà vu* and a false *déjà vu*?" (126). One notes, too, the numerous representations of television as a medium whose structures of signification are entirely "self-contained, self-referring" (51).

One sees perhaps the most overdetermined variation on this theme in the treatment of consumer packaging, especially in the supermarket, that definitive venue of white noise, the place that reveals the extent to which small-town and urban America are alike "awash" in advertising and media-shaped perceptions and appetites (36). The supermarket, a place where all is surface, where substance remains endlessly deferred, exemplifies postmodern reality. In the ubiquity of consumer enticement, John Frow suggests, DeLillo reveals a fundamental perversion of human values. The author links television and supermarket as the supremely important loci of a consumer economy. In his Marxist reading of the novel, Frow draws our attention to the passage in which Murray comments acerbically on how his students

> "are spinning out from the core, becoming less recognizable as a group, less target-able by advertisers and mass-producers of culture. Kids are a true universal. But you're well beyond that, already beginning to drift, to feel estranged from the products you consume. Who are they designed for? What is your place in the marketing scheme? Once you're out of school, it is only a matter of time before you experience the vast loneliness and dissatisfaction of consumers who have lost their group identity." Then I tap my pencil to indicate time passing ominously. (*White Noise* 50)

Frow argues that Murray, in these remarks, "is stating the central, the deadly serious principles of a capitalist society," in which "the marketing scheme really does work . . . as the scheme of things: the whole social organization is geared to this equation."[41] But this is to mistake a target of opportunity for the main mission. It is also to mistake Murray for a genuine sage (an error made by a number of critics).[42] His "old sexual injury" notwithstanding, Murray is no Tiresias (293). His pronouncements parody the glib cultural analyses already, by the mid-eighties, making their way into scholarly discourse. Not that DeLillo wields the satiric scalpel indiscriminately or without due consideration of his own romantic leanings—for Murray's remarks burlesque the same Wordsworthian or neo-Platonic intimations the author develops in, for example, *The Names* (Tap's spiritualized energy), in *Ratner's Star* (the principle of "more advanced the deeper we dig," not to mention the linguistic threshold that every infant crosses), and in the present novel (Wilder's mystical innocence). Murray stops short of describing his students as trailing clouds of glory, but he affirms that daily they must travel farther from the resplendent east of a stable and predictable consumer identity.

But in the last analysis one understands DeLillo less through Marx than through someone like the Allen Ginsberg of "A Supermarket in California" (to which the title of a Thomas Ferraro article on this book points us).[43] Though he is no friend to American materialism, Ginsberg declines to measure it against a Marxist vision of utopia. Rather, it is mortality itself that the consumer fails to take into account. Ginsberg cruises—innuendo intended—his supermarket and imagines Walt Whitman as fellow-shopper. Both are homosexual, both poets, both great cataloguers. But no catalog can contain the American material plenty symbolized by—no, contained in—the supermarket. Testing this vision of abundance against the ultimate mortal reality, Ginsberg anticipates DeLillo: "What America did you have when Charon quit poling his ferry and you got out on a smoking bank and stood watching the boat disappear on the black waters of Lethe?"[44]

For DeLillo, too, the supermarket becomes a memento mori. On one occasion Murray reflects on the hermetic isolation of the Tibetan death chamber and makes a droll connection with the similarly sealed-off quality of the American supermarket: "Here we don't die, we shop," notes Murray. "But the difference is less marked than you think" (38). Sliding doors are Murray's image of transition to death (36), and he more or less explicitly equates them with the sliding doors through which one enters that place of antiseptic, sterile, well-lit white noise, the supermarket. Here, in scene after scene, Jack Gladney immerses himself in "the ambient roar" (326) and struggles to integrate an endless stream of aural *disjecta membra,* language put into a blender and reduced to slurry: "Kleenex Softique, your truck's blocking the entrance" (36), "Leon, parsley" (19), "Kleenex Softique, Kleenex Softique" (39).

More than a postmodern death-fane, the supermarket and its serried voices resound with the mystery of Babel—which brings me, for the last time, to Michel Serres's meditation, in *Genesis,* on the relation of language to multiplicity. Serres, too, contemplates the myth of Babel, which he strives to represent in positive terms even as he simultaneously suggests that language masks a void. "No logos without noise," he declares (7). "Before language, before even the word, the noise" (54). To be "immersed in the noise of the tongues" (127), however, is to reencounter, as *sound,* the mystery of being. "Babel is not a failure, it is at that very moment when the tower is dismantled that we begin to understand that one must understand without concepts" (123). In the end, seeing language as merely the temporary interruption of the primal state, Serres may go further than DeLillo, who seems to cherish an idea of the linguistic sublime. But DeLillo's hapless character, Jack Gladney, might well agree with Serres that just as white noise, the chaos of "un-differentiation" (Serres 34), is the beginning or genesis of all things, so is it their likely end.

Like a great symphony, DeLillo's novel ends with a triple coda: Wilder's tricycle ride, the contemplation of sunsets previously upgraded from "modern" to "postmodern" (61, 227), and—the true cadence—a last visit to the supermarket. I have already suggested that Wilder's ride is a symbolically minimalist life journey; and of the elegiac family contemplation at "the overpass" (324) one need only note Thomas Peyser's astute characterization of "these sunsets" as "a bit Spenglerian." [45] It is the valedictory supermarket scene, however, that requires a final observation. I do not believe anyone has noticed—in print— the way it modulates into a kind of allegorical tableau. To think of it in this way helps one understand the puzzling reference to "holographic scanners, which decode the binary secret of every item, infallibly. This is the language of waves and radiation, or how the dead speak to the living." The scanners occupy a liminal space: they equip "terminals" toward which the shoppers shuffle in portentous lock-step. "Regardless of age," they are on their way—though DeLillo is too subtle, too committed to understatement to use the phrase—to "check out." It is just on this cusp, of course, that all humanity continues to tergiversate between that which can be digitally quantified (the weight of food, the price, one's years) and that which cannot: the whole messy business of the unseen and painfully unknown.

6   **Convergence of the Twain** *Libra*

At the center of Hell, in Dante's great vision, Satan sits up to his waist in ice, endlessly masticating the three worst malefactors in history. The first of these, Judas, requires no explanation in the context of a Christian poem. But why does Dante see a couple of mere political assassins, Brutus and Cassius, as deserving punishment on the same scale as Christ's betrayer? Patriotic as well as pious, Dante dates the decline of Rome from the death of Julius Caesar. In the fullness of time the act of the conspirators would eventuate in a great civilization's collapse into the divided and warring city-states of Dante's Italy. Dante lives in the world that Brutus and Cassius made.

Lee Harvey Oswald made the world in which DeLillo lives. Like his great Italian ancestor, the author of *The Divine Comedy*, DeLillo contemplates the introduction of a deadly poison into the veins of a once-robust civilization. Like Dante, that is, the author of *Libra* seeks to understand his age and his own identity as artist by returning to and contemplating the act that brought both into being. As Dante allows historical and political elements to complicate or enrich an essentially religious poem, DeLillo allows—as will be seen—a curious religious dimension to emerge in his essentially historical and political novel. In the end DeLillo does not imagine an eternity for Kennedy's murderer in what Shakespeare's Kent, addressing another Oswald, calls Lipsbury pinfold. Rather, the assassin emerges as a man of sorrows whose career and passing the author represents as a kind of strange martyrdom, oddly suggestive of the West's supreme myth of redemptive suffering. Lastly, both Dante and DeLillo distinguish themselves by their distinctive language: as Dante establishes the Tuscan vernacular as the language of serious Italian literature, so does DeLillo establish his own distinctive idiom as the postmodern lingua franca.

"Before history and politics," DeLillo told Adam Begley, "there's language."[1] Admired for the precision with which he writes, this author recognizes that language, more than anything else in the economy of the postmodern, is the vehicle of late-twentieth-century affect. Seldom freighted with emotion, this language goes beyond the instinctive and inveterate irony of those modernists who, in the aftermath of the Great War, felt that language had been to some considerable degree the instrument of a civilization's betrayal. DeLillo, however, is of two minds about his medium, for on the one hand he writes a prose that is detached and ironic, resistant to emotional elevation. Yet the crafter of this idiom of zero at the bone is on record as believing that "language lives in everything it touches and can be an agent of redemption, the thing that delivers us, paradoxically, from history's flat, thin, tight, and relentless designs, its arrangement of stark pages, and that allows us to find an unconstraining otherness, a free veer from time and place and fate."[2] These contrasting ideas of language live together under the sign of Libra, as it were, for even as DeLillo expresses himself in the affectless idiom of the post-assassination world, he allows the language constantly to rise to extraordinary performative heights, as in the lyrical description of a U-2 pilot's bailing out or in the stunning monologues—*constructed*, not transcribed—of Marguerite Oswald.[3]

DeLillo's achievement here begins with his effort to synthesize the language of an assassin, and one notes in passing that Mailer, in *Oswald's Tale*, seems also to have defined his task as the creation of a language, a prose rhythm, evocative of his elusive subject. Especially artful in the Minsk sections of his narrative, Mailer contrives—without Boris-and-Natasha travesty—constantly to echo Russian locutions. DeLillo, on the other hand, focuses chiefly on native American inflections: "Once I found Oswald's voice—and by voice I mean not just the way he spoke to people but his inner structure, his consciousness, the sound of his thinking—I began to feel that I was nearly home free. It's interesting that once you find the right rhythm for your sentences, you may be well on your way to finding the character himself. And once I came upon a kind of abrupt, broken rhythm both in dialogue and narration, I felt this was the prose counterpart to not only Oswald's inner life but Jack Ruby's as well. And other characters too. So the prose itself began to suggest not the path the novel would take but the deepest motivation of the characters who originated this prose in a sense."[4]

Passionate yet impaired, the language of Lee Harvey Oswald lies at the other end of the spectrum of sensibility from DeLillo's fine-tuned awareness of the power in words. Poorly educated (he completed only a month of high school), Oswald could nonetheless be verbally quite articulate, as his radio appearances and the longer interview from which the first of these was excerpted reveal.[5] But with his lack of education and heterodox political views he could not be perceived—to use Foucault's phrase—as *dans le vrai*. A Marxist in a virulently anti-Marxist society, he lacked the standing that makes one heard. "None may enter into discourse on a specific subject," says Foucault, "unless he has satisfied certain conditions or if he is not, from the outset, qualified to do so."[6] Unsanctioned by the educational, political, and economic institutions that in mid-century America determined who might speak with authority, the historical Oswald's words carried no weight, and DeLillo captures the world's refusal to listen in that moment at Dallas Police Headquarters when *Libra*'s Oswald "tried to answer a question or make a statement but no one could hear him."[7] Nor does he fare better as listener: he hears the reporters' babble as something like the "charismatic speech" (417) that so troubles Tap's "tongue-tied" Orville Benton.

On the other hand, Oswald's attempts at hearing and being heard fare better, in the struggle to register as a presence within the American-capitalist order, than his attempts at writing, for he was badly crippled by "dyslexia or word-blindness" (166, 210), a condition not yet widely recognized and treated by the schools. Writing the Historic Diary, Oswald experiences "the pain, the chaos of composition. He could not find order in the field of little symbols. They were in the hazy distance. He could not clearly see the picture that is called a word. A word is also a picture of a word" (211). Yet however clinically specific his condition, Oswald becomes at such moments, like Melville's tragically balbulous Billy Budd, an emblematic figure of all who grapple with the intransigent mechanics of signification—with the endless chain of phonemes, letters, words, word-pictures, pictures of words, and pictures of word-pictures that represent or transcribe only the illusion of reality. DeLillo's Oswald struggles in the modern world, and with its lexicon, to manipulate words and pictures of words, to clothe identity in language, to enter the Symbolic Order of history itself.

Seeking to write history, he discovers that his subject matter cannot exist apart from its embodiment on the page or on the tongue. By the same token, those who would write the history made by Oswald have discovered the barb hidden in the last words of Freud's *Totem and Taboo:* "In the beginning was the deed."[8] The deed, historians find, remains swaddled in the word, in the language or narrative that attempts to represent it, and even so stark a deed as the Kennedy assassination—an event actually recorded on eight-millimeter film—has become an object lesson in the elusiveness of the historical signified. Oral or written, history is recorded in language; like the unconscious in Lacan's famous dictum,[9] moreover, history is *structured* like a language, its signifiers in perpetual freeplay, refusing to yield up stable meanings. History resists the desire for resolution of ambiguities because its semes can never be sufficiently purged of their nonce-status, can never be made truly foundational. The past is like the Lacanian Real—one knows that it exists, but one is constrained to represent it by means of an economy of signification that endlessly postpones referential closure.

The Turning Point

In a previous book I argued against seeing scrupulous accuracy in the depiction of the past (capturing "the way it was") as the summum bonum of the historical novelist. Rather, such accuracy complements depictions of the historical moment as either a "turning point" or what Barbara Tuchman famously calls a "distant mirror" of the present.[10] Indeed, at least one critic/practitioner—Lion Feuchtwanger—has argued that from Homer forward all historical fictions reflect and comment on the present of their writing and presentation to the public.[11] But Feuchtwanger misses the perennial fascination with the moment of an historical paradigm shift. Often elegiac, a turning-point fiction can emphasize any historical *terminus ad quem.* Mary Renault's *The Last of the Wine,* for example, concerns the conclusion of the Peloponnesian War and the last days of Athenian civilization. Other historical novelists, including the DeLillo of *Libra,* focus on the moment in the past when the shape of the present manifests itself. In his novel about the Kennedy assassination, published a quarter century after the event, DeLillo returns to the *terminus a quo* of late-twentieth-century American anxiety and paranoia. A consummate chronicler of the contemporary, the author makes the past his subject in *Libra.* Not a particularly distant past, perhaps, but in scrutinizing 1963 from the vantage of 1988, DeLillo addresses a question he had not previously raised: how did the present acquire its character?

If the Cuban missile crisis was "the purest existential moment in the history of mankind" (316), the death of Kennedy was the moment the century changed course. "In the popular and professionalized discourses of contemporary cultural history," as Thomas Carmichael reminds us, "the Kennedy assassination is often read as the first postmodern historical event." [12] Similarly, Christopher Mott characterizes *Libra* as "an investigation of the episteme born in the slow-motion bloodspray of the Zapruder film." [13] In re-creating this moment in history the author seeks better to understand the great turning point of America's twentieth century, the moment when the national myth and sense of purpose contracted a strange disease. As the inception of the American postmodern, the assassination is the terrible thing guiltily experienced long ago, the thing that, so difficult to integrate psychologically, has warped contemporary identity, made Americans fearful of trusting in a father so easily destroyed. Our infantile perceptions of paternal invincibility, our assumptions that the father would always be the rocklike fosterer of growth toward maturity, suffer a catastrophic collapse. If, further, the father's terrible death coincided with feelings of hatred or jealousy on the part of the collective child (i.e., the electorate's burgeoning anger at Kennedy's perceived failings), the resultant guilt might well foster the profound disinclination to trust the father's political successors that characterizes post-Kennedy American public life. The repudiation of political simplicity might take the form, too, of a widespread conviction that irrational violence lies beneath the surface of life, that every public mishap, every lunatic's desperate act, screens an elaboration of the hideous conspiracy that erupted as primal scene. Aware that culture shares the individual's susceptibility to psychopathology, DeLillo returns to the moment of original violence to explore the etiology of postmodern neurosis.

The assassination changed America, put an end to its innocent conviction of invincibility, gave birth to the culture of paranoia, the perception of history as "the sum total of what they're not telling us" (321). It has come to seem a short step from the toxic event in Dealey Plaza to the disastrous build-up in Vietnam, the racial conflict, the Watergate scandal, and especially the shootings of Bobby Kennedy, Malcolm X, Martin Luther King Jr., John Lennon, George Wallace, Ronald Reagan, perhaps even John Paul II. To Ann Arensberg, DeLillo observed: "The subsequent assassinations and attempted assassinations all seem part of the events of November 22nd." [14] The author made similar remarks to the interviewers for *Rolling Stone* and *Paris Review*. "Within *Libra* and all his other books," interviewer William Goldstein wrote in *Publishers Weekly*, "there is 'an element of unresolvability' that reflects the psychic confusion the assassination has precipitated in American life and which is 'absolutely . . . where my work all began.'" DeLillo goes on to suggest to Goldstein that "everything I've done has been building toward" the creation of Oswald, that "Oswald himself, the assassination itself, was the starting point of my work, although I didn't know it at the time. . . . It may be that everything I've been doing all along is unwittingly influenced by November 22, and particularly by Oswald." [15] In addition to an enquiry into the American century's climacteric, then, *Libra* is an act of professional self-exploration.

In these interviews DeLillo repeatedly makes the point that what happened in Dallas affected him as an artist, especially with regard to the shaping of his distinctive style. Without being psychoanalytically reductive, one can discern a relationship between that style and the trauma of the assassination. DeLillo writes in language cautious of emotion, "air-conditioned" in its affect. Language, after all, pulls toward feeling, and feeling brings one close to that dangerously powerful moment in the past—a moment of vulnerability and trust (even if the trust is discovered after the fact). Language is the vehicle of the unbearable in the wounded psyche, the medium of all that flows from the primal scene, the primal trauma, the primal sacrifice. Anything so powerful as to return one to the psychic watershed must be at once totemized, fetishized, sacred, taboo. Indeed, what is sometimes vaguely numinous in DeLillo's conceptualization of language is here more recognizably part of a dynamic— twisted yet psychologically aboriginal—of religious feeling.

Although one can make an argument for the special validity or reliability of imaginative art as vehicle of historical truth, DeLillo does not cut the Gordian knot that has grown up around "that moment in Dallas, the seven seconds that broke the back of the American century" (181). However scrupulous in rendering the historical moment, he lays no claim to the final word on the abiding mystery of the assassination. If he supplies accurate period detail (the political climate, the language spoken by the characters), and if he displays surprising gifts as a naturalistic writer (in *Underworld* and in the sections of *Ratner's Star* describing Billy Twillig's childhood, one sees that he must have learned a number of things when he read *Studs Lonigan*), DeLillo nonetheless pursues something more than simple verisimilitude. Capturing the way it was is the elusive goal of the pure historian, denied imaginative license, and DeLillo implicitly critiques this aspiration in the doomed enterprise of his character Nicholas Branch, trying hopelessly to craft a secret history of the assassination for the CIA. Like Tristram Shandy or Pynchon's Brigadier Pudding, who struggles with the manuscript of *Things That Can Happen in European Politics,* Branch steadily loses ground to a growing mountain of raw information.

Branch in his room full of assassination data is a masterful conceit—he encapsulates and focuses one's sense of the overwhelming tide of information, analysis, and speculation spawned by those infamous seven seconds in Dallas. DeLillo describes Branch as inundated with paper and data, "the endless fact-rubble of the investigations" (300), including "the Warren Report, with its twenty-six accompanying volumes of testimony and exhibits, its millions of words" (181), the "one hundred and twenty-five thousand pages" of FBI material (59), the "CIA's one-hundred-and-forty-four-volume file on Oswald" (378), not to mention "twenty-five years of novels and plays about the assassination . . . feature films and documentaries . . . transcripts of panel discussions and radio debates" (442). Branch's room full of metastasizing information is an image of any mind that has grappled with the facts of the case. Stuffed with these facts and the theories that attempt to order them, such a mind seems always frustrated in its quest for clarity about what really happened. Nor has this goal been much abetted by congressional passage (in 1992, four years after publication of *Libra*) of an act that called on all branches of government (and all private collectors) to make public their records of the assassination and its aftermath. In a kind of Chernobyl of information, over three million pages suddenly became public.[16]

One can, to be sure, imagine a different story of the Kennedy assassination—one in which a set of facts could be established and accepted. But one would err to imagine that such certainty would promote a sense of coherence in history. The act of a John Wilkes Booth or Gavrilo Princip does not make its consequence—Reconstruction, World War I—any easier to understand. If the assassination of Kennedy were finally understood as unambiguously as that of the Archduke Franz Ferdinand, the historical questions and ambiguities would be the same, only without the endless need to analyze and re-analyze the inaugural act. The significance of the event itself would shrink—while the ramifications of the event would remain to puzzle and confound the desire for historical order.

History relies on documents, "primary material," and commonly the historian can sift the record for facts, then build on them a structure of inference and logic. But here the primary material is too unruly and internally contradictory. Was the president shot from the front or back? How many shooters were there? What became of the president's brain? And what of the man apprehended, Lee Oswald? What were the political sympathies of this "marine recruit who reads Karl Marx" (319), a man for whom "left is right and right is left" (303)? One errs, says Glen Thomas, to think of history in *Libra* as some "hermetically sealed entity, waiting the arrival of the historian to simply 'tell what has occurred.'" Rather, it is "an ever-changing construct whose traces and definitions are unstable."[17] Much of the irreducible confusion stems from about twenty seconds of eight-millimeter footage, the most remarkable document of the assassination. Viewing the Zapruder film, one expects a simple factual record, surely real in some fundamental way. But in fact what one "sees" is not reality but its simulacrum. DeLillo describes the film, here and in the "American Blood" article, not as an artlessly objective record of reality but as "a major emblem of uncertainty and chaos" (441). It presents only lessons in perception, in epistemology, and in the unreliability of representational systems. Truth, in this footage, remains elusive.

Years would pass before the Zapruder film could be publicly screened and re-screened, but its lesson—that a visual record of an event does not make it understandable—could be learned as effectively from the footage of Jack Ruby's shooting of Oswald at the Dallas Police and Courts building on 24 November 1963. The televisual immediacy of this act, which became the first occasion for endless-loop television journalism, "does not translate into reliability," remarks Philip Simmons: "Seeing should not be mistaken for knowing." [18] DeLillo's acute understanding of this precept, implicit in *Libra*, receives even greater emphasis elsewhere, notably in the play *Valparaiso* and in the "Videotape" sequence of *Underworld*. Indeed, a small digression on the way the phenomenon of the sensational event on videotape figures in these later works will help to bring out its meaning in *Libra*.

In *Underworld* the author describes the videotaped murder of a motorist by a psychopath known as the Texas Highway Killer. Experienced from the perspective of an anonymous living room or den, the videotape, like the Zapruder film, shows a man shot in the head. DeLillo at once registers and interrogates the claims on reality of this "video homicide." [19] At the same time he presents readers with something cryptic, something that calls for interpretive collaboration. Constructing a reality as they construct a reading, they join the author in the creation, perhaps, of coherence and structuralist meaning, noting a kind of hidden binary within the story: the horror of random death versus child, family, home (as adumbrated in references to bathroom, breakfast cereal, wife, grandfather). A camcorder, a device for recording images of the real, links the two spheres. But the relation among the actuality (a highway murder), its representation on film, and the representation of the representation in the words of the author remains puzzling. The reader finds that neither the words nor the footage can compel the event to make sense. At every level, a terrible opacity prevails.

In a sketch originally running to fewer than four pages (six in *Underworld*'s larger type) the author weights certain words, makes them especially prominent through repetition and variation: *real* (three times), *truer-to-life* (once), *realness* (twice), *realer than real* (once), *superreal* (once), and *underreal* (once).

But other word patterns, notably the fourfold appearance of *layer, layers,* and *layered,* foster erosions of the viewer's initial idea that the footage represents a transcription of raw actuality—unless it be the actuality intimated in the dueling dictions of accident and fate: *random* (4), *aimless* (2), *accidental* (1), *chance* (1) versus *relentless* (2), *unrelenting* (1), *determined* (1). There are, finally, at least six variations on the pattern *jostl(ed)(ing), jolt(ed)(ing), startle*— words that also figure in *Libra,* where Oswald coolly notes the "startle reaction" of the man he has shot (398).

Such a tesseration of the vocabulary here alerts readers to issues of contingency vis-à-vis reality and its simulacrum. At no point in these pages does DeLillo describe the incident itself. He describes only the videotape of the incident. Again, one medium (words) represents another medium (video) that ostensibly represents reality. The video and its verbal description resemble each other: both compel attention, both promise a kind of unmediated encounter with something starkly real. By the same token, neither quite allows—at least on the surface—much real insight. But DeLillo privileges his own medium even as he allows it to replicate another. As he subtly differentiates representation in words from representation on videotape, he critiques the response of a nation of television watchers to the simulacra they take for reality:

> This is either the tenth or eleventh homicide committed by the Texas Highway Killer. The number is uncertain because the police believe that one of the shootings may have been a copycat crime.
>
> And there is something about videotape, isn't there, and this particular kind of serial crime? This is a crime designed for random taping and immediate playing. You sit there and wonder if this kind of crime became more possible when the means of taping an event and playing it immediately, without a neutral interval, a balancing space and time, became widely available. Taping-and-playing intensifies and compresses the event. It dangles a need to do it again. You sit there thinking that the serial murder has found its medium, or vice versa—an act of shadow technology, of compressed time and repeated images, stark and glary and unremarkable.
>
> It shows very little in the end. (159)

Here serial killing and serial re-playing of the footage seem to partake of the same economy of replication—as do "copycat crime" and the artful stylistic repetitions that parody the entire process: "a man at the wheel of a medium Dodge" (155), "a man alone in a medium Dodge" (157), "he . . . waves briefly, wagging a hand without taking it off the wheel" (156), "an abbreviated wave, stiff-palmed" (157). And one scarcely notices the steady, rhythmic, eightfold iteration of "it shows": "It shows a man driving a car," "it shows a man in a sport shirt at the wheel of his car" (155), "it shows a man in his forties wearing a pale shirt" (156), etc. In the end "it shows very little" other than the some-thing murderous in the medium itself.

This indictment becomes more explicit in DeLillo's 1999 play, *Valparaiso*. A caustic meditation on the much-noted fifteen minutes of fame, *Valparaiso* con-cerns the instant celebrity of one Michael Majesky, who, attempting to fly to a city in Indiana, ends up on a plane to a city of the same name in Florida, then on another plane that takes him to a country in South America with yet an-other city of that name. The media batten on Michael's story, which presently, as journalists of every stripe subject the hapless traveler to the same interview over and over again, confers on him a highly spurious and strangely eroticized fame. Were Michael Majesky to survive, he would no doubt repeat more or less forever the single interview that itself replicates the journey to one Valpa-raiso after another. Like *The Day Room*, then, *Valparaiso* exploits a plot that resembles a Möbius strip. As infinitely iterable as video or audio tape, Ma-jesky's story is buttressed by other images of recurrence in the play: Michael's wife, for example, does "demon repetitions"[20] on her exercise bicycle, and Del-fina Treadwell, the appalling talk-show hostess, "live[s] in a box in a state of endless replication" (94). More than a donnée, the mistaken journey is a met-aphor for a culture that, in perfecting and abusing a remarkable telecommun-ications system, actually takes *itself* to an undreamed-of destination, nominally a "vale of paradise," a Happy Valley—but in fact a vale of the pseudo-real, a Valley of the Shadow.

The journey acquaints us, too, with the "veil" that obscures our sense of identity. Like *The Engineer of Moonlight*, *Valparaiso* engages the imagery of reality cloaked, but this reality—the "soul" or "naked shitmost self" that is "unwordable" (91)—is not so much cloaked as smothered. Hence the recur-rent motifs of mask and hood, which adumbrate the thin, false, veiled self that is the media's creation—and sustenance. The play opens with the back-projected scene of Michael Majesky's attempted self-asphyxiation aboard the airliner en route to Santiago, Chile. This terrifying image recurs at the close, braced by the repetitions—the demon repetitions, as it were—of every airline crew's unwitting promotion of identity confusion:

Then place the mask   Then place the mask. (84, 85, 109, 110)

The powerful image of the veil-like bag over the head hints at the death-by-suffocation that the self has undergone in postmodern times, a death the media enable and, vampire-like, feed on.

The problem of media vampirism (ultimately reified in Delfina) is the prob-lem of "communications" gone malign, of an abuse of language that eviscer-ates identity. As the inexorable interviewing process continues, it leaches out the soul of its victim, deflates the pneuma, sucks air out of the self. "Who were you?" asks Delfina, and Michael observes that "it's a joke question. The answer's *Boo*. Because there's no considered response that's nearly so apt as babble" (101). The play comes to its surreal conclusion as Delfina forces a microphone down Michael's throat (in production, she wraps the microphone cord around his neck) to complete the deadly work of media lionization. "The fame-making apparatus," DeLillo remarks in his *New York Times Magazine* article, "confers celebrity on an individual so intense that he or she can't possibly survive. The quick and pitiless end of such a person's career is inherent in the first gathering glimmers of fame." [21]

Everything here—to bring this digression to a close—begins with Ruby and Oswald. "In his televised death, witnessed 'live' by millions of TV viewers," remarks John Johnston, Oswald "becomes part of American consciousness in a way unique to its history." [22] As Beryl Parmenter, along with the rest of the nation, sees Ruby shoot Oswald over and over again, "the horror became mechanical. . . . It was a process that drained life from the men in the picture, sealed them in the frame" (447). Still, "they kept on showing it and she kept watching" (446). The phenomenon represented by the repeated screening of Oswald's death would itself, in coming years, be endlessly repeated, as DeLillo notes in the Begley interview, where he links "Ruby shooting Oswald" with "the Rodney King videotape or the *Challenger* disaster" [23]—footage that investigators, juries, and especially television audiences must view repeatedly. DeLillo suggests that the element of ceaseless, unremitting repetition is central to whatever these films have to show their viewers. In a 1992 interview with Brigitte Desalm in the *Kölner Stadt-Anzeiger,* the author makes a rare public reference to a work of literary or cultural criticism when he wonders out loud whether the dynamics described in Benjamin's "Work of Art in the Age of Mechanical Reproduction" have been superseded: "Today, I believe, we are at a point where reality itself is being consumed, used up, and the aura is all we are left with . . . and reality is disappearing in a curious way. . . . We have become unable to grasp something unmediated." [24] Welcome to Dallas, M. Baudrillard.

Men in Small Rooms

In the Ur-conspiracy that DeLillo imagines in *Libra,* Win Everett and Larry Parmenter plot to stage an unsuccessful assassination attempt (27–28, 50–53) reminiscent of the one in Pynchon's "Under the Rose" (which became chapter three of *V.*). In the Pynchon story English operatives feign attempts on the life of the British consul-general in Egypt, Lord Cromer, to foreclose possibilities of the real assassination that, at the time of the Fashoda crisis between England

and France, might lead prematurely (and with the wrong antagonists) to World War I. In *Libra* this "assassination theater," as Frank Lentricchia calls it, will supposedly be perceived as Castro's greatest enormity—and mobilize public support for action more determined and purposive than the disastrous Bay of Pigs invasion.[25] Everett and Parmenter start from the idea that they can create a would-be assassin, "put him together. A far-left type. . . . Tie him to Cuban intelligence. Possibly even place him at the scene. If he thinks he's operating on the left, pro-Castro, pro-Soviet, whatever his special interest, we'll help him select a fantasy" (75). Insofar as they propose to manipulate the signifiers of identity and commitment, they demonstrate how intelligence was always already postmodern in its premises. But insofar as they think they can control or arrest this protean process, they reveal their own hopeless bondage to a naive "construction" of the signifying chain. "We'll help him select a fantasy" is one of the most chilling lines in the novel, but one can take some comfort in the recognition that, at this moment, Everett and Parmenter are themselves selecting a fantasy regarding the possibility of marrying any signifier to its signified. It is ultimately inconsequential whether there is a separate, real-life Oswald, with his own political valences and aspirations. The dynamics of identity, history, and linguistic meaning share the same endless fluidity.

Like his surrogate, Nicholas Branch, DeLillo takes as his "subject . . . not politics or violent crime but men in small rooms." Branch sees that "after Oswald, men in America are no longer required to lead lives of quiet desperation. You apply for a credit card, buy a handgun, travel through cities, suburbs and shopping malls, anonymous, anonymous, looking for a chance to take a shot at the first puffy empty famous face" (181). Such men have come out of nowhere to shape both history and consciousness, especially as it informs a widespread contemporary paranoia, and DeLillo seeks, without denying the paranoia, to offer what he characterizes as fictive consolation, a story that "rescues history from its confusions."[26] That is, he devises but does not privilege a conspiracy narrative that artfully blends and to some degree reconciles seemingly contradictory facts. As he explains in interviews, he bases his plot on certain plausible elements in the historical record: the dangerously concurrent anger of disgruntled CIA operatives, Bay of Pigs survivors, and mobsters yearning for a return to the Havana paradise from which Fidel had expelled them.

Readers, then, are ultimately to understand the book not in terms of this or that theory affirmed, nor as an argument for or against the lone-gunman hypothesis, but rather as a sense-making of history centered on the role of the irrational and its instrument, the man who, as DeLillo told Ann Arensberg, "stepped outside history and let the forces of destiny move him where they would—nonhistorical forces like dreams, coincidences, intuitions, the alignment of the heavenly bodies, all these things."[27] Thus Oswald, however marginalized, is at once the book's viewpoint character and real subject, along with the historical phenomenon he introduces: the more or less gratuitous assassination of the charismatic leader. His characterization of Oswald notwithstanding, DeLillo sees the fundamental irony of the outsider's eventual success in violently broaching history, placing himself inside at last. DeLillo's research and his cunning embrace of the Oswald persona lead him to the recognition that the most significant element in the bottomless mystery of Kennedy's murder was the emergence on the historical stage, from which they had been excluded, of hitherto faceless men who had spent their lives dreaming of their affinities with principled, notorious, or merely intellectual or scholarly dwellers in small rooms: revolutionaries such as Trotsky and Castro, spies such as Francis Gary Powers (Oswald looks in on him in a Kremlin cell), historians (Nicholas Branch, last glimpsed in "the room of growing old, the room of history and dreams" [445]), and writers such as DeLillo himself. "What a sense of destiny he had, locked in the miniature room, creating a design, a network of connections. It was a second existence, the private world floating out to three dimensions" (277).

"At times," DeLillo observes in the *Rolling Stone* article, Oswald's "career has the familiar feel of those lives of dedicated and obsessed men who undergo long periods of isolation, either enforced or voluntary, who live close to death for the sake of some powerful ideal or evil, and who eventually emerge as great leaders or influential thinkers, outsized figures in the history of revolution and war."[28] One thinks of Yeats's image, in "Easter, 1916," for the ideologue: an unyielding stone in the midst of life's stream. But this is a modernist archetype, and DeLillo knows that Kennedy's assassin represents another, postmodern model of the person in the small room. Neither Hitler nor Mandela, Oswald is merely a nonentity whose violent resentments, coalescing around mail-order weapons and fantasies of pseudonymous intrigue, set the pattern for Sirhan Sirhan, James Earl Ray, Arthur Bremer, John Hinckley, et al.

Of the right and of the left, though with little real coherence in their thinking or their acts, those who emerge from their small rooms share at most a sense of betrayal by the consumerist dream that, with its "artificial and dulling language," as DeLillo remarks in "American Blood," merely "makes people lonely."[29] Jack Ruby, another nonentity who stumbles into history, helps to define this new breed. He and Oswald share a miserable youth, absentee fathers, sexual ambivalence, the bleak experience of being "a truant, a ward of the state," and "living in foster homes" (445). By the same token, the inchoate thoughts of Ruby define for the reader "what it means to be nothing, to know you are nothing, to be fed the message of your nothingness every day for all your days, down and down the years" (445). Fated to end his days in another small, carceral room, the delusional Ruby becomes not "the man who killed the president's assassin" but "the man who killed the president" (445). Driven by an anger and a desperation they do not understand, such individuals are much given to undigested scraps of one extremist ideology or another. But what really figures here is neither political conspiracy nor coherent individual purpose (however murderous the intent). Rather it is the workings of dreams, coincidence, astrology—all that lies outside systems of historical logic. Only the "language of the night sky" can express the truth behind Oswald's act, but it is an astrological "truth at the edge of human affairs" (175).

Structuring an entire novel around a single astrological emblem, DeLillo resourcefully exploits the sign of Libra for its associations with doubling, tergiversation, and a host of self-contradictory gestures. Subsumed hereunder are numerous motifs of unstable or frangible dichotomy. Attempting to recruit Oswald as an FBI informant, for example, Agent Bateman observes that ostensible political loyalties have become fluid in New Orleans, where "black is white is black" (310). DeLillo portrays General Walker, too, as a person whose mental categories are subject to reversal, a person "who mind-wanders into the midst of the other side" (284). Elsewhere one reads about anti-Castro militants wanting to look like Che Guevara (296). Guy Banister loves to read about "Red Chinese troops . . . massing" in Mexico: "He wanted to believe it was true. He did believe it was true. But he also knew it wasn't" (352). Bobby Dupard, asked by his cellmate if he set fire to his bunk, replies: "I could like verbalize it either way. . . . I could go either way and be convinced in my own mind" (98). The confused and contradictory Jack Ruby seems also to function under the sign of Libra. A last, uncanny detail puts even Kennedy himself into the Libran economy, for at his death he carries (and has carried for some time, apparently) a scrap of paper with a slight misquotation from Shakespeare: "*They whirl asunder and dismember me*" (393). The line is from *King John,* where Blanch of Spain describes her painfully divided loyalties before a battle whose opposing forces include her husband and father-in-law on one side, her uncle and grandmother on the other:

> The sun's o'ercast with blood: fair day, adieu!
> Which is the side that I must go withal?
> I am with both: each army hath a hand;
> And in their rage, I having hold of both,
> They swirl asunder and dismember me. (3.1.326–30)

Oswald, like Blanch, experiences profoundly divided thoughts and emotions. He exhibits personality traits appropriate to one born, as he was, under the zodiacal sign of Libra. David Ferrie characterizes Oswald's thinking as scrambled. His mind is "like a fucking car wash" (353). More charitably, he calls Lee "a man who harbors contradictions. . . . 'This boy is sitting on the scales, ready to be tilted either way'" (319). For Oswald, thinks Mackey, "left is right and right is left" (303). In other words, something like the scales dictates Oswald's mental reality. As DeLillo told DeCurtis, Oswald "was a living self-contradiction."[30] He can serve the interests of the political left if by chance he assassinates General Edwin Walker—or those of the political right if by chance he assassinates President Kennedy. "This boy played Ping-Pong in his head," thinks Kirilenko, the KGB agent who handles Oswald during the period of his defection to Russia (167). David Ferrie has a stateside role similar to Kirilenko's. "Why," he asks Oswald, "do you want a job doing undercover work for the anti-Castro movement when it's clear to me that you're a Castro partisan, a soldier for Fidel?" (316). Clay Shaw notes that just as Libra implies a balancing act, so are there "positive" and "negative" exemplars of the sign: "balanced" and "levelheaded" on one side, "unsteady and impulsive" on the other. "Poised to make the dangerous leap" yet "easily influenced," Oswald is the wrong kind of Libran (315).

Like Othello hesitating between Desdemona and Iago, like Dr. Faustus prompted now by the Good Angel, now by the Bad, DeLillo's Oswald yearns for Fidel yet acts with Alpha, the sinister organization committed to ending the Cuban experiment in communism. Not that coherent volition dictates his ultimate act, for as David Ferrie observes in one of the book's most important passages, he becomes subject to and controlled by deeply nonrational forces:

> "Think of two parallel lines," he said. "One is the life of Lee H. Oswald. One is the conspiracy to kill the president. What bridges the space between them? What makes a connection inevitable? There is a third line. It comes out of dreams, visions, intuitions, prayers, out of the deepest levels of the self. It's not generated by cause and effect like the other two lines. It's a line that cuts across causality, cuts across time. It has no history that we can recognize or understand. But it forces a connection. It puts a man on the path of his destiny." (339)

Ostensibly so remote from each other, Kennedy and Oswald share that destiny. They resemble the ocean liner and the iceberg in Hardy's lines on the *Titanic* disaster. Ship and iceberg come together there "by paths coincident"[31]—and resemble what Bill Millard refers to as the concurrence of "engineered events and happenstance" that, in DeLillo's novel, frames the near impossible likelihood that Oswald will be in a position to shoot at Kennedy.[32] The drama that unfolds in "Convergence of the Twain" itself converges on the word "cleaving," which appears in the middle of the line at the middle of the poem, where it signals ironic "consummation" of the familiar marital figure in Matthew: "For this cause shall a man leave father and mother, and shall *cleave* to his wife: and they *twain* shall be one flesh" (19.4–5). Though DeLillo occasionally opts for such symmetries (both *End Zone* and *Ratner's Star* unfold as twinned or balancing mirror-narratives), here he simply makes the scales, the astrological sign of Libra, a dominant conceit. Like Hardy, nonetheless, he struggles to reconceptualize the idea of fate or destiny as a distillate of accident and necessitarian law.

For the loner, the man with three first names and a squint (as DeLillo says in his *Rolling Stone* article), the problem is to force himself into the sweep of events. Paradoxically, that is, he hopes to achieve a sense of self by submerging it in history. DeLillo compounds the irony when he imagines Oswald, just before his death, as momentarily picturing a "cell with books about the case. He will have time to educate himself in criminal law, ballistics, acoustics, photography. Whatever pertains to the case he will examine and consume" (435). His mission accomplished, in other words, Oswald will return to his small room as incarcerated historian—a figure ironically realized by Nicholas Branch, surrogate for the scholar/writer who, like the assassin he studies, spends his life in cramped quarters and grapples with history from a position at its periphery. In his brief vision Oswald seems even to anticipate the factual superfluity that will glut the small rooms to which his chroniclers will be sentenced.

DeLillo, then, counterposes what Nicholas Branch thinks of as "deft men and fools" (441): "men who," like Everett and Parmenter, "believed history was in their care" and "men in small rooms," men who break into history from "outside" (127). A president or other such old-style maker of history, meanwhile, has little chance between these two brands of folly and psychopathology. The political equivalent of the terrorists who displace the literary artist (in the trenchant analysis of *Mao II*'s Bill Gray), these individuals swiftly transform the nation's charismatic and humane leader into an excerebrate corpse.

Totem, Taboo, and the Breakdown of Metanarrative

The Kennedy assassination—"the murder of some figure out of deepest lore"[33]—was always the stuff of myth, but DeLillo suggests that Oswald's fate is also mythic, that in their twinned deaths Kennedy and Oswald share an identity familiar to psychoanalysis and anthropology. In "American Blood" DeLillo calls Oswald "Jack Kennedy's secret sharer" (24), and in his skewed imagination the Oswald of *Libra* fancies that he and Kennedy have things in common. "Lee was always reading two or three books, like Kennedy. Did military service in the Pacific, like Kennedy. Poor handwriting, poor speller, like Kennedy. Wives pregnant at the same time. Brothers named Robert" (336). "He enjoys foreign travel, just like the president" (355).

Oswald's having been stationed at the airfield at Atsugi, in Japan, provides DeLillo with one of his most important motifs: the u-2 spy plane, an aircraft of surpassing grace on high but, like Baudelaire's albatross, clumsy on the ground. In one of the finest passages in the novel a pilot ejects and floats earthward as the reader slowly realizes that what is being poetically evoked is the shooting down of the Icarian u-2 pilot Francis Gary Powers, who will become, like Oswald, a lone American in Russia, a man in a small room of the Kremlin, a man who comes to be known, always, by all three of his names: "Once you did something notorious, they tagged you with an extra name, a middle name that was ordinarily never used" (198). As one of Lee's co-workers at a photography studio with important government contracts remarks, the plane's name suggests a pun: "I thought they were saying you-toos, like there's me-too and you-too" (274). Subsequently DeLillo imagines that Oswald will recall this conceit at the moment of his death. As consciousness fades, "it is the white nightmare of noon, high in the sky over Russia. Me-too and you-too. He is a stranger, in a mask, falling" (440). Long a stranger to himself, Lee Harvey Oswald joins Francis Gary Powers and John Fitzgerald Kennedy in the select company of the triple-named. But the "me" and the "you," hitherto in flux as Oswald and his various pseudonymous identities, may at last be arrested as the Oswald and Kennedy who converge in life, in death.

In *Libra* the author brings together the primal slaying of the father (the president) and the sacrifice of the son (Oswald). Psychoanalytically, the violent death of the presidential father is a terrifying reenactment of the crime that Freud, building on the speculations of Darwin, Frazer, and Robertson Smith, sees as giving rise to primitive ideas of the sacred. In *Totem and Taboo* and again in *Moses and Monotheism* Freud examines the "primal horde," ruled by "a violent and jealous father who keeps all the females for himself and drives away his sons as they grow up." Eventually the resentment of the brothers takes on a murderous intensity: "One day the brothers who had been driven out came together, killed and devoured their father and so made an end of the patriarchal horde."[34] Subsequently, the feast became ritualized, and its fare became a latter-day symbol of the father—the totem animal that was taboo in the "antithetical" sense that so fascinated Freud. The totem animal was perceived, that is, as at once tutelary and forbidden, at once the godlike protector and, once a year, a scapegoat. In time, a more sophisticated theology, with its god or gods, displaces this totemism to complete the transmogrification of terrible father into deity and cannibal feast into Seder or Eucharist. A primal guilt remains, but Freud contests the doctrinaire definition of Original Sin. "There can be no doubt that in the Christian myth man's original sin was one against God the Father. If, however, Christ redeemed mankind from the burden of original sin by the sacrifice of his own life, we are driven to conclude that the sin was a murder." The Christian messiah, says Freud, "sacrificed his own life and so redeemed the company of brothers from original sin." [35]

What happens in Dallas on 22 and 24 November 1963 telescopes this theological declension. In *Moses and Monotheism* Freud argues that Moses, an irascible and jealous tyrant, eventually drove the Israelites to murder him—to repeat, that is, the primal transgression and its cultural sequel. "Fate had brought the great deed and misdeed of primaeval days, the killing of the father, closer to the Jewish people by causing them to repeat it on the person of Moses, an outstanding father-figure." [36] With substitutions for two key terms, the preceding sentence reads: "Fate had brought the great deed and misdeed of primaeval days, the killing of the father, closer to the American people by causing them to repeat it on the person of Kennedy, an outstanding father-figure." If later hagiography does not obscure memory, the electorate was—not unlike the primal horde—widely disaffected with its leader. Some deplored his Catholicism, others his position on civil rights for Negroes, others his recklessness during the Cuban missile crisis, others his failure to smash Castro. When Oswald, seeming to act on the collective anger, commits the archetypal crime and is in his turn cut down, the country embarks on an epochal orgy of self-recrimination, mistrust, paranoia, and guilt, meanwhile elevating the erstwhile father to quasi-divine status. If DeLillo stops short of elevating the son in like manner, he nonetheless registers the ironic and mythopoeic valence of his scapegoating at the hands of a Jew, Ruby, much exercised by the unjust reputation of the Jews as Christ-killers. Small wonder, in any event, that Mailer, in his own anatomy of the Oswald pathos, calls him our "First Ghost": "Can there be any American of our century who, having failed to gain stature while he was alive, now haunts us more?" [37]

Father. Son. Ghost.

As Nicholas Branch says, "There is much here that is holy" (15). DeLillo's readers, accustomed to the rhetoric of martyrdom in discussions of Kennedy's untimely death, probably encounter with little surprise Jack Ruby's reflection on this calamity as "an event that had the possibility of being bigger in history than Jesus. . . . It was almost as though they were reenacting the crucifixion of Jesus" (428). Yet Kennedy must divide the martyr's crown with Oswald, who realizes, scant hours before his own fated death, that "he and Kennedy were partners. The figure of the gunman in the window was inextricable from the victim and his history" (435). Indeed, it is the final days of *Oswald*, the filial

Judas, that offer the strangest resonances, the most suggestive echoes. Marina Oswald told the Warren commission that on the eve of the assassination her husband asked that they end their separate living arrangement: "He repeated this not once, but several times, but I refused." [38] In the DeLillo novel, however, the refusals become more numerically suggestive. "Three times he'd asked her to live with him in Dallas. Three times she'd said no" (390, 425). The interment of Oswald, exactly three days after *Kennedy*'s death (which takes place on the archetypal Friday), plays like Easter in Alice's—or "Alek's"—looking-glass world. Instead of culminating at an empty tomb, it *begins* with an empty chapel. ("The body was not there" [448].) Though "an executive of the Council of Churches" speaks at graveside (451), the assassin's real eulogy is spoken by Marguerite Oswald, who sees herself as Mater Dolorosa in the Passion of the Son: "If you research the life of Jesus, you see that Mary mother of Jesus disappears from the record once he is crucified and risen" (453).

What is this all about? It is an especially dramatic and concrete instantiation of the fundamental proposition advanced by Lyotard in *The Postmodern Condition* (1984). Lyotard suggests that throughout the modern period of history we have subscribed to a variety of "grand récits" or "metanarratives" about human destiny and the human condition. He identifies "incredulity" toward these metanarratives as an essential feature of the new paradigm. Lyotard is not quite as clear as one might wish in explaining what metanarratives are and just when they are supposed to have ceased being credible. I believe, though, that he is describing a process that has been cumulative throughout the late phase of modernism: the breakdown of certain overarching narratives about history, more than anything else—the idea that humanity was moving toward greater and greater social justice, for example (the vision that animates the Marxian paradigm and, behind it, the ideal of Truth as something in which to ground any local political or social narrative). More and more, humanity must live without any such absolute sanction. "We no longer have recourse to the grand narratives—we can resort neither to the dialectic of Spirit nor even to the emancipation of humanity as a validation for postmodern scientific discourse." Meanwhile, "the little narrative *[petit récit]* remains the quintessential form of imaginative invention." [39]

In his inchoate or fragmented narrative of the Passion, then, DeLillo trenchantly documents an emergent incoherence or breakdown of myths that in many ways manifests itself first and most starkly in the Kennedy assassination. The reader is teased with archetypal possibility, but the mythemes—the triple denial, the ritual murder, the grieving mother, the bodiless obsequies, the three-day interim—refuse to coalesce in any of the familiar metanarratives of suffering, sacrifice, and redemption. Who is the divine figure here—Kennedy or Oswald? How is it that the three days issue not in the presidential scapegoat's resurrection but in the powerfully imagined interment of his Judas? How can this Judas participate in (indeed, be at the center of) the narrative of the empty tomb? Is he also, three times denied, a sacrifice? These elements "swirl asunder and dismember" the familiar Christian story. They announce the postmodern recognition that myth and historical paradigm have become immiscible.

Because he can be seen as advancing yet another theory purporting to resolve the mysteries surrounding the crime, DeLillo has been reproached—by George Will and Jonathan Yardley, most vehemently—for his alleged irresponsibility, his "literary vandalism" or "bad citizenship."[40] But DeLillo does not embrace the paranoia he distills.[41] Nor does he advance his conspiracy-propelled version of the assassination as some kind of superior analysis of such facts as have been determined. To do so, he seems to understand, would be to produce what Lyotard calls a *grand récit,* the very "metanarrative" no longer viable in the postmodern period that actually begins with the death of Kennedy. Thus he devises a *petit récit,* a little narrative, a plot that will serve novelistic ends—and he invites his readers to recognize that *no* account of the assassination can be more than *petit récit.* Troubled by DeLillo's apparent embrace of a theory of the assassination with a second shooter and a conspiracy of CIA, Alpha, and the mob, those who think like George Will dismiss the author as a paranoid leftist, but it is *they* who yearn for the grand narrative that will explain all. DeLillo, on the other hand, sees that no such narrative exists any more— only the little narratives, no one of which is more foundational than any other. From 1963 forward, all plots are equally true. Like Jack Gladney in *White Noise,* however, Win Everett recognizes the "tendency of plots to move toward death" (221)—death that cannot, as in Dante, be redeemed by some divinely comedic or tragic metanarrative.

7   "Our Only Language Is Beirut"   *Mao II*

Writers have perished on the page before: Broch's Virgil, Mann's Aschenbach, Harry Street in Hemingway's "Snows of Kilimanjaro." But in *Mao II*, as in Auster's *City of Glass*, one encounters a writer's passing framed, as it were, by the postmodern resonance of the phrase "death of the author." Second only to *The Names*, *Mao II* (1991) involves DeLillo with subject matter interestingly parallel to or contemporaneous with the age's most tendentious thinking about language and its erstwhile master, the author. Though on record as believing in the continuing viability of the novel (even—indeed, especially—as written "in the margins"), DeLillo undertakes an unflinching exploration here of authorial disability during the reign of simulacra.[1] But rather than issuing warnings about the fate of a world indifferent to or unable to conceptualize authorial autonomy, DeLillo affirms that reports of authorial death have been greatly exaggerated. Rather than defer to a cliché of current theory, a neo-scholastic premise that exercises only a handful of academics, he marshals the full power of language to anatomize the age, its discourse, and its apprehensions of apocalypse.

Though somewhat less foregrounded than in DeLillo's other novels, the language theme still figures importantly here. One hears or hears about the language of the streets, the language of evangelical fervor, the language of the media, the language of terrorism, the language of art, the language of the totalitarian state. But as these languages come under scrutiny for their diversity and viability, the vision is less of healthy, democratic, Bakhtinian heteroglossia than of a Darwinism of discourse: some dialects—notably those that nourish "the language of self" (8)—survive precariously on this or that linguistic Galapagos, while others (discourses of media, consumption, capital) proliferate like starlings.

In his own sentences, DeLillo goes among these competing languages to expose their metastases or to gauge their attenuation. As Mark Osteen says, this author "imitates the discourses he aims to deconstruct and thereby generates a dialogue with those cultural forms that both criticizes their consequences and appropriates their advantages."[2] From time to time the dialogue becomes explicit. Thus Brita Nilsson can wonder about "a secret language" known only to writers. Chatting with Bill Gray as she photographs him, she regrets that she cannot "converse in the private language, the language that will mean something to you" (37). Bill himself, working "the old spare territories of the word" (142), remarks that "every sentence has a truth waiting at the end of it." Struggling to get to that truth, the writer "matches with language" (48). Karen Janney suspects that "everything she saw was some kind of vernacular." Momentarily an Emersonian eyeball, she discovers a visual language, "a dialect of the eye" (175). Among street people, she hears "a language everywhere that sounded like multilingual English" (149), for "it is hard to find a language for unfortunates. One word out of place and their eyes call up a void" (145). As she tries to speak with this derelict population, Karen finds that she cannot understand their language: "The woman spoke . . . in raven song, a throttled squawk. . . . It was a different language completely, unwritable and interior, the rag-speak of shopping carts and plastic bags, the language of soot" (180).[3] Yet at times Karen herself thinks and speaks the barbaric pidgin embraced by followers of the Reverend Sun Myung Moon: "They have God once-week. Do not understand. Must sacrifice together. Build with hands God's home on earth" (7).

In his scrutiny of language DeLillo seems to delight in "the uninventable poetry" of vernacular speech (216), the paronomasic possibility of certain artless phrases that, redolent of proliferating instabilities, often function motivically to declare and enact thematic meanings. One of the more suggestive (and comic) of these phrases, "the line that says everything" (170), comes from "the Sears Roebuck Catalog" (201): "Measure your head before ordering" (216). In addition to "see what size your head is before ordering a hat," this can mean "see if your head is big enough before issuing orders" or "see if the desire to give orders is merely the product of a big head." Perhaps, too, if you are Chairman Mao, Abu Rashid, or the Reverend Sun Myung Moon, you may need to measure the *contents* of your head. Brita's observation about Beirut, "Everybody's nowhere" (239), is only slightly less polysemic. The apostrophe can signal a contraction of "everybody is nowhere" or a genitive that characterizes the shattered city as "the nowhere of all souls." "Nowhere" thus has its denotative meaning—no place—and its colloquial meaning: a locus, metaphorical or otherwise, for those without agency. The phrase, like Melville's "sinister dexterity," is double-edged, self-interrogating. But the mother lode of these locutions is, again, the "rudimentary English" of the Moonie lexicon, where words "take a funny snub-nosed form" (8)—at once, in other words, cartoonish, unhandsome, and deadly. The Moonies "speak a half language, a set of ready-made terms and empty repetitions" (7): "Heart of God is only homeland. Pali-pali. Total children of the world. . . . For there is single vision now. Man come to us from far away. God all minute every day. Hurry-up time come soon" (193). From unintentional echoes of Coca-Cola advertising ("children of the world") to unwitting admissions of tunnel-mindedness ("single vision"), these catchphrases rehearse a linguistic victimization that may be the most terrible thing about cult-think. The concluding phrase in the preceding litany, in any event, provides a last example of the double and triple meanings under review. It speaks of a temporal acceleration ("hurry-up" is adjectival) appropriate to a sense of apocalyptic anxiety. But one can also read it as the hortative apostrophe of those who yearn for the Last Days: hurry *up*, time.

The language of apocalyptic expectation links groups as disparate as the Moonies of Korea and America, the Shiite mullahs of Iran, and the followers of Abu Rashid, the Middle Eastern terrorist who also wants to hurry time. "The force of nature runs through Beirut unhindered," he declares, "and it must be allowed to complete itself. It cannot be opposed, so it must be accelerated" (234). DeLillo has remarked that "true terror is a language and a vision,"[4] and here he characterizes Beirut itself as language, its squalor, suffering, torture, civil war, and endless, violent death all giving tongue to the misery of the "nowhere" population that keeps its head down but still lifts an inarticulate cry from doorways and bombed-out cellars. Brita, in the closing paragraphs, listens to this cacophony of "machine gun fire," "dark rumbles," "boxy clatter," and "radios perched on balconies" (238):

Radio voices calling all around her. Beirut, Beirut. They crowd in toward her, pressing with a mournful force. People calling from basement shelters, faces in shadow, clothing going dark with heavy sweat, sleeping children curled around their war toys. All the hostages, pray for them stashed in their closets and toilets. All the babies, pray for them lying in rag hammocks. All the refugees, pray for their dead and wait for the shelling to subside. The war is so fucking simple. It is the lunar part of us that dreams of wasted terrain. She hears their voices calling across the leveled city. Our only language is Beirut. (239)

Again, the equivocal terms. A "lunar part" is an empty part—yet this curious metaphor for war seems also to invoke a kind of satellite to consciousness, a mental companion world that teases us with a vision of the societal collapse that will "bring hurry-up time to all man" (146). Beirut's suffering citizens have only their doomed city to talk about, only the communal suffering out of which to compose discourse, make a language. Yet a larger citizenry, in the crosshairs of the millennium, may find itself obliged to speak this language as well. *Our* only language is Beirut.

Death of the Author

DeLillo evinces a certain anguish in suggesting that only an effete writer—Bill Gray—here stands in opposition to the mentality of crowds, the meretricious glamor of terrorism, the consumerist imperative, and the hegemony of the image. "I'm playing the idea of death," says Bill, with more irony than he quite intends (42). In *Mao II* he in fact plays the author-protagonist whose literal death completes a process of diminution at once personal and cultural. That is, his ability to write fails him just as the "species" to which he belongs ceases to have importance for his society and its collective consciousness. Yet this writer, however weakened or blocked, at least understands the forces his culture arrays against independent thinking. Struggling to affirm the validity of the individual imagination, he wrestles with forms of ideological coercion at once subtle and immensely powerful.

To gauge the actual meaning of Bill Gray's ostensibly postmodern death, one can compare it to a modernist antecedent, the passing of Hemingway's Harry Street. Harry's long reverie before death exemplifies the modernist emphasis on consciousness. The story also reaffirms the moderns' bleak understanding of the human condition, in which nothing finally gainsays our mortality. Human beings die painfully, their bowels spilled in the barbed wire—or painlessly, of gangrene. But they die, and perishing by accidental thorn scratch suggests the triviality of death in any absolute scale. As modernist writer, Harry refuses to make peace—even on his deathbed—with the unimaginative society so inimical to his art. Harry cannot, however, shock the bourgeois while flat on his back, so he does the next best thing, baiting the woman who represents the materialistic values that have destroyed his artistic soul. Though he has apparently lost his edge as a writer, having become the husband of a rich socialite, Harry manages still to express the disgust with middle-class culture that modernism shares (uneasily before the Depression and the Spanish Civil War) with Marxism. Written in 1936, at the height of Hemingway's own left sympathies, "The Snows of Kilimanjaro" seems tentatively, like *To Have and Have Not* (which came out the following year), to embrace the Marxist vision one might characterize as the last of those historical and political metanarratives that, according to Lyotard, remained viable—if steadily diminished—throughout the centuries of the modernist project.

As a good modernist Hemingway could, like Pound, imagine a social and cultural order in which art would have its honored place. He could believe that one index to the good society would be its regard for and fostering of great art. His story, then, concerns the horrific rot—gangrene is an effective metaphor—that dooms the modern artist. Yet Harry continues faithful to his artistic calling, and at the very moment of his death he dreams of approaching the snowy summit of his African Parnassus, the Mt. Kilimanjaro that the Masai call "the house of god." Pitting the hideous reality of death by gangrene against this image of ideal, numinous stasis, the story affirms the validity of a transcendent artistic vision.

One discerns, as expected, a somewhat different meaning in DeLillo's story of a moribund author. Bill perishes first in the simple exhaustion of his talent. But, more insidiously, he suffers death as the victim of societal indifference or cultural forces that turn him and the books he writes into commodities. "In the West," as DeLillo observes in his trenchant testimonial for the incarcerated Chinese poet Wei Jingsheng, "every writer is absorbed, turned into breakfast food or canned laughter."[5] Indeed, Bill's resistance to commodification must owe something to a recognition of the price Hemingway paid for becoming a household name, the familiar face on all those magazine covers. In *Mao II* this process of commodification frames and politically contextualizes the much discussed death of the author—the absorption of the authorial function in intertextual dynamics, in the tendency of texts to reproduce or integrate other texts—that Barthes and Foucault have described. Some link this authorial dissipation to the death of authority in its most general sense, the death that comes about with the undermining, in poststructuralist thought, of every foundational principle. This crisis of authority can sometimes seem a bit of an academic parlor game, but it speaks, as a concept, to the many concrete breakdowns of order in the late twentieth century: the collapse of civility, the violence in the American inner city, the accelerating political chaos of the civil wars one sees in Beirut and elsewhere in the Levant, not to mention both East and West Africa.

Both Bill Gray and Harry Street embark on a night-sea journey—in Bill's case, a literal one. Harry, benighted, imagines the morning sun on Kilimanjaro; Bill voyages "morningward toward the sun" (216). Whether the stifling environment be conceived as "bourgeois values" or culture of the simulacrum, Harry Street and Bill Gray come together in the ultimate failure of their art. Where the modernist fails to redeem the wasteland, the postmodernist fails to matter at all to a world that responds only to the acts of terrorists or to the daily image bombardment of popular culture. As Steffen Hantke observes, Bill's "anonymous and unrecognized death is a symptom of the hopeless imbalance of ideological powers in favor of postmodern society."[6]

It is instructive to note who promotes and who resists Bill's professional death. The parasitic Scott Martineau, for example, is to some degree redeemed by his faith in literary genius. One of the most deft sequences in the novel has him obsessively cleaning the typewriter of the absent Bill, blowing into the keys over and over again (six times, in all) until one recognizes in his labor the unconscious attempt to fill the word machine with the afflatus that has departed (139 ff.). Like Propertius keeping his erasers in order, Scott will keep ready the tools needed to temper or deflate the illusions of what Pound called "the distentions of empire."[7] The well-meaning Brita Nilsson, by contrast, contributes to Bill's demise. She calls her project of photographing writers "a work-in-progress" (26), but like Bill's abortive third novel, it will be abandoned. On her way to meet the reclusive writer, Brita remarks, "I feel as if I'm being taken to see some terrorist chief at his secret retreat in the mountains" (27). The irony, of course, is that she will presently visit the secret retreat of a real terrorist chief, Abu Rashid. This progression defines contemporary journalism, and the transfer of her professional focus bears out Bill's bitter pronouncements on the displacement of novelists by terrorists. "She does not photograph writers anymore. It stopped making sense" (229). When she abandons this project, Brita seems to declare the larger authorial death far advanced. A sympathetic and even heroic character, she loses faith with literature, declares it finished. But all along, by making glossy black-and-white photographs of authors, she has accelerated their co-optation within a culture that, increasingly indifferent to the books such authors write, embraces only simulacra. The unsettling corollary to her retirement from photographing authors is that, in converting them into images, she has retired *them*.

Not that one denies the complex dynamics of her confrontation with Abu

Rashid and his henchboys. Four times the terrorist asks her if she thinks him crazy (233, 234, 236), and perhaps one recalls Owen Brademas's remark, in *The Names*, that "in this century the writer has carried on a conversation with madness."[8] The "conversation" that takes place in the closing pages of *Mao II* ought, that is, to be between Abu Rashid and Bill Gray, between the terrorist and the person whose views have been shaped by and expressed through books, not pictures.[9] DeLillo himself, while noting his own keen interest in photography and other visual arts, his own intensely visual imagination, has emphasized the fundamental distinction: "A picture is like the masses. . . . A book on the other hand, with its linear advance of words and characters seems to be connected to individual identity. I think of a child learning to read, building up an identity, word by word and story by story, the book in its hand. Somehow pictures always lead to people as masses. Books belong to individuals."[10] And Brita, to do her justice, seems intuitively to grasp this distinction between scales of identity, for, even as she makes pictures of a famous terrorist and his milieu, she insists—at considerable personal risk—on unmasking the individual concealed by a hood and an image of the leader.

The camera promises a dubious glamor, desired by Abu Rashid, despised by Bill Gray. Calling himself "a bad actor" (42), Bill signals his discomfort before the lens. The striking of poses does not come naturally to him, for he has only truths to represent. There is also a rueful claim for being a "bad actor" in the vernacular sense—an outlaw, a bull for all the china shops of polite society. But this sense has been usurped by those new "bad actors," the terrorists, who leave Bill to bibulous impersonations of a violent or dangerous disposition— as at the dinner table with Karen, Scott, and Brita or in his almost wistful assertion that "the state should want to kill all writers" (97). Such a desire on the part of the state, however reprehensible, is a valid measure of the threat they pose. The only thing worse than the state's hostility and persecution, of course, is the indifference that, in the West, signifies impotence. DeLillo is fully aware of the irony that makes western writers comparative nonentities, while their colleagues under repressive regimes are hunted down and jailed (one, a *fatwa* the literal price on his head, goes in fear of his life). A further irony of Bill's failure is that, conceivably, his becoming hostage in the Swiss poet's place might have worked as the consciousness-raising gesture that literary artists can no longer effect through writing alone. But more likely is the boomerang effect Douglas Keesey imagines as the consequence of a successful public reading of the poet's work by Bill: "It may end up furthering the very forces of terrorism and totalitarianism that he as an independent writer is sworn to combat."[11] Were either of these gestures successfully to refurbish the influence of the artist, it would also, according to the inexorable logic of spectacle, promote the media profile and thus the power of the terrorist hydra. Part of the horror here is that the artist would have surrendered himself to the global exchange in which terrorists and the media do business. Had he survived to confront Abu Rashid, Bill would have discovered himself outbid in the marketplace of terrorism, for a hostage, too, is a commodity. As Abu Rashid tells Brita, "We sold him to the fundamentalists" (235).

The serious writer, Bill fears, is little more than an anachronism, a dinosaur, a dying breed. Indeed, Brita speaks of her photographic project as a "species count" (26). Bill makes a number of sententious remarks during his session with Brita: "Years ago I used to think it was possible for a novelist to alter the inner life of a culture. Now bomb-makers and gunmen have taken that territory. They make raids on human consciousness" (41). Later, Bill expands on this idea in a conversation with an urbane apologist for terrorism, George Haddad: "For some time now I've had the feeling that novelists and terrorists are playing a zero-sum game. . . . What terrorists gain, novelists lose. The degree to which they influence mass consciousness is the extent of our decline as shapers of sensibility and thought. The danger they represent equals our own failure to be dangerous" (156–57). Here and in the earlier scene with Brita, Bill bitterly echoes the language with which Norman Mailer had once (in 1959, to be exact—the thirty-year interim coincides with the period since Bill's last session with a photographer) announced literary ambitions on a grand scale: "The ambition of a writer like myself is to become consecutively more disruptive, more dangerous, and more powerful." Mailer added that he could "settle for nothing less than making a revolution in the consciousness of our time."[12]

George embraces and expatiates on Bill's lugubrious analysis, but DeLillo's embattled author firmly resists every tendentious step, refusing, for example, to call terrorists "the only possible heroes for our time." Persisting, George articulates perceptions that are hardly limited to terrorist sympathizers like himself:

> In societies reduced to blur and glut, terror is the only meaningful act. There's too much everything, more things and messages and meanings than we can use in ten thousand lifetimes. Inertia-hysteria. Is history possible? Is anyone serious? Who do we take seriously? Only the lethal believer, the person who kills and dies for faith. Everything else is absorbed, the artist is absorbed, the madman in the street is absorbed and processed and incorporated. Give him a dollar, put him in a TV commercial. Only the terrorist stands outside. The culture hasn't figured out how to absorb him. (157)

George wants to romanticize the terrorist as the one "we take seriously," the one who "stands outside" and speaks "the language of being noticed, the only language the West understands" (157). Bill's "angry" resistance to these propositions is forensically unimpeachable, for he adduces the traditional values of human rights, democracy, and creative individualism. But he knows that what he opposes is oceanic in its vastness and power. Like Cuchulain, he cannot prevail against this tide.

Happily one does not mistake Bill Gray for Don DeLillo. Though he recognizes that art has been marginalized by terrorism and its media confederates, DeLillo remains true to his calling—remains, as functioning artist, the world's faithful mirror and conscience. Unlike Bill Gray, DeLillo continues to write. Unwilling to surrender to a world that responds only to the acts of terrorists or to the daily image bombardment of popular culture, he testifies against cultural entropy and defends the validity of individual perceptions. As he explained to Desalm, "*Mao II* . . . depicts a fight for human imagination— between persons representing individuality, and the anonymous masses."[13] Indeed, the Jerusalem Prize, which he won in 1999, goes biennially "to a writer whose work expresses the theme of the freedom of the individual in society."

"Nothing happens until it's consumed"

"The crowd," says Kierkegaard, "is untruth. Therefore was Christ crucified."[14] But as the twentieth century gives way to the twenty-first, individual identity sustains itself with increasing difficulty. "This is what you fear," George Haddad remarks to Bill Gray, "that history is passing into the hands of the crowd" (162). Impatient to swallow all individuality, this crowd already threatens to become global. One recognizes in it a kind of textuality within which individuals, like authors, engage in a doomed struggle to resist the intertextual undertow.

Consciously or unconsciously engaged in furthering the politics of mass will, the crowds that DeLillo depicts in this novel—cultists, soccer fans, Chinese communists, Shiites mad for Khomeini, TV audiences, even certain kinds of mass-market readers—variously seek to deny or repress individual subjectivity. They express, too, a millennial desire to escape from the present, from the self, and from history. At the same time, paradoxically, they are the response to the postmodern evisceration of these terms. "Is history possible?" asks George Haddad (157), an unsympathetic character who speaks, nonetheless, for the many who weep at the proliferation of the homeless and the crazy, the many who stare dumfounded at urban decay, cults, terrorism, and bloodletting from Lebanon to Liberia, from Port-au-Prince to Priština. Small wonder that the masses wax apocalyptic, "thinking of the bloodstorm to come" (7).

The masses embrace the charismatic figure—the Reverend Sun Myung

Moon, for example—who promotes a corrupt vision of millenarian expectation. Thinking the Korean evangelist has "come to lead them to the end of human history" (6), those who follow the Reverend Moon embrace a debased version of the West's linear and transcendental model of Apocalypse, with its messianic return, its final battle between good and evil, its thousand years of peace. DeLillo hints at the imaginative bankruptcy of this model in representing its appeal to cultists marrying en masse in Yankee Stadium, beyond which "the tenement barrens stretch, miles of delirium, men sitting in tipped-back chairs against the walls of hollow buildings, sofas burning in the lots, and there is a sense these chanting thousands have, wincing in the sun, that the future is pressing in, collapsing toward them, that they are everywhere surrounded by signs of the fated landscape and human struggle of the Last Days" (7).

Similarly, in the Middle Eastern cradle of millennial fantasies such as these, the novel depicts a deranged terrorist who, embracing the equally corrupt Maoist vision, presides over another ruined city, another apocalyptic *mise en scène*. Abu Rashid seeks to replicate Mao's public relations feat (not to mention that of the Reverend Sun Myung Moon) by having his murderous followers wear hoods and announce their identity in the image pinned to their chests: the face of Abu Rashid. This desire to lose the self in the personality of the charismatic leader, DeLillo suggests, differs little from one demagogue to another: faceless and anonymous, the followers of Abu Rashid or the Ayatollah Khomeini flow into the crowds around the Reverend Sun Myung Moon. However ideologically friendly or opposed to the communist leader whose name provides DeLillo's title and crops up repeatedly in his narrative, all such crowds derive from the same totalitarian template.

That contrasting ideologies should so embrace and defer to the tyranny of the image is only one of the abundant ironies assembled here. One notes in passing that a political vision ostensibly at odds with capitalism and its methods achieves its ends almost routinely by means—images of mass desire—familiar to anyone in the capitalist West. The Chinese dictator, in other words, effected something ironically identical to the dream of every marketing and sales manager, creating instant "product recognition" and putting his name and ideas into the mouths of millions. "In the streets of Beirut," notes Peter Brooker, "Brita sees towering red 'Coke II' signs that run together the iconography of American consumerism with echoes of the cultural revolution." [15] Terrorists, too, strive for saturation effect, and DeLillo seems aware that advertising, terrorism, and the cult of political personality in a totalitarian state offer images that function in much the same way. There is a disturbing coalescence of spheres once thought to be separate. Now political ideology, art, show business, advertising—all prove to be part of a larger economy or grammar of the image.

Modern advertising and the consumer consciousness it shapes make of the many one—one in taste, one in appetite, one in vision, one in values. The subject, in other words, is subjected. To use the terminology of Althusser, the subject is interpellated or "hailed" by ideological police who never even have to manifest themselves to consciousness.[16] Ironically, this standardization of an ideological unconscious, the supreme accomplishment by which the culture of the image manifests and validates itself, effects something very much like that most powerful Maoist vision: the transformation of human nature.

Partly through state-sanctioned art, Mao strove, like Hitler, to produce assembly-line human beings, and in *Mao II* DeLillo problematizes such replication in a number of ways. For example, he engages and subverts the totalitarian vision of universal conformity by implicitly comparing it to pop art's cookie-cutter Maos and Marilyns. He parodies this aesthetic of mechanical reproduction in his own quasi-lithographic scenes of thematic iteration and reiteration. At the same time, insofar as his juxtaposed scenes often seem disjunct, he parodies or reprocesses or copies a gesture characteristic of his literary predecessors. At his most original even as he seems to imitate, DeLillo reconfigures a modernist technique to map postmodernity. The modernist practice of juxtaposing images or fragments without connective material— one sees it often in DeLillo's proclivity to verbless constructions—depends for its effectiveness on the reader's collaborative effort. Amid the fragments shored against ruins one discerns a shadowy coherence nostalgically grounded in the larger order of older, less troubled civilizations. Discrete, seemingly unrelated elements in *Mao II* discover a less nostalgic and less tendentious logic even as the fragments prove isomorphic, each the thematic echo of its neighbor. Like the modulation that proceeds as nuanced repetition in the music of Philip Glass or John Adams, the progression from one DeLillo scene to its seeming thematic clone disguises subtle variations in subtext. The modulation becomes palpable only gradually—fully realized only in larger movements, as, most obviously, from prologue to epilogue. That is, the thematic material of the novel's opening pages—nuptials, explosions, photography, and wasteland landscape—emerges at the end in something like an altogether different key. But perhaps a look at the technique in miniature should precede discussion of this larger thematic metamorphosis.

The two scenes with which the narrative proper gets under way—Scott Martineau goes to a bookstore, then to a museum or gallery—make the same (or at least complementary) points about the problematic status of contemporary art. This transition from books to paintings seems natural enough—one follows a young man who likes graphic as well as literary art. But DeLillo improves on mere plausibility. In the progression from bookstore to art museum to pictures of a dictator, DeLillo presents pieces of a larger puzzle—a puzzle that subsumes civil war in Beirut, that "millennial image mill" (229), and the chiliastic fantasies of organizations like the Reverend Sun Myung Moon's Unification Church. As will be seen, this novel's vision will integrate seemingly disparate scenes in bookstore, art museum, Yankee Stadium, and wasteland Beirut. As one may err to make simplistic connections between one kind of civil collapse and another, so may one err to read the transition from Borders or Barnes and Noble to the Museum of Modern Art as either a simple parallel between types of art or a simple contrast between an old-fashioned aesthetic medium (books) and its postmodern successor (pop art).

Though described with DeLillo's trademark detachment, the experience in the bookstore gratifies neither aesthetic nor intellectual expectation. For who has not walked into a large, sumptuous, and hitherto unvisited bookstore—only to find it exactly like every other bookstore in the land? In this one Scott sees "books on step terraces and Lucite wall-shelves, books in pyramids and theme displays. He went downstairs to the paperbacks, where he stared at the covers of mass-market books, running his fingers erotically over the raised lettering. Covers were lacquered and gilded. Books lay cradled in nine-unit counterpacks like experimental babies. He could hear them shrieking *Buy me*" (19). Noting the extent to which even books can be made to fuel consumer desire, the creator of this scene emphasizes not bibliophilia but merchandising. Hardly a temple consecrated to the unique and holy work of literary art, this is the bookstore as Disneyfied simulacrum. Whatever aura exists here (and it extends even to an erotics of book covers) is co-opted by commercial calculation.

When a deranged and ragged street person stumbles in, declaring "I'm here to sign my books" (20), one recognizes him, however outlandish, as a version of the cranky and idiosyncratic individual who actually writes the books marshaled here for maximum consumer titillation. In fact, the dereliction of this crazed intruder anticipates that of Bill Gray, the author presently seen stumbling about in a Levantine backwater before suffering his inglorious postmodern death. Like an impotent Jesus among the moneylenders, this authorial specter is a walking reproach to those who have commercialized the word—at least until someone in uniform restores the premises to the safe hawking of the latest Danielle Steel and Stephen King to consumers who, in their undiscriminating throngs, share a herd instinct with soccer fans, Chinese Communists, followers of the Ayatollah, nuptial couples chanting *mansei* in Yankee Stadium, and the other vast crowds that trouble the imagination of a serious writer like DeLillo.[17]

From books, then, to pictures by that high priest of pop art, the Andy Warhol who, undermining the distinction between serious art and popular culture, denying depth, denying "authority," denying uniqueness and aura in the work of art, became one of the inventors of postmodernism.[18] Topical references in the book suggest that Scott visits the Museum of Modern Art, which held a major Warhol retrospective in 1989 (present time in the novel—the year of the Hillsborough Stadium disaster, the death of Khomeini, and the Tiananmen Square massacre—all described in the course of DeLillo's narrative).[19] In the museum Scott contemplates a 1963 picture called *Crowd* and several of the versicolor Mao canvases Warhol executed between 1972 and 1974. Warhol's multiple images of Mao are mechanically reproduced, two-dimensional salutes to an iconicity, as Warhol's related portraits suggest, indistinguishable from that of Troy or Liz or Elvis or Jackie. DeLillo makes this point himself in an interview in the *Chicago Tribune*:

> What Warhol was doing was sort of ironic, distanced, even comical in a way. . . . And it worked. It's evocative. What he did with Mao in particular was to float this image free of history, so that a man who was steeped in war and revolution seems in the Warhol version to be kind of a saintly figure on a painted surface, like a Byzantine icon. In a way, this was another bit of perverse genius on Warhol's part, because there's no difference in the Warhol pantheon between Mao and Marilyn, or Mao and Elvis.[20]

One might think that an original, the man himself, exists for all representations of the Chinese leader. But Mao, DeLillo suggests, has long since become iconic, dispersed into his endlessly replicated likeness, unvarying as a Big Mac or Coke. Warhol called his studio "The Factory," and he produced images there as standardized as anything Henry Ford ever dreamed of. In the selection of Maos that appears on DeLillo's dust-jacket, one can see that the same image recurs in assorted hues and variously accessorized—rather as Detroit's products come in different colors, with more or less chrome, and with different "options."

As a manipulator of crowds, as a terrorist of global ambition, and as a focus of apocalyptic desire, Mao is also the natural subject of a new art. Moreover, he is himself an artist in the new mode. His "Little Red Book of Quotations" is the ultimate bestseller (162), a book that enjoys a new kind of "aura" (to use the term that DeLillo often favors, though usually in a somewhat different sense than Benjamin). It is the bible of ultimate conformity, the icon of crowd mentality. "The cult of Mao was the cult of the book," says George Haddad. "It was a call to unity, a summoning of crowds where everyone dressed alike and thought alike" (162). Through the book Mao "became the history of China written on the masses" (161).

In his references to the founder of the People's Republic of China, DeLillo points to a compelling yet cryptic emblem of postmodern identity. The novel's enigmatic title derives specifically from the souvenir Scott brings home to Karen from the museum or gallery he visits before meeting Brita Nilsson for the first time: a "reproduction of a pencil drawing called *Mao II*" (62). Though mass-produced for sale in the museum shop, *Mao II*, as a *drawing*, may seem to differ from the pop art norm of multiple images, commonly silk-screened or lithographed. The image Karen eventually unrolls and contemplates has, after all, an original. But Warhol's 1973 drawing of Mao is itself a second version and, like its predecessor (not to mention all the silkscreens), has clearly been executed with the aid of an opaque or slide projector, for the mature Warhol, contemptuous of classical standards of draftsmanship, seldom drew freehand. Moreover, all of Warhol's images of Mao (this drawing included) are the same picture, based on the one that appears "as the frontispiece"—itself reproduced by the millions—"to *Quotations from Chairman Mao Tse-tung.*"[21] The modest joke of a painter who, unlike many of his contemporaries, seldom appended numerical suffixes to his titles (only two or three such titles appear in *Andy Warhol: A Retrospective,* the massive chronicle of the MOMA show), this idea of a *second* drawing of Mao—amid literally hundreds of other such representations by Warhol—participates in the larger irony of an iconography that remains endlessly static and unvaried.

The author seems to intend the numerical suffix in the title to work by paronomasic suggestion, hinting that the subject—Mao—was himself part of a series: Mao I, Mao II, Mao III, and so on. Indeed, any manifestation of iconic presence—whether one speaks of a literal likeness or some more rarified transmogrification of totalitarian ethos, savvy marketing, and groupthink—is "Mao too." One sees an especially stunning example of this dynamic in the derivative picture that catches the eye of Brita Nilsson at a gallery opening. This canvas, *Gorby I,* sums up much of what DeLillo has to say about the much discussed work of art in the age of mechanical reproduction. A further instance of what I have called thematic iteration, it also exemplifies the "symmetries, repetitions, and juxtaposed obsessions" that Joseph Tabbi sees as "crucial to DeLillo's postmodern aesthetic" here. "The multiple parallels, symmetries, and recursive patterns in the novel," Tabbi says, "enable the author to find the places where language converges with the real, the unpresentable, everything that does not conform to formal pattern and syntax."[22]

In *A Portrait of the Artist As a Young Man,* one recalls, Stephen Dedalus's surly friend Lynch says of an aesthetic theory that it "has the true scholastic stink."[23] Such an acute olfactory sense might discern in *Gorby I* the true odor, so to speak, of postmodernism:

> It took her a while to reach the picture that had attracted her. A silk screen on canvas measuring roughly five feet by six feet. It was called *Gorby I* and showed the Soviet President's head and boxed-off shoulders set against a background of Byzantine gold, patchy strokes, expressive and age-textured. His skin was the ruddy flush of TV makeup and he had an overlay of blond hair, red lipstick and turquoise eye shadow. His suit and tie were deep black. Brita wondered if this piece might be even more Warholish than it was supposed to be, beyond parody, homage, comment and appropriation. There were six thousand Warhol experts living within a few square miles of this gallery and all the things had been said and all the arguments made but she thought that possibly in this one picture she could detect a maximum statement about the dissolvability of the artist and the exaltation of the public figure, about how it was possible to fuse images, Mikhail Gorbachev's and Marilyn Monroe's, and to steal auras, Gold Marilyn's and Dead-White Andy's, and maybe six other things as well. Anyway it wasn't funny. She'd taken the trouble to cross the room and look closely at this funny painted layered photo-icon and it wasn't funny at all. Maybe because of the undertaker's suit that Gorby wore. And the sense that these were play-death cosmetics, the caked face-powder and lemon-yellow hair color. And the very echo of Marilyn and all the death glamor that ran through Andy's work. Brita had photographed him years ago and now one of her pictures hung in a show a few blocks down Madison Avenue. Andy's image on canvas, Masonite, velvet, paper-and-acetate, Andy in metallic paint, silk-screen ink, pencil, polymer, gold leaf, Andy in wood, metal, vinyl, cotton-and-polyester, painted bronze, Andy on postcards and paper bags, in photomosaics, multiple exposures, dye transfers, Polaroid prints. Andy's shooting scar, Andy's factory, Andy tourist-posing in Beijing before the giant portrait of Mao in the main square. He'd said to her, "The secret of being me is that I'm only half here." He was all here now, reprocessed through painted chains of being, peering out over the crowd from a pair of burnished Russian eyes. (134–35)

In this passage, a *mise en abîme* of the larger fiction, the author presents a textbook example of the simulacrum, the copy without an original. The imagery—gold field, Byzantine iconicity—recalls that with which, in the *Chicago Tribune* interview (quoted above), DeLillo described Warhol's multiple Maos. In this pseudo-Warhol one encounters a meditation on the signifying chain. As a simulacrum, complete with pretentious numerical suffix, it has much to say about the economy of signification as deconstructively defined. How ironic that, "only half here" in life, Warhol is so completely present in *Gorby I*, looking out through the eyes of an epigone's cheerful conflation of Russian orthodox icon, Soviet premier, and silver screen's supreme sex symbol. Indeed, as Andy looks out through the eyes of Gorby, the reader looks through the eyes of Brita. Gaze meets gaze in an unrepresentable "illustration" of the poststructuralist argument that subjectivity itself is a fiction. The image repeats what was earlier said about the mass identity of Karen and her fellow cultists: Moon "lives in them like chains of matter that determine who they are" (6). More than the linked signifiers that, in the Lacanian Symbolic, forever preclude a true knowledge of self, the phrase "painted chains of being" also recalls the cosmological conceit of the Great Chain that, as Arthur O. Lovejoy showed some years ago, dominated the West's philosophical picture of the universe for centuries—the chain from God down through all the forms of creation.[24] Fully unpacked, the phrase may even glance sardonically at Joyce's idea of "the artist, like the God of the creation," as divine apex, anchor of art's catenary. Indeed, this substitution, so familiar to modernist self-fashioning, finds echoes elsewhere in the text. "When a writer doesn't show his face," says Bill, "he becomes a local symptom of God's famous reluctance to appear" (36). Later, half drunk at dinner, he remarks that "in many ancient languages, God's name has four letters" (69). The observation seems meaningless, unless one reflects that both "Bill" and "Gray" are versions of the Tetragrammaton. The painter of *Gorby I*, however, is a demiurge, for the artistic god—whether by that phrase is meant "Andy Warhol" or the whole Joycean/modernist idea of the artist as divine creator—is dead. Yet the iconicity achieved in life survives undiminished in death, for "Andy" survives as product, fully commodified as the image on "postcards and paper bags, in photomosaics, multiple exposures, dye transfers, Polaroid prints," etc.

One would never confuse the creator of *Gorby I* with the Don DeLillo who describes "the writer as the champion of the self."[25] Authors write, DeLillo told Jonathan Franzen, to deliver themselves from mass culture. Moreover, "if serious reading dwindles to near nothingness, it will probably mean that the thing we're talking about when we use the word 'identity' has reached an end."[26] As *Mao II*'s single most famous sentence has it, "The future belongs to crowds" (16). Thus DeLillo punctuates his tale of a moribund writer with one stunning crowd scene after another, all taken from the headlines. The reader's last, indirect view of Bill Gray is especially chilling. One looks over the shoulders of Scott and Karen as they examine Brita's contact sheets, each filled with serried images of a Bill Gray now existing only as simulacrum: "The differences frame to frame were so extraordinarily slight that all twelve sheets might easily be one picture repeated" (222). Bill Gray I, Bill Gray II, Bill Gray III. . . . Insofar as the central character here, an author of apparently no small gifts and integrity, perishes at the periphery of cultural and political history, a reader might legitimately see the book's conclusion as offering little hope for the cause of letters. Yet another author, neither blocked nor dead, looks to the looming millennium with precisely the kind of energy Bill Gray seems to lack. Taking as his subject the death of *an* author, DeLillo himself embodies the still viable will to create, which his character Bill Gray cannot sustain.

Within the larger culture, that will may be embattled, but it remains, perhaps, the sleeping seed of the fresh creation that will take back the future from its crowds. Some such augury figures, I think, in DeLillo's concluding his novel with a recapitulation of the ceremony with which it began. Each of these ceremonies takes place amid ordnance (the firecrackers of slum mischief-makers in the Bronx, the mortar and small-arms fire of Beirut) and photography (parents snapping away in Yankee Stadium, the magnesium flash that Brita momentarily mistakes for an explosion). In the urban decay that surrounds one scene and in the street fighting and civil war of the other, a seemingly apocalyptic desolation reigns, though neither ceremony bears much resemblance to the marriage with which, in the vision of St. John the Divine, the apocalypse culminates. Yet despite its ostensible despair for humane culture, the book seems to end on a positive note. Laura Barrett may be right to argue for an element of optimism in the epilogue, notably in "the final reproduced photograph of the novel, which overturns the previous association of photography and loss of individuality by presenting a different kind of image: three children, two of whom are holding up peace signs, play in the war-torn city of Beirut. The face of the third boy is clear, unobstructed by crowds, flailing arms, or wire fencing, and we are left, oddly enough, with a sense of hope for the resurgence of the individual." [27]

As Willa Cather once remarked, "Whatever is felt upon the page without being specifically named there—that, one might say, is created." [28] If one reads the mass wedding at the beginning of *Mao II* as emblematic of the institution's debasement to the crowd ethos, perhaps one can read the wedding at the conclusion as emblematic of some sacramental resilience in the midst of a general collapse. As celebrations of fulfillment and new life, weddings traditionally provide comedic endings, restoring lives subject to terrible dislocations. One can hope for some such sanguine possibility here. Indeed, the novel's bracketing in hymeneal imagery may even signal the larger geographical and cultural wedding that capped 1989, the fateful, crowd-troubled year that began in February with the *fatwa* against Salman Rushdie and the Andy Warhol retrospective, continued with the Sheffield soccer disaster in April, and seemed to culminate, in June, with the massacre in Tiananmen Square and the appalling spectacle of the Ayatollah Khomeini's funeral. But just as the last photograph in *Mao II* does not depict another frenzied horde, so does DeLillo invite his readers to remember the triumphant gathering that, in November of that year, provided powerful symbolic contrast to the many ugly crowd scenes that had gone before. In Berlin a different kind of crowd danced at the demolition of the Wall, proclaiming a new nuptial for East and West. In this novel's epilogue, then, readers may experience something "felt upon the page without being named there": an augury of renewal.

Part Three   **"The word beyond speech"**

8   For Whom Bell Tolls   *Americana*

Americana (1971) represents a rethinking of the identity or alienation theme that had figured with particular prominence in the quarter century since World War II. These themes persist in DeLillo, but the self becomes even more provisional. The changing social conditions and imploding belief systems that alienate a Meursault, a Holden Caulfield, or a Binx Bolling do not constitute so absolute an epistemic rupture as the gathering recognition—corroborated by post-Freudian psychology—that the old stable ego has become permanently unmoored. Whether or not he would embrace Lacanian formulations of psychological reality, DeLillo seems fully to recognize the tenuousness of all "subject-positions." He knows that postmodern identity is not something temporarily eclipsed, something ultimately recoverable. DeLillo characters cannot, like Hemingway's Nick Adams, fish the Big Two-Hearted to put themselves back together. Thus David Bell, the narrator of *Americana,* remains for the reader a slippery, insubstantial personality—even though he claims to be able to engage with his self whenever he looks in a mirror. Bell in fact stumbles through life, waiting for some change, some new dispensation, to complete the displacement of the old order, in which the fiction of a knowable, stable identity enjoyed general credence.

In psychoanalytic theory one's sense of self originates, at least in part, in the early relationship with the mother. DeLillo, like Freud or Lacan, extends this idea beyond individual psychology. He knows that Americans collectively define themselves with reference to a land their artists frequently represent, in metaphor at least, as female. In *Americana* DeLillo represents this female land as maternal—a trope common enough in Europe (where nationalists often salute "the Motherland") but seldom encountered on this side of the Atlantic. The author thereby makes doubly compelling the theme of the land violated, for he presents not the familiar drama of rapacious Europeans despoiling a landscape represented as Pocahontas, but the more appalling tragedy of the American Oedipus and his unwitting violation of a landscape the reader gradually recognizes as Jocasta.[1]

By means of these and other allegorizing identifications, DeLillo participates in and wields a certain amount of control over the profusion of images by which America represents itself. More than any other contemporary writer, DeLillo understands the extent to which images—from television, from film, from magazine journalism and photography, from advertising, sometimes even from books—determine what passes for reality in the American mind. Unanchored, uncentered, and radically two-dimensional, these images constitute the discourse by which Americans strive to know themselves. DeLillo's protagonist, a filmmaker and successful television executive, interacts with the world around him by converting it to images, straining it through the lens of his sixteen-millimeter camera. He attempts to recapture his own past by making it into a movie, and much of the book concerns this curious, Godardesque film in which, he eventually discloses, he has invested years. Thus one encounters—two years before the conceit structured *Gravity's Rainbow* (1973)— a fiction that insists on blurring the distinctions between reality and its representation on film. Film vies, moreover, with print, for readers must negotiate a curiously twinned narrative that seems to exist as both manuscript and "footage"—and refuses to stabilize as either. *Americana,* the novel one actually holds and reads, seems to be this same narrative at yet a third diegetic remove.

In his scrutiny of the mechanics of identity and representation in the written and filmed narratives of David Bell, especially as they record an Oedipal search for the mother, DeLillo explores the America behind the Americana. What the author presents is a set of simulacra: manuscript and film and book mirroring a life and each other, words and images that pretend to mask a person named David Bell. But of course David Bell is himself a fictional character—and six years too young to be a stand-in for DeLillo (though one can recast the conundrum here as the attempt of this other subject—the author—to trick the simulacra into yielding up a modicum of insight into the mysteries of the ego's position within the Symbolic Order). DeLillo makes of his shadow play a postmodernist exemplar, a dazzling demonstration of the subject's inability to know a definitive version of itself. Thus Bell's film begins and ends with a shot of Austin Wakely, his surrogate, standing in front of a mirror that reflects the recording camera and its operator, the autobiographical subject of the film. A perfect piece of hermeticism, this shot announces an infinite circularity; it suggests that nothing in the rest of the film will manage to violate the endless circuit of the signifying chain. It suggests, too, the complexity—indeed, the impossibility—of determining the truly authentic subject among its own proliferating masks.

"An image made in the image and likeness of images"

One can resolve some of the difficulties of DeLillo's first novel by searching for coherent elements amid the larger obscurity of its action and structure. The central events of the narrative evidently take place some time after the Kennedy assassination and before the Vietnam War had begun to wind down. Recollecting the second year of his brief marriage, terminated five years previously, Bell remarks that the conflict in southeast Asia "was really just beginning" (38/35),[2] and subsequently the war is a pervasive, malign presence in the narrative. Inasmuch as the hero is twenty-eight years old and apparently born in 1942 (his father in the film mentions that the birth occurred while he was overseas, shortly after his participation in the Bataan death march), the story's present would seem to be 1970. Yet occasionally Bell intimates a much later vantage from which he addresses the reader. He seems, in fact, to be spinning this narrative at a considerable remove in time, for he refers at one point to "the magnet-grip of an impending century" (174/166). He is also remote in space: like another great egotist who embodied the best and worst of his nation, Bell seems to have ended up on an "island" off "the coast of Africa" (16/14, 137/129, 357/347).

DeLillo structures the novel as a first-person narrative divided into four parts. In the first of these Bell introduces himself as a jaded television executive in New York. He describes the funny yet excruciating corporate world in which he moves, a world in which one jockeys endlessly for position while never actually doing any work (people attend meetings, play trash-can basketball, tryst at the lunch hour, and plot the downfall of their rivals). In a flashback, Bell fills the reader in on his marriage and the love affairs before, during, and since. This section ends as he collects three companions and sets out on a cross-country trip—ostensibly to meet a television film crew in the Southwest, but really to look in the nation's heartland for clues to himself and to the American reality he embodies. In part 2 the reader learns more about Bell's relations with his family (mother, father, two sisters) and about his past (childhood, prep school, college). In part 3 he stops over in Fort Curtis, a Midwestern town, and begins shooting his autobiographical film with a cast composed of his traveling companions and various townspeople recruited more or less at random. This part of the story climaxes with a long-postponed sexual encounter with Sullivan, the woman sculptor he finds curiously compelling. Subsequently, in part 4, he abandons his friends and sets off alone on the second part of his journey: into the West.

Bell's "post-Kerouac pilgrimage," as Charles Champlin calls it,[3] takes him from New York to Massachusetts to Maine, then westward to the sleepy Midwestern town of Fort Curtis, in a state he vaguely surmises to be east (or perhaps south) of Iowa. After his stay in Fort Curtis he undertakes a "second journey, the great seeking leap into the depths of America, wilderness dream of all poets and scoutmasters, westward to our manifest destiny, to sovereign red timber and painted sands, to the gold-transfigured hills, westward to match the shadows of my image and my self" (352/341). A hitchhiker now, picked up "somewhere in Missouri" (358/348), he travels with the generous but sinister Clevenger, himself a remarkable piece of Americana, through Kansas, through "a cornerpiece of southeastern Colorado," across New Mexico, and on into Arizona. Significantly, he never gets to Phoenix. Instead, he visits a commune in the Arizona desert before rejoining Clevenger and heading "east, south and east" (372/362), back across New Mexico to the west Texas town of Rooster (where DeLillo will locate Logos College in his next novel, *End Zone*). Parting with Clevenger for good, he hitchhikes to Midland, where he rents a car and drives northeast, overnight, to Dallas, honking as he traverses the ground of Kennedy's martyrdom. In Dallas he boards a flight back to New York.

In his end is his beginning. Seeking the foundational in self and culture, Bell travels in a great circle that is its own comment on essentialist expectations. His circular journey seems, in other words, to embody the signifying round, impervious to a reality beyond itself. In this circle, too, readers may recognize elements of a more attenuated symbolism. As an emblem of spiritual perfection, the circle suggests the New World promise that Fitzgerald and Faulkner meditate on. As an emblem of final nullity, it suggests America's bondage to historical process—the inexorable *corsi* and *ricorsi* described by Vico (whom Bell briefly mentions). DeLillo teases the reader, then, with the circle's multiple meanings: vacuity, spiritual completeness, inviolable link in the chain of signification, historical inevitability.

That history may be cyclical affords little comfort to those caught in a civilization's decline. Like his friend Warren Beasley, the Jeremiah of all-night radio, Bell knows intimately the collapse of America's ideal conception of itself. He speaks of "many visions in the land, all fragments of the exploded dream" (137/129). The once-unitary American Dream, that is, has fallen into a kind of Blakean division; and DeLillo—through Bell—differentiates the fragments embraced by "generals and industrialists" from what remains for the individual citizen: a seemingly simple "dream of the good life." But this dream, or dream fragment,

> had its complexities, its edges of illusion and self-deception, an implication of serio-comic death. To achieve an existence almost totally symbolic is less simple than mining the buried metals of other countries or sending the pilots of your squadron to hang their bombs over some illiterate village. And so purity of intention, simplicity and all its harvests, these were with the mightiest of the visionaries, those strong enough to confront the larger madness. For the rest of us, the true sons of the dream, there was only complexity. The dream made no allowance for the truth beneath the symbols, for the interlinear notes, the presence of something black (and somehow very funny) at the mirror rim of one's awareness. This was difficult at times. But as a boy, and even later, quite a bit later, I believed all of it, the institutional messages, the psalms and placards, the pictures, the words. Better living through chemistry. The Sears, Roebuck catalog. Aunt Jemima. All the impulses of the media were fed into the circuitry of my dreams. One thinks of echoes. One thinks of an image made in the image and likeness of images. It was that complex. (137–38/130–31)

This passage is an especially good example of the DeLillo style and the DeLillo message. DeLillo's writing, like Pynchon's, is keyed to the postmodern moment. Inasmuch as this is prose that strives to become as uncentered and as shadow-driven as the peculiarly American psychological and social reality under scrutiny, one glosses it only at the risk of violating the author's studied indirection. But one can—again, without pretending to exhaust its ambiguity and indeterminacy—hazard a modest commentary.

"Almost totally symbolic," the dream of the good life is subject to "complexities" from which powerful ideologues are free. Focused, single-minded, exempt from doubt, the military and industrial powerful confront the "larger madness" of political life in the world (and especially in the twentieth century) with a singleness of purpose that, however abhorrent, at least enjoys the distinction, the "harvests," of "purity" and "simplicity." The reader who would convert these abstractions into concrete terms need only recall how for decades a Darwinian economic vision and a passionate hatred of Communism made for an American foreign policy that was nothing if not "simple." The irony, of course, is that simplicity is the last thing one should expect of dealings between nations, especially when those dealings take the form of war. But DeLillo evinces little interest in attacking the monomania of Lyndon Johnson and Robert McNamara or Richard Nixon and Melvin Laird. By 1971, their obtuseness had been exposed too often to afford latitude for anything fresh in a literary sense—and DeLillo has the good sense to know the fate of satiric ephemera like *MacBird!* (1966) and the contemporaneous *Our Gang* (1971). In *Americana,* by contrast, DeLillo explores the far-from-simple mechanics of life in a culture wholly given over to the image. The citizen of this culture, however seemingly innocent and uncomplicated, exists as the cortical nexus of a profoundly complex play of advertisements, media bombardments, and shadow realities that manage, somehow, always to avoid or postpone representation of the actual, the "something black . . . at the mirror rim of one's awareness." DeLillo, then, chronicling this "existence almost totally symbolic," sees the American mass brain as "an image made in the image and likeness of images."

But the real lies in wait, says the author, whose thesis seems to complement Lacanian formulations of the subject position and its problematic continuity. The subject cannot know itself, and language, the Symbolic Order, discovers only its own play, its own energies, never the bedrock reality it supposedly names, glosses, gives expression to. Hence DeLillo actually echoes Lacan— not to mention Heidegger, Derrida, and others—in speaking of "interlinear notes" to the text of appearances, a presence at the edges of mirrors, a "truth beneath the symbols." *Americana* is the record of an attempt to break out of the endlessly circular signifying chain of images replicating and playing off each other to infinity. As such it is also the record of a growing awareness of the complexity with which a consumer culture imagines itself. For the author, this awareness extends to knowledge of the social reality beneath what Thomas Pynchon, in *The Crying of Lot 49,* characterizes as "the cheered land." [4]

Part of the agenda in the Pynchon novel, one recalls, is to bring to the surface of consciousness the disinherited or marginalized elements of the American polity. *The Crying of Lot 49* functions in part to remind readers that enormous numbers of Americans have been omitted from the version of the country sanctioned by the media and other public institutions, and this is one way to understand what DeLillo is doing when a reference to Aunt Jemima follows a cryptic remark about "the presence of something black (and some-how very funny) at the mirror rim of one's awareness." For years, one encoun-tered no black faces in that cornucopia of middle-class consumerism, the Sears, Roebuck catalog, but the semiotics of breakfast-food merchandising could ac-commodate a black domestic like Aunt Jemima. The reference to a familiar and venerable commercial image affords a ready example of a reality the six-ties, in one of the decade's more positive achievements, had brought to con-sciousness—the reality of an American underclass that for years could be rep-resented only as comic stereotype. Thus the reader who needs a concrete referent for what DeLillo is talking about here need go no further than a social reality that was, in 1970, just beginning to achieve visibility.

Aunt Jemima metonymically represents the world of advertising, a world dominated by that especially resourceful purveyor of the image, Bell's father (the familial relationship reifies the idea that television is the child of advertis-ing). The father's pronouncements on his calling complement the book's themes of representational form and substance. He explains that advertising flourishes by catering to a desire on the part of consumers to think of them-selves in the third person—to surrender, as it were, their already embattled positions as subjects. But the person who laments "living in the third person" is his own son (64/58), this novel's narrating subject. "A successful television commercial," the father remarks, encourages in the viewer a desire "to change the way he lives" (281/270). This observation mocks and distorts the powerful idea Rilke expresses in his poem "Archäischer Torso Apollos": "Du mußt dein Leben ändern."[5] The poet perceives this message—"you must change your life"—as he contemplates the ancient sculpture. He suggests that the work of art, in its power, its perfection, and (before the age of mechanical reproduc-tion) its uniqueness, goads viewers out of their complacency. The artist—Rilke or DeLillo—confronts torpid, passionless humanity with the need to seek a more authentic life; the advertiser, by contrast, confronts this same humanity with a spurious, even meretricious need for change. The impulse behind this narrative, interestingly enough, is precisely that need to change a life one has come to see as empty—the need to return from the limbo of third-person exile, the need to recover, insofar as possible, a meaningful subjectivity.

Like the questers of old, then, Bell undertakes "a mysterious and sacramen-tal journey" (214/204): he crosses a threshold with a faithful band of compan-ions, travels many leagues, and descends into a Dantesque underworld with the Texan, Clevenger, as cicerone. Indeed, the nine-mile circumference of Clevenger's speedway seems palpably to glance at the nine-fold circles of Dante's hell (especially as Bell imagines, back in New York, a "file cabinet marked *pending return of soul from limbo*" [345/334]). When, from here, Bell puts in a call to Warren Beasley, who has "foresuffered almost all" (243/232), he modulates from Dante to Odysseus, who learns from Tiresias in the underworld that he must "lose all companions," as Pound says, before the completion of his quest. Alone and empty-handed, without the boon that traditionally crowns such efforts, Bell is a postmodern Odysseus, returning not to triumph but to the spiritual emptiness of New York before ending up in solitude on a nameless island that would seem to have nothing but its remoteness in common with Ithaca. Indeed, announcing toward the end of his story that he will walk on his insular beach, "wearing white flannel trousers" (358/348), he dwindles finally to Prufrock, the ultimate hollow man.

In attempting to understand the reasons for Bell's failure, the reader engages with DeLillo's real subject: the insidious pathology of America itself, a nation unable, notwithstanding prodigies of self-representation, to achieve self-knowledge. The novelist must represent the self-representation of this vast image culture in such a way as to reveal whatever truth lies beneath its gleaming, shifting surfaces. But the rhetoric of surface and depth will not serve: America is a monument to the ontological authority of images. DeLillo seeks at once to represent American images and to sort them out, to discover the historical, social, and spiritual aberrations they embody or disguise.

Mothercountry

DeLillo focuses his analysis in the character of David Bell, a confused seeker after the truth of his own tormented soul and its relation to the larger American reality. One makes an essential distinction between DeLillo's engagement with America and that of his character, who becomes the vehicle of insights he cannot share. Marooned among replicating images, Bell loses himself in the signifying chain, as doomed to "scattering" as Pynchon's Tyrone Slothrop. In his attempts to recover some cryptic truth about his family and in his manipulation of filmic and linguistic simulacra, Bell fails to see the extent to which he embodies an America guilty of the most abhorrent of violations—what the Tiresias-like Beasley calls the "national incest." David Bell's existential distress seems to have an important Oedipal dimension, seen in his troubled memories of his mother and in his relations with other women in his life. I propose to conclude, therefore, with a consideration of just how the relationship between David Bell and his mother extends symbolically into the life of a nation.

Throughout his narrative Bell strives to comes to terms with some fearsome thing having to do with his mother—something more insidious, even, than the cancer that takes her life. She grapples with a nameless anomie that becomes localized and explicable only momentarily, as in her account of being violated on the examining table by her physician, Dr. Weber (one recalls the similarly loathsome gynecologist in *The Handmaid's Tale,* Margaret Atwood's meditation on another rape of America). Neurasthenic and depressed, Bell's mother evidently lived with a spiritual desperation that her husband, her children, and her priest could not alleviate. Bell's recollections of his mother and his boyhood culminate as he thinks back to a party given by his parents, an occasion of comprehensive sterility that owes something to the gathering in Mike Nichols's 1968 film *The Graduate,* not to mention the moribund revels of Joyce's "The Dead." The party ends with the mother spitting into the ice cubes; subsequently, the son encounters her in the pantry and has some kind of epiphany that he will later attempt to re-create on film. This epiphany concerns not only the mother's unhappiness but also the son's Oedipal guilt, for Bell conflates the disturbing moments at the end of the party with his voyeuristic contemplation, moments earlier, of a slip-clad woman at her ironing board— a figure he promptly transforms, in "the hopelessness of lust" (117/109), into an icon of domestic sexuality. "She was of that age which incites fantasy to burn like a hook into young men on quiet streets on a summer night" (203).

Perhaps the remark of Bell's sister Mary, who becomes the family pariah when she takes up with a gangland hit man, offers a clue to this woman's misery: "There are different kinds of death," she says. "I prefer that kind, his kind, to the death I've been fighting all my life" (171/163). Another sister, Jane, embraces this death-in-life when she opts for Big Bob Davidson and suburbia. Bell's father completes the pattern: like the man he was forced to inter in the Philippines, he is "buried alive" (296/285). The death that his mother and sisters and father know in their different ways is also what David Bell, like Jack Gladney in *White Noise,* must come to terms with. The pervasive references to mortality reflect the characterization of death in the line from St. Augustine that Warburton, the "Mad Memo-Writer," distributes: "And never can a man be more disastrously in death than when death itself shall be deathless" (23/21). Later, when Warburton glosses these words, he does not emphasize the spiritual imperative represented by death so much as the simple fact itself: "Man shall remain forever in the state of death" because "death never dies" (108/101).

Bell's charm against death and social paresis may be his recurrent recollection of Akira Kurosawa's 1952 film *Ikiru,* especially the famous scene in which its protagonist, an old man dying of cancer, sits swinging in a nocturnal park amid drifting snowflakes.[6] Though he does not mention it, Bell must know that *ikiru* is Japanese for "living." Certainly he understands in the image something redemptive, something related to the fate of that other victim of cancer, his mother. In his own film he includes a sequence in which Sullivan, playing her, sits swinging like old Watanabe. In another, the amateur actor representing his father recalls that during his captivity in the Philippines the prisoners had filed by an old Japanese officer who sat in a swing and, moving to and fro, seemed to bless them with a circular motion of his hand. This detail may reflect only Bell's desire to graft certain intensely personal emblems onto the imagined recollections of his father, but he seems in any event curiously intent on weaving Kurosawa's parable into his own story of familial travail.

The submerged content of DeLillo's Kurosawa allusions suggests the larger meanings here. Kurosawa's character struggles within an enormous, implacable bureaucracy to drain a swamp (symbol of Japanese corruption and of his own part in it) and build a children's park. Similarly, when David Bell speaks of "the swamp of our own beings" (122), DeLillo hints at the personal element in a whole culture's corruption. Like Kurosawa, too (or for that matter St. Augustine), DeLillo understands that *ikiru*, living, can never be pursued outside the process of dying. The power of Kurosawa's conclusion, in which, dying, the protagonist sits in the swing, has to do with just how much his modest achievement has come to signify: it is what one can do with the life that gives the film its title. But this insight remains inchoate for Bell, who seems half-fatalistically to relish the knowledge that his own culture clears swamps only to achieve greater regularity—more straight lines, more utilitarian buildings—in a landscape progressively purged of graceful features that might please children. As an American, he knows that the clearing of "what was once a swamp" merely facilitates erection of some monument to transience and sterility: the "motel in the heart of every man" (268/257).

The reification of this place, a motel near the Chicago airport, provides the setting in which Bell and his ex-wife's cousin, Edwina, commit what she refers to as "some medieval form of incest" (273/261). This jocular reference contributes to a more substantial fantasy of incest at the heart of the book, a fantasy or obsession that figures in other fictions of the period, notably Louis Malle's witty and daring treatment of incestuous desire, *Un souffle au cœur* (1971), and the starker meditations on the subject in Mailer's *An American Dream* (1965) and Roman Polanski's *Chinatown* (1974). If *Americana* had been written a generation later, at the height of controversy over repressed-memory retrieval, it might, like Smiley's *A Thousand Acres,* involve the revelation of literal incest. Bell, however, seems guilty of transgressing the most powerful of taboos only in spirit.

But he transgresses it over and over, nonetheless, for almost every woman he sleeps with turns out to be a version of his mother. In his relations with women he enacts an unconscious search for the one woman forbidden him, at once recapitulating and reversing the tragically imperfect Oedipal model: as he was rejected, so will he reject successive candidates in what occasionally amounts to a literal orgy of philandering and promiscuity. Meanwhile, he suffers the ancient Oedipal betrayal at the hands of one surrogate mother after another. Thus when Carter Hemmings steals his date at a party, Bell spits in the ice cubes—a gesture that will make sense only later, when Bell describes his mother's similar (and perhaps similarly motivated) expression of disgust. Bell thinks Wendy, his college girlfriend, has slept with Simmons St. Jean, his teacher. Weede Denney, his boss, exercises a kind of seigneurial *droit* with Binky, Bell's secretary. And even Sullivan turns out to have been sleeping with Brand all along.

In Sullivan, at once mother and "mothercountry," Bell recognizes the most significant—and psychologically dangerous—of these surrogates. When she gives Brand a doll she replicates a gesture made by Bell's mother on another occasion. To Bell himself she twice tells "a bedtime story" (332/320, 334/322). He characterizes three of her sculptures as "carefully crafted afterbirth" (114/106). Her studio, to which Bell retreats on the eve of his journey westward, was called the Cocoon by its former tenant; swathed in a "membranous chemical material" (116/108) that resembles sandwich wrap, it is the womb to which he craves a return. Here he curls up, goes to sleep, and awakens to the returning Sullivan, "a shape in the shape of my mother . . . forming in the doorway" (118/110), "my mother's ghost in the room" (242/230). Bell's attraction to this central and definitive mother figure is so interdicted that it can only be described in negative terms; indeed, the climactic sexual encounter with Sullivan, a "black wish fulfilled" (345/334), is remarkable for its sustained negative affect: "Mothercountry. Optional spelling of third syllable" (345). "Abomination," he keeps repeating, for symbolically he is committing incest (331/319, 344/333).

Sullivan's narratives, the bedtime stories she tells the filial Bell, represent the twin centers of this novel's public meanings—the heart of a book otherwise wedded to superficies and resistant to formulations of psychological, sociological, or semiotic depth (here the play of simulacra retreats to an attenuated reflexivity: one story is told *in* Maine, the other *about* Maine). Sullivan's first story concerns an encounter with Black Knife, aboriginal American and veteran of the campaign against Custer; the other concerns the discovery of her patrilineage. The subject of these stories, encountering the Father, complements the larger narrative's account of coming to terms with the Mother.

Black Knife, hundred-year-old master ironist, describes the strange asceticism that drives Americans to clear their world of annoying, wasteful clutter: "We have been redesigning our landscape all these years to cut out unneeded objects such as trees, mountains, and all those buildings which do not make practical use of every inch of space." The idea behind this asceticism, he says, is to get away from useless beauty, to reduce everything to "straight lines and right angles" (126/118), to go over wholly to the "Megamerica" of "Neon, fiber glass, plexiglass, polyurethane, Mylar, Acrylite" (127/119). Black Knife hopes that we will "come to terms with the false anger we so often display at the increasing signs of sterility and violence in our culture" (127/119)—that instead we will "set forth on the world's longest march of vulgarity, evil and decadence" (128/120). These imagined excesses would reify a vision like that of the Histriones in Borges's story "The Theologians" or the Dolcinians of Eco's *The Name of the Rose*—heretics who seek to hasten the Apocalypse by committing as many sins as possible. Black Knife looks to the day when, "having set one foot into the mud, one foot and three toes," we will—just maybe—decide against surrendering to the swamp and pull back from our dreadful course,

> shedding the ascetic curse, letting the buffalo run free, knowing everything a nation can know about itself and proceeding with the benefit of this knowledge and the awareness that we have chosen not to die. It's worth the risk . . . for . . . we would become, finally, the America that fulfills all of its possibilities. The America that belongs to the world. The America we thought we lived in when we were children. Small children. Very small children indeed. (128–29/120–21)

We would, that is, repudiate the swamp in favor of an environment friendly to children—a park like the one created by that Japanese Black Knife, the Watanabe of Kurosawa's *Ikiru*.

The second bedtime story, which parallels the interview with Black Knife, concerns Sullivan's misguided attempt to recover her patrimony. In a sailing vessel off the coast of Maine, Sullivan and her Uncle Malcolm contemplate "God's world" (336/324), the land the Puritans found when they crossed the sea: America in its primal, unspoiled beauty. The voyage, however, becomes Sullivan's own night-sea journey into profound self-knowledge—knowledge, that is, of the intersection of self and nation. The vessel is the *Marston Moor*, named for the battle in which the Puritans added a triumph in the Old World to complement the success of their brethren in the New. The vessel's master is himself an avatar of American Puritanism, with roots in Ulster and Scotland. What Sullivan learns from her Uncle Malcolm immerses her—like Oedipus or Stephen Dedalus or Jay Gatsby or Jesus Christ—in what Freud calls the Family Romance. The child of a mystery parent, she must be about her father's business. She dramatizes the revelation that Uncle Malcolm is her real father in language that evokes by turns Epiphany and Pentecost and Apocalypse—the full spectrum of divine mystery and revelation.

The imagery here hints further at Sullivan's identification with the American land, for the heritage she discovers coincides with that of the nation. Described originally as some exotic ethnic blend and called, on one occasion, a "daughter of Black Knife" (347/336), Sullivan proves also to be solidly Scotch-Irish, like so many of the immigrants who would compose the dominant American ethnic group. In that her spiritual father is a Native American, her real father a north-country Protestant, she discovers in herself the same mixture of innate innocence and passionately eschatological Puritanism that figures so powerfully in the historical identity of her country.

The perfervid description of the wild Maine coast and the travail of the seafarers recall nothing so much as the evocations of spiritualized landscape in Eliot's *Four Quartets* (Sullivan is not so many leagues distant from the Dry Salvages, off Cape Ann). In the present scene as in Eliot, the reader encounters a meditation on the way eternity subsumes the specific history of a place, a meditation in which deeply felt religious imagery intimates meanings that strain the very seams of language. Yet the mystery proves ultimately secular, and the only direct allusion to Eliot is from "Gerontion," one of his poems of spiritual aridity. Her shipmate, appalled at the absence of "Christ the tiger" (342/330) in the apocalyptic scene into which he has steered, also sees into the heart of things, and an unquoted line from the same poem may encapsulate both their thoughts: "After such knowledge, what forgiveness?"

The allusion to "Gerontion," like the other Eliot allusions in *Americana*, recalls the reader to an awareness of the spiritual problem of contemporary America the book addresses. The climax of the sailing expedition occurs when a boy with a lantern appears on the shore: he is a sign, a vision at once numinous and secular. He disappoints Uncle Malcolm, who seems to have expected a vision more palpably divine. In Sullivan's explanation, his shining countenance reveals certain truths about the human bondage to entropy—yet he also embodies an idea of innocence and the generative principle: "the force of all in all, or light lighting light" (342/330). He is, in short, the child that America has long since betrayed, the principle of innocence that sibylline Sullivan, glossing Black Knife's parable, suggests America may yet rediscover—and with it salvation.

DeLillo conceived *Americana* on a visit to Mount Desert Island, a place that moved him unexpectedly with its air of American innocence preserved.[7] Sullivan and her companion are off the island when the boy with the lantern appears. Though the moment bulks very small in the overall narrative, it will prove seminal as DeLillo recurs in subsequent novels to an idea of the redemptive innocence that survives, a vestige of Eden, in children. The boy with the lantern, an almost inchoate symbol here, will turn up again as the linguistically atavistic Tap in *The Names* and as Wilder on his tricycle in *White Noise*.

When Sullivan, in her valedictory, calls Bell "innocent" and "sick" (348/

336), she describes the American paradox that he represents, but DeLillo defines the canker that rots the larger American innocence in terms considerably stronger. Bell's sister Mary, as played by Carol Deming in the film, remarks that "there are good wombs and bad wombs" (324/312), and the phrase recurs to Bell as he contemplates the southwestern landscape from Clevenger's speeding Cadillac (363/353). In other words, the mother he repeatedly violates is more than flesh and blood. DeLillo conflates and subverts a familiar icon of American nationalism: mother and country. In doing so he augments and transforms the traditional symbolism of the American land as the female victim of an ancient European violation. Fitzgerald, in *The Great Gatsby,* reflects on Dutch sailors and "the fresh green breast of the New World." Hart Crane, in *The Bridge,* and John Barth, in *The Sot-Weed Factor,* imagine the land specifically as Pocahontas. But DeLillo suggests that the real violation occurs in an Oedipal drama of almost cosmic proportions: not in the encounter of European man with the tender breast of the American land but in the violation of that mother by their Oedipal progeny. "We want to wallow," says Black Knife, "in the terrible gleaming mudcunt of Mother America" (127/119). Indeed, a character in a later novel will describe the "extreme regions" of America as "monstrous and vulval, damp with memories of violation."[8] Like Oedipus, then, Bell discovers in himself the source of the pestilence that has ravaged what Beasley calls "mamaland" (243/231). The American Oedipus, seeking to understand the malaise from which his country suffers, discovers its cause in his own manifold and hideous violations of the mother, the land that nurtures and sustains. Physical and spiritual, these violations take their place among the other Americana cataloged in DeLillo's extraordinary first novel.

This chapter was first published in slightly different form as "For Whom Bell Tolls: *Americana.*" *Contemporary Literature,* 37, no. 4 (winter 1996): 602–19. Copyright © 1996 The University of Wisconsin Press.

9   "More Advanced the Deeper We Dig"   *Ratner's Star*

Illusion, DeLillo suggests in *Ratner's Star* (1976), dogs all scientific aspirations to objectivity. Attempting to decode a message ostensibly from the celestial body named in the title, the scientific community imagined by DeLillo eventually discovers that the cryptic transmission in fact emanates from the earth, from an ancient civilization wholly unknown to history and archaeology. This discovery of a message that encodes the transmitting self becomes emblematic of all systems of analysis and thought. DeLillo characterizes the vaunted detachment of science as, to borrow a phrase from Sir Thomas Browne, a dream and folly of expectation. He suggests, too, that no matter how frequently scientists remind themselves of Gödel's theorem (that all systems falter in the ultimate lability of their postulates), they merely struggle, Laocoöns of the Enlightenment, in the toils of subjectivity.

DeLillo's premise will be appreciated by anyone who may have experienced difficulty with the microscope in introductory biology. Squinting through the eyepiece, one is duly thrilled to observe the promised paramecium, its effulgent nucleus and gently splayed cilia. But then recognition dawns: the image in the eye of the beholder is in fact the eye of the beholder, caught in the mirror designed to reflect light into the apparatus. Such an experience lodges in the mind as a parable of perception: perhaps human intelligence always finds what it wants to find, some image of itself. In *Ratner's Star* the parable grows to epic length, as DeLillo examines the claims of mathematics to be "what the world is when we subtract our own perceptions."[1] At the same time the author refracts and scrutinizes almost the full spectrum of scientific knowledge, asking, in effect, whether the sciences that mathematics might seem to sanction or enable—physics, astronomy, chemistry, biology—really manage any greater insight into the human condition than do such "soft" sciences as psychology, linguistics, and archaeology. Indeed, is there really a difference, asks DeLillo, between the rationalism of mathematics and hard science, on the one hand, and, on the other, the various forms of systematic irrationalism with which humanity has always sought to negotiate the unseen?

The author devotes the first half of *Ratner's Star* to an entertaining survey of the eccentric geniuses—they include thirty-two Nobel laureates—in residence at the vast think tank called Field Experiment Number One. Little in the way of plot development occurs, but this static quality signals the eventual revelation regarding the star message: it originates from earth—not from "out there." DeLillo's protagonist and viewpoint character in this first part (and sporadically in the second, concluding part) is fourteen-year-old Billy Twillig, a recent recipient of the Nobel Prize in mathematics. Comically passive, Billy functions as the screen on which, one after another, the denizens of Field Experiment Number One shadowgraph obsessions that range from the plausible to the absurd. Billy encounters twelve or so staff members and some forty-five of his fellow researchers—with such droll names as Viverrine Gentian, U. F. O. Schwarz, Rahda Hamadryad, Timur Nüt, Shirl Trumpy, Othmar Poebbels, Desilu Espy, Siba Isten-Esru, Orang Mohole, Cheops Feeley, and Schlomo Glottle.

The scientists air one extravagant but intellectually islanded premise after another. Mimsy Mope Grimmer, "an expert on infantile sexuality" (29), wants to discuss Billy's "genital organization" (35). A man named D'Arco investigates "stage-four-sleep," in which "you connect with your own racial history" (264). Father Verbene, an old Jesuit, studies the "semifluid secretions" of red ants. The "secretions teach us that pattern, pattern, pattern is the foundational element by which the creatures of the physical world reveal a perfect working model of the divine ideal" (157–58). Unfortunately one descries no such pattern in the multifarious research going on at Field Experiment Number One.

Although every character has a specialization, a theory, and a jargon, no over-arching system integrates the various technologies of knowing. Indeed, part of the research here involves a committee's attempt "to define the word 'science,'" but the proposed definition, as committee member Cyril Kyriakos informs Billy, remains incomplete at "some five hundred pages" (30).

In the second part of the novel, "Reflections: Logicon Project Minus-One," the character population shrinks to eleven, only five of them central. Billy Twillig's unsavory teacher and mentor, Rob Softly, assembles an elite team that he charges with devising "a logistic cosmic language based on mathematical principles" and suited to communicating with the Ratnerians, whom he proposes to call—in a first step toward denotative precision—"ARS [artificial radio source] extants" (273, 274). Softly's word "logistic" is the adjectival form derived from "logicism," the philosophical attempt to ground language, including the language of mathematics, in logic. "Think of it. A transgalactic language. Pure and perfect mathematical logic. A means of speaking to the universe" (274). He therefore salutes Gottlob Frege, the German mathematician who did groundbreaking work in logicism, as the true founder of the Logicon Project. Because he includes in the project the goal of developing a "metalanguage" that will enable scientists to gauge the precision of their invented language, Softly must be aware of the logistic cautions issued by Gödel and by such Frege-influenced theorists as Bertrand Russell and the Wittgenstein who asserts that "to represent logical form"—to speak of it or picture it, in other words—"we should have to be able to station ourselves with propositions somewhere outside logic, that is to say outside the world." [2] But Softly's breezy assurance betrays a failure to grasp the dubiousness of his enterprise: "What we've got to do is . . . submit our mathematics . . . to a searching self-examination. In the process we'll discover what's true and what's false not only in the work before us but in the very structure of our reasoning" (275).

He might just as well propose assembly of a perpetual motion machine, DeLillo suggests—or a tower reaching to heaven, for the Logicon Project aims to reverse the linguistic disaster of Babel. Indeed, it represents the attempt to devise an *artificial* Logos, a *factitious* Word. Supremely logocentric, the project offers only a profound violation of the medium a Logicon team member characterizes as "undoubtedly female" (330). DeLillo reveals the fallacy behind Softly's vision in a text that, like language itself (including the most scrupulous scientific or mathematical language), constantly embodies a kind of referential circularity. It does so from sentence to sentence as well as on broadly structural and thematic levels. Thus one hears, early in the narrative, of the proposition said to have caused "the MIT language riots" (31): "What there is in common between a particular fact and the sentence that asserts this fact can itself be put into a sentence" (33). The statement itself exemplifies the point being made. Similarly, the reader encounters more than one reference to the boomerang—the primitive missile that functions reflexively, rounding on the one who deploys it. Like boomerangs, the various technographic conceits canvassed here come flying back at those who deploy them. Indeed, the message that propels the plot of DeLillo's novel proves to have arrived, boomerang-like, at its point of origin. As noted previously, the narrative's static quality complements the recognition that eventually comes to the researchers of both Field Experiment Number One and the Logicon Project: "We get back only what we ourselves give. . . . We've reconstructed the ARS extant and it turns out to be us" (405).

Thus when the great scientific project chronicled in *Ratner's Star* enacts a movement from the aboveground part of Field Experiment Number One to its subterranean "antrum" or cave, it recapitulates the similar earthward migration of the frustrated researcher Henrik Endor. Defeated by the task of interpreting the message from Ratner's star, Endor has retired like an anchorite to a hole in the ground, whence he speaks—reflexively—of "man's need for metaphysical burrows that lead absolutely nowhere" (90). Thereafter, in a variety of ways, the various characters (including the author's surrogates, Billy Twillig and the journalist Jean Sweet Venable) find themselves retreating to their rooms, their beds, their closets, their hastily devised snuggeries beneath tables draped with blankets—and even, in the case of Rob Softly, to the hole within Endor's hole. Here, in the closing paragraphs of the story, panicked by the "unscheduled total eclipse of the sun" (419) predicted in the message originally thought to emanate from Ratner's star, Softly burrows past Endor's worm-covered body in a flight that parodies the desperate attempt of Dr. Faustus ("Earth, Gape!") to escape the consequences of knowledge.[3]

"The importance of the message from Ratner's star, regardless of content," Endor tells Billy, "is that it will tell us something of importance about ourselves" (91). This prophecy is realized in more ways than one. Sent into the future, the 1979 in which the novel is set (273), the message eventually reveals itself as having emanated from planet Earth—presumably from an advanced civilization of such antiquity as to be wholly unknown. It foretells the eclipse that violates astronomical science, and because it is "unscheduled" it announces an appalling breakdown, the collapse, even, of scientific pretensions to understanding of the phenomenal world. Evidently the ancient senders of the message saw, too, the absorption of the terrestrial corner of the universe into a "mohole," defined as "part of a theoretical dimension lacking spatial extent and devoid of time value" (181). As the earth and its environs go "mohole-intense" (410), becoming subject to "Moholean relativity" (180), space and time become immeasurable and unquantifiable.

In the "value-dark dimension" of a mohole (180, 357), humanity will find all knowing—not just mathematically based science—brought low by a kind of ultimate demonstration of Gödel's theorem. According to Gödel, the validity of any system cannot be established so long as one operates only within the premises of that system. The "noncognate celestial anomaly" in *Ratner's Star* represents the intrusion of a reality the human mind cannot comprehend because it comes from outside the system in place (420, 434). Along with astronomy and physics, psychology now implodes. All along, the reader has perhaps wondered at the discontinuity, in the latter half of DeLillo's story, between the frequent appearance of first person in the section titles and the unvarying third person of the narration they punctuate. This perspectival fluidity becomes more pronounced in the closing pages, where from paragraph to paragraph, then within paragraphs and even within sentences, the narrative shifts out of one consciousness and into another. Here DeLillo allows the text itself to become a mohole, a space in which identity, answerable to no coherent law, enters its own value-dark dimension. This gradually more prominent feature of the narration disorients readers, preparing them for the novel's bizarre dénouement, in which science and mathematics surrender their vaunted precision to enter the messy realm always already occupied by art and the humanities, the realm of imprecision in which history and literature and philosophy have, these many centuries, taken their solitary way. This breakdown, embodied in the eclipse and in the failure of night to fall on schedule (433), drives the increasingly disturbed Softly to flee, to try for some absolute burrowing away from the horror of the ideational apocalypse.

One of the more engaging demonstrations of DeLillo's point is the subplot concerning the spelunking archaeologist Maurice Wu, who discovers (evidently helped along by the drug or "intensifier" Softly slips him) that the sophistication of the artifacts found in an archaeological dig does not diminish continually. At a certain point, the artifacts begin to be more sophisticated—begin, indeed, to reveal, at the deepest levels, the most developed civilization: "Man more advanced the deeper we dig" (321, 360). One is reminded here of what Bucky Wunderlick, the protagonist of *Great Jones Street,* calls a "counter-archaeology." In the future, Bucky imagines, humanity will live underground and undertake its archaeology *upwards:* "Back in their universities in the earth, the counter-archaeologists will sort their reasons for our demise, citing as prominent the fact that we stored our beauty in the air, for birds of prey to see, while placing at eye level nothing more edifying than hardware, machinery and the implements of torture" (209). The similar conceit of *Ratner's Star* represents yet another reflexive parallel to the story's climactic revelation: the message initially thought to have emanated from extraterrestrial intelligence has really been sent from earth in the remote past—and by a civilization more advanced than the present one.

Whether in archaeology or in astronomy, one ends up finding oneself. As a character in a cult film of the 1980s famously says, "No matter where you go, there you are." Presently, then, Wu appears diagramming a stellated twilligon—Billy has, many pages earlier, noted that the figure "resembled a boomerang" (118)—in the powdered dung of the cave floor where he has found an ancient mirror, traditional symbol of vanity, shallow replication—and unsparing truth. At the bottom of the archaeological trench, as at the furthest astronomical reaches, the eyes that gaze back are the inquirer's own. Wu passes the artifact on to the obsessive, manipulative, and significantly mirror-phobic mathematical Svengali, Rob Softly. This mirror, however, its reflecting surface ruined, will not oblige him to recognize his folly. Only the eclipse, the "noncognate celestial anomaly," can do that.

However disinterested, Wu's nosing into caves represents a further elaboration of the burrowing theme already noted. Just as human sophistication waxes the deeper one digs, so in the present does humanity move inexorably toward some kind of devolution, some neo-trogloditism inspired, in the phrase that so haunts the journalist Jean Venable, by "fear itself" (338, 348, 396). This phrase, too, becomes self-referring, or at least echoic, appearing now as "fear itself fear itself fear itself" (362), now as "fear itself itself itself" (381). It reveals, too, another counterintuitive etiology, for anyone consulting a dictionary of quotations—any archaeologist of locutions, as it were—discovers that it was not invented, as most Americans think, by Franklin Delano Roosevelt. Before him it was used by Thoreau, by the Duke of Wellington, by Bacon, by Montaigne, and by the Old Testament author of Proverbs. More advanced the deeper we dig.

Though most keenly felt by Jean Venable, this "primal fear" (338) eventually claims as its chief victim Rob Softly, who panics at the advent of the celestial anomaly and burrows into the womblike "hole's hole" (438) to which Endor had previously fled. This mole-like progress ("he crawled . . . he scratched" [438]) is somehow related to the burrowing of the "earliest . . . artists" who, Jean Venable reflects, "descended to the most remote parts of caves and applied their pigments to nearly inaccessible walls, the intricate journey and the isolated site being representative perhaps of the secret nature of the story told in the painting itself." These artists produce pictorial fiction, and "all fiction, she thought, all fiction takes place at the end of this process of crawl, scratch and gasp, this secret memory of death" (394). The making of stories, then—on the walls at Lascaux and Altamira or between the covers of books—originates in the secret self, at a level that exhibits an affinity with nonbeing, death, or (for

Softly) the collapse of "something . . . essential to the spiritual fact that bracketed his existence" (435). Fiction, in short, *starts* with the insight so painfully achieved by the mathematicians and scientists of *Ratner's Star*. The writer of fiction, in fear and trembling, burrows to the bottom of the cave (a poet called it "the foul rag and bone shop of the heart") to begin that manipulation of symbols whereby human creativity works with rather than against the medium—language—that mocks scientific reductionism.

Another of DeLillo's projections of artistic impotence, sister to the failed pornographer Fenig in *Great Jones Street* and to the increasingly marginalized Bill Gray in *Mao II*, Jean Venable never completely frees herself from Rob Softly, nor, despite recurring on three different occasions to "having herself been a character in someone else's novel" (362, 310, 396), does she ever realize that she is a character in *this* novel. Only the occasional Nabokov character manages that insight—and here DeLillo wants one more demonstration of how blind we are to whatever lies outside our epistemic systems. Nevertheless, she begins to operate with greater independence once she decides that the book she has undertaken to write will be a novel. In a conversation with Billy Twillig, she notes that fiction may have an affinity with Billy's field: "I plan to make strict rules that I plan to follow. Reading my book will be a game with specific rules that have to be learned. I'm free to make whatever rules I want as long as there's an inner firmness and cohesion, right? Just like mathematics, excuse the comparison" (352). Ironically, her book—or DeLillo's, with which it becomes conflated—may be a version of the needed metalanguage, "the alternate system that we can use to analyze the consistency of the original system" (375). Perhaps fiction, among its many virtues, promises some liberation from the endless circularity predicated by poststructuralist linguistics and Gödel's mathematics alike.

The Two Cultures

Just as the accurate forecasting of eclipses was among the earliest triumphs of science, so is the scientific community's failure to anticipate the celestial event that provides DeLillo's climax imagined as a kind of epistemic death knell, a paradigm shift like no other. In *Ratner's Star*, then, DeLillo envisions a darkly ironic reconciliation of a notorious cultural dichotomy. "Literary intellectuals at one pole—at the other scientists," observes C. P. Snow. "Between the two a gulf of mutual incomprehension."[4] Jacob Bronowski and Bruce Mazlish, in their 1960 study *The Western Intellectual Tradition*, reframe that famous observation: "Every thoughtful man who hopes for the creation of a contemporary culture knows that this hinges on one central problem: to find a coherent relation between science and the humanities."[5] DeLillo imagines such an ideational bridge in the principle of radical uncertainty, which, in the twentieth century, bedevils mathematics, science, and humanistic thought alike.

Fiction and mathematics—both are symbol-systems, exercises in signification that supposedly differ in their precision. Both economies afford DeLillo the opportunity to gauge the capacity of any language to accommodate a reality construed as something of extraordinary complexity, something that keeps presenting the human investigator with fresh, paradigm-confounding data. The point of "pure mathematics" has always been "its precision as a language" (13). Thus "there is no reality more independent of our perception and more true to itself than mathematical reality" (48). "Free from subjection to reality," the mathematician is answerable only for "the deft strength of his . . . reasoning" (117), which, however, "gradually reveals its attachment to," among other things, "reality itself" (118).

Fiction, too, boasts a simultaneous, paradoxical exemption from and responsibility to reality. Historically novelists have defined theirs as a preeminently "realist" genre—even when, as in the modern novel, they sought to represent such pictorially resistant realities as consciousness and time. In the postmodern period, the commitment to mimesis supposedly breaks down in favor of what Brian McHale characterizes as an overwhelmingly "ontological" project—not the representing of *the* world but the making of *a* world. But DeLillo, an exemplary postmodernist, problematizes mimesis without departing altogether from a perceived responsibility to probe whatever realities may exist beneath the surface of—and perhaps be misrepresented by—our systems of signification. He remains within the larger novelistic tradition insofar as, being now wholly unrealistic romance, now an account of something profoundly true that never actually happened, fiction has always sustained a ludic relationship with reality. At once engaged with and divorced from the real, fiction does in fact resemble mathematics, which can be pure or applied. The novelist is as "free from subjection to reality" as the mathematician is said to be. "The only valid standard" of Billy's work in pure mathematics, the author says, "was the beauty it possessed" (117). Billy's zorgs sound very much like a metaphor for art as famously defined by Oscar Wilde: the truest art is "quite useless." It is *only* beautiful. The surprise comes when the phenomenal world becomes to some degree understandable in terms (zorgs, postmodernist fiction) originally conceived as immune to practical application. "The physical universe," says Mainwaring, "tends to provide an arena for the utilization of totally abstract mathematical ideas long after these ideas are developed. Happens time and again" (354). That the aesthetic purity of his kind of mathematics proves always, sooner or later, to model some reality is a datum to which Billy reacts ambivalently, and he is shocked to discover that his special branch of mathematics, the study of beautiful but supposedly useless zorgs, turns out to have at least one real-world instantiation. The identification of a mohole, late in the story, is facilitated by the very category of mathematics (Billy's zorgs) said to be exemplary in their useless beauty and elegance.

DeLillo deepens his critique of scientific thought by references to the development of mathematics and science over the centuries. Thus the reader encounters mini-dissertations on the origins of the zero on the Indian subcontinent and the system of counting by units of sixty (instead of ten) devised by the ancient Sumerians. Also pervasive are names from the history of mathematics. Myriad, the beautiful wife of Cyril Kyriakos, is a walking biographical dictionary of the great mathematicians from Nils Henrik Abel to Ramanujan, Hermite, Cardano, Dedekind, Lobachevski, Poncelet, and Évariste Galois (model, one recalls, for the character Weed Atman in Pynchon's *Vineland*). Myriad asks Billy "whether mathematics has a muse" (257)—a role for which she might be a candidate. She stands out, in any event, as an attractive character amid so many obsessives. One infers her discrimination when, perhaps significantly, she omits from her catalog that important presence in DeLillo's novel (if not its presiding spirit), the Gottlob Frege who, in attempting to ground mathematics in logic, promoted the idea that a system of conceptual notation might, conceived rigorously enough, become some kind of universal medium of expression, free of ambiguity, semantic slippage, and what modern information theorists characterize as redundancy and "noise."

Because this notion had its origins in the Enlightenment, DeLillo appropriately borrows and extends the images and rhetoric with which the great eighteenth-century satirists mocked it. Throughout *Ratner's Star,* in fact, one hears echoes of the satirical treatments of science in the Age of Reason, the age that, in the West, saw the stupendous effort to make the physical world answerable to the human hunger to understand and control it. The satire of DeLillo's novel seems often informed by the now bracing, now tragic wit of similar narratives by Voltaire, Swift, and Dr. Johnson. Thus Billy Twillig, another Candide or Gulliver or Rasselas, travels across the world to a think tank whose corridors he strolls and into whose "antrum" he descends to encounter a staggering array of eccentrics, each displaying her or his exemplary obsession, each astride some figurative hobby horse.

DeLillo's emphasis on the element of illusion in the modern world's romance with science, mathematics, and technology reframes the Christian-stoic premises of Dr. Johnson's great parable, *Rasselas.* The eponymous hero of that fiction, one recalls, leaves the Happy Valley (a name that recurs in DeLillo's fiction) with his tutor, Imlac, and searches through the world for the ideal mode of living. He visits and observes and interviews numerous sages but finds none of them content, however philosophical or scientific. Toward the end of his story, he and his companions meet a distinguished astronomer who seems to embody what they seek: a way of life deeply gratifying to the intellect and the moral sense. Their enthusiasm is checked, however, when the great man of science reveals that, in his meteorological investigations, he has become convinced that he can control the weather. Rasselas and company sadly realize that their last, best model of virtue has been completely unhinged by his obsessive studies.

Dr. Johnson emphasizes the delusiveness of hope in this life. In *Rasselas* he demolishes, one after another, the sanguine visions engendered by philosophy and science among those "who listen with credulity to the whispers of fancy, and pursue with eagerness the phantoms of hope; who expect that age will perform the promises of youth, and that the deficiencies of the present day will be supplied by the morrow." DeLillo seems to hear in this famous period a prophetic resonance. Thus his own story promotes recognition that Johnson's words concern more than the foolish dreams and illusions of individuals: those seduced by "the whispers of fancy" include whole civilizations.

In his youth and sexual naïveté, however, Billy Twillig is closer to Candide than to Rasselas. Billy's mentor, Rob Softly, is less the wise Imlac than the dubious—and libidinous—Pangloss. Like Pangloss Softly embodies a philosophical position that the author exposes as misguided. Softly's sexual relations with Jean Venable may derive in part from the similar Panglossian venery. In the first chapter of Voltaire's fable Cunegonde sees Pangloss "in the bushes, giving a lesson in experimental physics to . . . a very pretty and docile little brunette. Since Lady Cunegonde was deeply interested in the sciences, she breathlessly observed the repeated experiments that were performed before her eyes. She clearly saw the doctor's sufficient reason, and the operation of cause and effect." [6]

Johnson and Voltaire for the most part pillory pretentious philosophy, leaving subversion of science per se to the unsparing satire of their predecessor, Jonathan Swift. Thus it is with *Gulliver's Travels* (especially the third voyage) that *Ratner's Star* has the most marked affinity. Field Experiment Number One, in fact, resembles Swift's Flying Island of Laputa at a number of points. DeLillo shares with Swift what Norman O. Brown calls "the excremental vision": each writer deploys scatology to deflate scientific pretension. Swift imagines his scientists attempting to convert excrement back into food, and DeLillo recurs often to the economics of guano harvesting by the consortium headed by the sinister Elux Troxl, "nonabstract proponent of actual living shit" (413). Billy Twillig, by the same token, is haunted by a piece of invective from his Bronx childhood: "K.b.i.s.f.b." ("Keep believing it, shit-for-brains" [18, 27, 167, 258, 297, 369, 436, etc.]).

Swift observes that dwellings in Laputa "are very ill built, the Walls bevil, without one right Angle in any Apartment."[7] Similarly, in DeLillo the walls of Billy's quarters "were slightly concave and paneled in a shimmering material decorated with squares and similar figures, all . . . distorted by the concave topography. The optical effect was such that the room seemed at first to be largely devoid of vertical and horizontal reference points" (17). By the same token, the "Changes . . . in the Celestial Bodies" so dreaded by Swift's Laputans (164) sound very much like the apocalypse—the "noncognate celestial anomaly"— that descends on DeLillo's hapless characters. As the director of the "mathematical school" at the Grand Academy of Lagado attempts to inculcate his subject by having his students ingest wafers on which formulae have been inscribed, so does Rob Softly feed Maurice Wu and Walter Mainwaring a "high-grade synthetic intensifier" that "enhances insight" (327, 358, 401). DeLillo even arranges for Billy to meet a latter-day Struldbrugg: the incredibly decayed old scientist Shazar Lazarus Ratner. "At Ninety," Swift's unhappy immortals "lose their Teeth and Hair; they have at that Age no Distinction of Taste, but eat and drink . . . without Relish or Appetite. The Diseases they were subject to, still continue without increasing or diminishing" (213). Old Ratner, moored to elaborate life-support systems, suffers a comic encyclopedia of afflictions: "Swollen tooth sockets. Brown eye. Urinary leakage. Hardening of the ducts. Hormone discolor. Blocked extremities. Seepage from the gums" (208–9).

Scientists of the Enlightenment anticipated Gottlob Frege and Rob Softly by calling for a language of precision, a language stripped of rhetorical ornament, a language appropriate to scientific discrimination. Himself a practitioner of the plain style, Swift could not resist lampooning such linguistic naïveté. Thus the academicians of Laputa attempt to dispense with all words except nouns, then with words altogether. They attempt to obviate spoken language on the naive theory that words merely name things—and therefore one need only hold up the things themselves to communicate. Gulliver describes Laputan "sages" who improve on language by carrying heavy packs from which they solemnly produce such items as they wish to discuss. These linguistic reductionists and their *nullius in verba* project live again in DeLillo's pages, for like Swift this author attacks as misguided any effort to reduce or arrest the infinite fluidity and suppleness of language in its natural state.

It was the Age of Enlightenment, of course, that saw comprehensive consolidation of the physical sciences that had, in the preceding century, freed themselves from alchemy and magic. It saw the publishing of the great French *Encyclopedia*, for example, and the Royal Society, founded in the 1660s, now came into its own as supporter of scientific enquiry and disseminator of the new knowledge. The Society's collections were intended eventually to contain one of everything in the world (a project suggestive of the ultimate goal of science itself: to chart, map, or describe—and explain—all physical phenomena). DeLillo's Field Experiment Number One seems similarly to contain one of every species of scientist—from more or less likely-sounding mathematicians, astronomers, and computer modelers to increasingly outré mystics, shamans, lapsed anthropologists, and outright crackpots. "The characters," as the author explains in an interview, "keep bouncing between science and superstition."[8] Yet even this familiar binary proves unstable: in *Ratner's Star,* the more respectable the field, the wackier its representatives. Outright mystics, on the other hand, come in a variety of flavors, from Gerald Pence ("Mutuka") and his whirling aborigine to assorted practitioners of kabbalism, geomancy, gematria, onomastic spiritualism, and alphabetical and numerological divination. Such mysticism, disparaged by Softly as "science's natural laxative" (262), proves nonetheless a mental economy that, as another character observes, "tends to become progressively rational" (36). DeLillo's joke is that Freud's unsparing assessment of the "oceanic" feeling that the mystic mistakenly takes as exterior to the unconscious promptings of the perceiving mind proves ultimately to apply, mutatis mutandis, to even the most respectable forms of scientific striving.

System Interbreak

Thus another of the characters spared the author's contumely is Logicon team member Edna Lown, who begins to play with a mysticism of language not so far from DeLillo's own. Toward the end Edna is surprised to find that her notes and jotted musings strike her as cogent in ways not achieved in the more focused work she has done on the logistic language. Even at their least scientific or empirical, Edna's notes are pregnant with insight. Although they take up what seem to be disparate subjects—sex, language, play, the end of childhood, logistic "undecidability" (392)—these jottings gradually begin to cohere around ideas about the linguistic threshold crossed in infancy. They also help to explain certain curious elements in DeLillo's narrative—elements that grow more insistent and more puzzling. Why, for example, the emphasis on Billy's maladroit expressions of sexual curiosity—his spying on Una Braun in the bath (40–43), his request of Thorkild, another bather, that she show "some thigh" (163), and his general fascination with "female hair down there" (320)? Why do Rob Softly's unromantic couplings with Jean Sweet Venable receive so much attention? Why, at the same time, the seemingly contradictory emphasis on Softly's infantilism—the diminutive child's body, the self-absorption, the fondness for games and nonsense, the thumb-sucking? Why does the otherwise sober Lester Bolin expose himself to Jean Venable and demand: "Show me your fuzzy wuzzy" (375)? Why, in short, do adult characters like Softly and Bolin begin to act as loopy about sex as their fourteen-year-old colleague, Billy Twillig?

Some of these questions appear to have easy answers. In Billy's breathless wonder one discerns the familiar comedy of hormonal hyperbole. In the asinine behavior of Bolin and the infantilism of Softly, DeLillo satirizes the technologue as sexual Yahoo. In Jean's erotic bondage, on the other hand, readers may recognize some symbolic representation of the deference to science and technology on the part of journalism in our time. Softly and his colleagues attempt, after all, to appropriate language itself, the very medium of journalism and, more broadly, the humanities. This symbolism becomes even more disturbing as, repeatedly "screwed" by the technological elite, Jean modulates from journalist to novelist.

More intriguing answers lie in Edna's notes, however. When she pauses over the idea that "human speech derived from . . . the mating calls of animals" (a reversal of the conceit behind Frost's poem "Never Again Would Birds' Song Be the Same"), Edna sees that "words became a playful analog of sexual activity." For the individual, she understands, the intimate relationship between sex and language originates in infancy. As ontogeny recapitulates phylogeny, so does the individual's learning of language rehearse that of the human race. "We imagine the . . . child learning to speak in the arms of its mother. Here we have the essence of play. Mother and child. Language and sexuality" (330).

Edna arrives at a Wordsworthian insight highly characteristic of DeLillo, that "the erotic content of language begins to dissolve" (331) as one leaves childhood behind. "The codes to language contained in play-talk are the final secrets of childhood," she muses. "When . . . taught how to use words," the child crosses a boundary "in the wrong direction." Perhaps, then, "play-talk" is "a form of discourse *about* language," and "babbling is metalanguage" (365). Tracing linguistic sophistication back to infantile babble, one reaches not the zero degree but the point of contact with some infinitely mysterious dimension of language, something like Hermann Broch's "word beyond speech" (which DeLillo invokes in the LeClair interview).[9] An archaeologist of the tongue, Edna moves toward a recognition parallel to that of Maurice Wu. Both characters make discoveries that counter the further-back-is-more-primitive assumption of all linear thinking.

As an adult, one can reapproach the primal, erotically cathected threshold of language in moments of sexual transport. "'To mate,'" Edna reasons, is linguistically to regress, "to pass beyond words as we know them" (332). In effect, she endorses the narrator's observation that lovers exhibit, in intercourse, a "failure (or instinctive disinclination) to produce coherent speech" (280). Jean Venable bears this out when, in the act of love, she "began to speak as though in tongues . . . to utter fabricated babble" (320).

As should be obvious, certain kinds of linguistic inquiry, in bringing the male researcher (Rob Softly, Lester Bolin) close to the language threshold, will also bring him into a state of eroticized infantilism. Edna's reflections explain the thematic relevance of Bolin's silliness and the arrested development of Softly, not to mention the seemingly paradoxical fierceness of his sexual activity with Jean Venable. According to Edna's thesis, the closer one gets to the essence of language, the closer one gets to an infantile memory of the sexually liminal prelinguistic state. DeLillo imagines a special, linguistic dimension to Freud's polymorphous perverse.

One begins to understand why the author makes his central character fourteen years old. In pubescent transition between childhood and adulthood, Billy Twillig is Softly's reluctant playmate in travesties of childhood pastimes. Billy is not, then, the typical DeLillo child—not an innocent savant like Tap, in *The Names,* or the Wilder of *White Noise* (another novel that ends with a child on a tricycle). The most that can be said is that, in his reluctance to participate in Softly's antrum project, Billy may sense his own situation as adolescent suspended between two models of the desiderated metalanguage—the babbling that Edna intuits as its infantile version and the ideal of perfect transparency sought in mathematical symbolization by his adult colleagues.

Softly's regressive behavior, on the other hand, figures as an ironically distorted approximation of infancy, the state in which one may actually remember a transcendent language. DeLillo has on more than one occasion commented on his sense that language neither begins nor ends with corporeal life. "Is there another, clearer language? Will we speak it and hear it when we die? Did we know it before we were born?"[10] In *Ratner's Star,* however, he intimates that the quest for linguistic essence can return one only to a simulacrum of childhood ingenuousness. Blind to this dynamic, Softly remains ever childish, never childlike.

Hitherto the mastermind of Logicon's dual quest for a perfectly logical language and the metalanguage that will guarantee its accuracy and truth-content, Softly is reduced, in the end, to a kind of poststructuralist, deconstructive extreme. Like all true believers when faced with the breakdown of their cherished ideas, that is, he embraces the opposing ideological position. From the outset he has accepted the idea that the first step toward achieving his "totally logical system of discourse" would depend, to use the phrasing of Chester Greylag

Dent (a Nobel laureate not present at the think tank), on his having "drained the system of meaning" (347). This should come naturally to someone in the habit, as Softly is, of "talking in quotes." Billy, annoyed, sees this practice as "isolating an object from its name" and, ultimately, "trying to empty an entire system of meaning" (334). But when, at the end, Softly puts *all* words in quotes, he transforms what has hitherto been an exercise in irony into an admission of the infinite gap between reality and the sign systems by which human beings attempt to represent it. "Each word," as Glen Scott Allen remarks, "is thus partitioned by an ironic valence even from its immediate, syntagmatic context."[11] The effect is to compound, from a deconstructive point of view, the original irony. Softly seems to have understood, at last, the eternal, immutable slippage between the phenomenal world and the symbols—verbal, mathematical, scientific—by which he and his kind attempt to represent it. He admits the defeat of his efforts to devise a mathematical language wholly congruent with physical reality.

Thus DeLillo characterizes the man behind the Logicon Project as king of the hollow men destined to whimper at world's end. Presently aware of "the shadow speeding toward him" (434), Softly experiences the full terror of what Eliot calls "death's twilight kingdom":

> Between the idea
> And the reality
> . . . .
> Falls the Shadow.

Idea and reality, signifier and signified, word and thing, language and the world—all subject to and sundered by *différance,* the gossamer shadow never to be rent. What could be more terrible than this estrangement from the real, this exile in a Symbolic Order that mathematics, however pure, can never circumvent?

The inexorably advancing umbra, like the terminator of darkness that sweeps across the planet's face in *Gravity's Rainbow,* creates a space in which to hear the author's "prayer" to the ARS extant, that "creature of our own pretending." One of the most stunning passages in DeLillo, the five dense pages of the "system interbreak" at the end of *Ratner's Star* offer a kind of summing up of this novel's themes (429). The "system" interrupted here is that of the novel itself, and the "you" addressed is, first, the reader situated "Outside" the text. But the "you" is also a "hypothetical ARS extant"—the entity that, having "outgrown" one "frame of logic and language" (430–31), is responsible for the message that anchors DeLillo's plot. Such a being, with "the benefit of an omnidirectional viewpoint" (430), takes a godlike view of time and space—yet can and does, DeLillo imagines, choose the view from the time-bound, human inside. "To redirect yourself from the Outside, as you're able to do, . . . is the equivalent of entering once more your outgrown frame of logic and language. Having dismantled the handiwork of your own perceptions in order to solve reality, you know it as a micron flash of light-scattering matter in a structure otherwise composed of purely mathematical coordinates" (430–31). One is somewhat baffled here as to whether, for the extra-systemic intelligence apostrophized, mathematics remains "what the world is when we subtract our own perceptions" (432). Can it be that "things make sense," as the narrator observes, "at the contact line of nature and mathematical thought" (431)? Evidently not—this entity merely accepts mathematics as she, he, or it remembers, reorients to, or reenters the "inside" world of "human experience" (430, 433). Thus statements that seem unironically to valorize mathematics remain system-bound, valid only from the limited perspective of "your earthly study of the subject" (432).

Of course the "you" addressed here is also "we." Only the *y* differentiates "your" from "our." The narrator imagines that the entity has attempted to communicate its understanding—notably regarding mathematical insight into "a painless 'nonexistence'"—to time-bound, future humanity. "And so you beamed into the heavens a clue to the limitations not only of (y)our science but of human identity as well" (432). It is this limitation of identity, I think, that DeLillo speaks of when characterizing Rob Softly's frantic reaction to the unscheduled eclipse. The sense of self as discrete reality is the "something . . . essential to the spiritual fact that bracketed his existence" (435).

Spiritual fact. In the end it is to a hypothetical deity that DeLillo addresses his strange prayer, and he repudiates such transcendence as can be imagined from that divine perspective "Outside" human time and space:

> You see our rapt entanglement in all around us, the press to measure and delve. There, see, in annotated ivory tools, lengths of notched wood, in the wave-guide manipulation of light and our nosings into the choreography of protons, we implicate ourselves in endless uncertainty. This is the ethic you've rejected. Inside our desolation, however, you come upon the reinforcing grid of works and minds that extend themselves against whatever lonely spaces account for our hollow moods, the woe incoming. Why are you here? To unsnarl us from our delimiting senses? To offer protective cladding against our cruelty and fear? The pain, the life-cry speak our most candid wonders. To outpremise these, by whatever tektite whirl you've mastered, would be to make us hypothetical, a creature of your own pretending, as are you. (432–33)

The candid wonders of pain and life-cry. Such anguish makes us human—the "message" James Axton will hear again when, in *The Names*, he takes to the Acropolis his offering of language. And that linguistic oblation, we realize, is what separates us from the "painless 'nonexistence'" researchers approach as they trace language to its threshold. It was from their knowledge of this same nonbeing—or death—that the artists of Jean Venable's reverie decorated the deepest, most remote walls of their caves with primitive stories told in a simple language of childlike symbols. Yet the death or nonbeing seen by cave artist and ARS extant alike remains problematic and mysterious for an author so given to reflections on the genesis of language, the primal link in the signifying chain. His fiction, his message, the pictures on the walls of his cave—all concern a vision that, however harrowing, remains breathtaking in its mystery, its beautiful liminality.

Ratner's Star, then, represents an important stage in DeLillo's unfolding theory of language. He steers a course, here and hereafter, between two extreme positions—the one associated with Gottlob Frege (language can be grounded in the precision of logic and mathematics) and the one many of his readers would identify as poststructuralist (language as infinite regression, mocking the desire of its users to "name" reality). Though DeLillo's text embodies both positions by turns, and though his story ends in the flight of its protagonist and his mentor, he holds out the possibility that language harbors some unrecognized richness for those prepared to contemplate the extraordinary insight of Maurice Wu and Edna Lown: the idea of something "more advanced the deeper we dig."

This chapter was first published under the same title but in slightly different form in *Modern Fiction Studies,* 45, no. 3 (fall 1999): 600–620. Copyright © 1999 The Purdue Research Foundation.

10   **"The Deepest Being"**   Language in *The Names*

One discovers in *The Names* (1982) the book of a writer who thinks almost obsessively about language as the medium by which human beings encounter reality—or assemble it. Predictably, DeLillo challenges traditional, naive ideas about referentiality in language, but he also raises questions about the newer thinking that, from de Saussure and Peirce to Derrida and Lacan, has ushered in a much discussed crisis of representation. DeLillo recognizes in language the defining gift of human existence, and in *The Names* he breaks down, anatomizes, and "parses" it, examining the phonemic schematization of alphabets and the larger systems of grammar whereby one "does things with words," to paraphrase a noted philosopher. As his title implies, he lays particular emphasis, in rude isolation, on names and naming, but even as he suggests (following Plato in the *Cratylus*) that these fundamental linguistic elements subsume all others, he goes on, like Wittgenstein in *Philosophical Investigations,* to problematize nomination and to play ever more complicated language-games. Though he grapples with and deconstructs the myths of Babel and Pentecost, he leaves unimpaired the larger idea that language, in its mysterious plenitude, defies all attempts to treat it reductively. Language reveals itself, in DeLillo's seventh novel, as "the deepest being,"[1] something infinitely precious, something the human race might even, according to one cryptic intimation, lay on an altar.

DeLillo invites readers to meditate on the varied meanings of his title, which refers at once to a murderous cult and to what may be its founding perception: that language, the essential condition of all attempts to conceptualize the real, is compromised by the radical superficiality of "naming," the applying of signifiers like packing stickers to the world's phenomena. Thus the author seems to construct the book as an edifying tease, an elaborate demonstration of a familiar postmodernist precept: try as we may, we cannot capture the world in its substantiality so long as it can exist for us only in language. As reality escapes language, so will final information about the cult elude Axton and the reader. By the same token, any tour of the title motif in DeLillo's novel, any attempt to "name" the theme of names and naming, must prove an ultimately circular catalog of signifiers that refer to and modify only each other—like certain entries in the index to Nabokov's *Pale Fire*. Such a tour fails to yield up the meaning one seeks, for "naming" refers only to an endless declension, the ultimately fruitless attempt to fix words to their referents. Like Pynchon's Oedipa Maas speculating on the discoveries, the category-piercing recognitions, of the epileptic undergoing a seizure, we can get only approximations of epiphany regarding the cult, whose members seem to hover between recognition of the divorce between language and the world—and mystical assertions about the secret power of naming.

One errs, however, to look in DeLillo for casual impugning of language as reality vehicle. The idea here requires cautious expression (any lack of subtlety will cause the thing sought to evaporate), but perhaps, by following DeLillo's exploration of language, the thoughtful reader will discover something other than the already clichéd message of postmodernism's looped circuitry. Certainly the "power of naming" seems—from *Ratner's Star* to *Running Dog* to *Mao II*—to occupy a prominent place in this author's imagination. In *End Zone,* for example, a character quotes the passage from Rilke's ninth Duino elegy that registers the strange poetry of simple, uninflected catalogs. Whether for Rilke's dead or for DeLillo's defeated football players, the naming of house, bridge, olive tree, and so forth proves curiously comforting. Among DeLillo's most characteristic gestures as stylist, in fact, are all-noun sentences (and even paragraphs) as elaborate, in their way, as George Herbert's wonderful sonnet

"Prayer," which achieves cosmic heights of predication without benefit of verbs. Thus the narrator of *The Names* will at times pause briefly, without comment or explanation, to catalog objects. In the moment after one of Owen Brademas's more shocking conclusions about the cult and its murders, the narrator can proffer only a Rilke-like, paragraph-length askesis of the verb:

> The twig broom. The muted colors of the pillows and rugs. The angles of arranged objects. The floorboard seams. The seam of light and shade. The muted colors of the water jug and wooden chest. The muted colors of the walls. (308)

Walt Whitman observes that "folks expect of the poet to indicate more than the beauty and dignity which always attach to dumb real objects. . . . They expect him to indicate the path between reality and their souls."[2] With what philosophical or spiritual meaning, then, does DeLillo freight such forays into verblessness?

Juxtapositions such as those in DeLillo's unverbed sentences are familiar from modernist practice, where they embody themes of fragmentation even as they invite acts of integration on the part of readers. Such an aesthetic presumes a recoverable wholeness of meaning and value—and in fact the adjustment of reading habits called for by modernist writers tends to be rewarded by nostalgic vistas. Readers who come to terms with Cather's "unfurnished" fiction, or with Hemingway's scrupulous economy (whereby, according to his figure of the iceberg, he overtly expresses only one-tenth of what he means), or with Eliot's shored fragments, or even with Pound's cobbling together of scraps of Homeric hymn, Andreas Divus, Nemesianus, Sigismundo di Malatesta, Thomas Jefferson, Confucius, and a host of others—such readers recover pictures of history and art imagined still to afford the means to present cultural amelioration.

But postmodern discontinuity is more radical—it is not susceptible to integration. When DeLillo writes a paragraph full of verbless nouns, as in the example above, he expresses something more than a nostalgia for lost cultural wholeness; he invokes ideas of presence that cannot, as Derrida has shown, coexist with expression in the deceptive and misleading medium of standard grammatical structures. One must look, then, to the all-nominative construction—Wittgenstein calls it the "elliptical" or "degenerative" sentence[3]—and to whatever binds noun to noun or name to name therein (*name* and *noun* do not differ etymologically: both derive from Latin *nomen*, Greek *onoma*). According to philosophers of language, this universal binding ingredient is still, as in standard sentences, the copula—but a copula that derives special force from being effaced, elided, under erasure.

Heidegger, in *An Introduction to Metaphysics,* offers some intriguing thoughts on the relation between 'to be,' the humble, near-meaningless infinitive, and its grandiose but also near-meaningless lexical cousin: 'Being.' Heidegger traces the copula and its inflected forms to their Latin, Greek, Sanskrit, and Indo-European stems. This etymological exploration reveals, in the philosopher's words, "three initial concrete meanings: to live, to emerge, to linger or endure" (72).[4] In the surviving lexical unit, however, this semantic multiplicity dwindles to the vague approximation of 'to exist.' The original meanings have become "extinct" or "effaced." He argues, further, that in its primal state the copula must have contained more, semantically, than utterance could accommodate: "Even the root meanings (live, emerge, dwell) invoke something more than indifferent particulars in the sphere of the sayable"—something that, "by naming," they "first disclose." Heidegger, then, remains fascinated with the idea that language, investigated phenomenologically, can provide a window on Being, a term hitherto murky, "its meaning a vapor," but potentially understandable as "whole and fundamental" (73, 74). As he remarks in the Hölderlin essay, "Language has the task of making manifest in its work the existent, and of preserving it as such."[5]

For direct comment on the *omitted* copula, one turns to Heidegger's agonistic apostle Derrida. In "The Supplement of Copula," in which he critiques the discussion of this subject by Benvéniste, Heidegger, and others, Derrida ponders the relation of language to "the transcendental value of 'Being'" and argues (characteristically) that certain forms of reality can only be present when linguistically absent (195).[6] "The absence of the verb 'to be,' the absence of this single lexeme, is absence itself," he observes. "The lexical-semantic value of 'to be,'" then, depends on the "semantic value of *absence*" (201). Thus in verbless constructions he descries intimations of precisely the semantic fullness whose loss Heidegger laments. This presence, which absconds when "named," is Being itself, which Derrida has characterized (in Benvéniste's words) as "the condition of all predicates" (195).

For DeLillo as for Heidegger, language affords insight into Being, and DeLillo, like Heidegger, may see that "what we usually mean by language, namely, a stock of words and syntactical rules, is only a threshold of language" ("Hölderlin" 301). Like Derrida, DeLillo seems to construe as transcendental and even spiritually enabling the idea of presence that cannot be represented directly. It may be, then, that DeLillo's paragraph of nominative sentences allows one to think in new ways about the familiar modernist problem of connecting ("Andreas," asks a character in The Names, "is it absolutely necessary to know verbs? *Must* we know verbs?" [63]). At the same time, more importantly, it engages the postmodern problem of representation. DeLillo, that is, recognizes an important affinity between the gap-ridden mechanics of signification and

the essential feature of literary art—its indirection. This capacity (require-
ment, actually) of art to transcend its medium is implied, I think, in the un-
tended box camera that Axton sees when he finally makes his visit to the
Acropolis:

> The old box camera remains untended on its tripod, the black hood lifted in a breeze.
> Where is the photographer, the old man in the battered gray jacket with sagging
> pockets, the man with the sunken face, dirt in his fingernails? I feel I know him or
> can invent him. It isn't necessary for him to appear, eating pistachio nuts out of a
> white bag. The camera is enough. (331)

DeLillo faithfully renders the scene at the Acropolis on any day of tourist visits:
the ancient stone, the crowds, the box camera (which, as those who have been
there know, is as much a fixture as the Erechtheion). That the unattended
camera is aimed at the Parthenon seems richly suggestive. Is this "the most
photographed barn in Greece," to anticipate a set-piece in a later DeLillo
novel? A camera is commonly the means of creating an illusory presence: it is
the means of producing the sign of something absent, a photograph. But this
camera is itself a sign, the sign of the absent photographer. Aimed at a work of
art that exemplifies the old idea of uniqueness and "aura" (a word DeLillo is
fond of), it is also the emblem of "art in the age of mechanical reproduction."

In the ontologically gravid mysteries of absence (photographer/photo-
graphed/elided copula), as in James Axton's inspired description of language
as "the deepest being," readers glimpse the phenomenological element in *The
Names.* Indeed, even in the recent *Underworld* one encounters emphasis on
acts of naming that lead to similar moments of phenomenological—and specifically Heideggerian—insight. Father Paulus, the reformatory priest of that
novel, makes Nick Shay "name the parts" of a boot, catechizing him on "the
physics of language." "You didn't see the thing because you don't know how to
look. And you don't know how to look because you don't know the names."[7]
Father Paulus embodies *Sorge* (care, concern), a virtue desiderated by Heidegger, and his message to Nick Shay concerns defeat of the everydayness, the
Alltäglichkeit, that, for modern humanity, precludes spiritualized perception.
The minor scene in *Underworld* helps one recognize the influence of Heidegger
in *The Names,* which builds toward and culminates thematically in Axton's
moment of spiritual perception on the Acropolis at the end. This epiphany
takes place in the golden light of Heideggerian *phainesthai*—that transcendent
showing forth or deep knowing in which the subjective-objective split col-
lapses, along with the very distinction between Being and being-known. It is
on this occasion that DeLillo's narrator speaks of language as an "offering"
(331), a medium of exchange with eternity. Language, that is, is divine, for we

give unto the gods what is always already theirs. Heidegger prompts us to an appropriate gloss from Hölderlin: "Signs to us from antiquity are the / language of the gods" ("Hölderlin" 311). Axton, on the Acropolis, stands before the definitive assemblage of such theoglossal signs.

DeLillo's foregrounding of the noun/name, then, along with his stylistic gestures toward verblessness, asyndeton, simple juxtaposition may, of course, have nothing to do with what Derrida unblushingly calls "transcendental" import. The significance of these features can also be construed in deeply negative terms. After all, the cult's similar acts of primal juxtaposition—initials of place name and initials of victim name—partake of no such elided lexical or spiritual fullness. Every murder is itself a nominative sentence that says, simply, "HM [place] is where HM [person] ceases to be." Thus one can interpret the cult's "signature" act as the expression of a desire, on the one hand, to arrest the lexical fullness that gives rise to linguistic ambiguity and, on the other, to suppress all possibility of seeing in language intimations of the spiritual.

DeLillo takes the cult's implicit nihilism fully into account—and gives it the lie by deconstructing the mock-pentecostal question the cultists like to ask: how many languages do you speak? In effect he counters their question with a counter-question: How many language-games do you play? Can you, that is, differentiate primitive ideas of language from more advanced, complex ones? Do you know the city of language, to borrow Wittgenstein's figure, from the palings of its first settlement out to its modern suburbs?

From phoneme to alphabet to complete grammar, in fact, DeLillo probes every aspect of language. He perpends even the vexed relation of speech to writing. In the end, I argue, he invites his readers to join in discovering a way to reconfigure or reconceptualize a notorious prison house as cosmic playground. The figure of the playground hints at language as sphere of childlike diversion, and, not for the first time, DeLillo introduces a child as the mighty prophet, the seer blest. Like the character in *Ratner's Star* who defines a child as "a person who hasn't strayed too far from his archaic collective memories," Axton eventually recognizes in his son Tap a kind of Wordsworthian ephebe.[8] Experiencing Tap's naive wordplay as deeply refreshing, Axton glimpses, in language, what Melville calls the very axis of reality.

The Perils of Epigraphy

DeLillo does, however, do full justice to the prison-house aspect of language. This reductive idea receives its major amplification in the linguistic obsessions of the cult, but it also figures in James Axton's twenty-seven depravities (his list of the faults he imagines himself guilty of in the eyes of his estranged wife) and in the inscribing of political good and evil by terrorists. Somewhat surprisingly, it comes most fully into focus in the character of Owen Brademas, with his passionate interest in inscriptions. Owen devotes himself to what theorists would call grammatology—a term proposed by Derrida to suggest that writing, not speech, is the true model for all structures of signification, all semiotic difference, all language. Weltering in a sea of inscriptions, Owen drowns in waters notoriously without depth.

Owen is by profession an archaeologist, but he seems less and less engaged with or committed to his calling. Even the generous Anand Dass calls him "the worst field director in my experience. This is Owen. He digs like an amateur" (255). Owen's progressive estrangement from archaeology is symptomatic of a larger retreat. Archaeology is the book's trope for the idea of penetrating surface phenomena to get at the originary penetralia (for the root here, *archê*, as some of Derrida's usages remind us, means not merely "ancient" but *original*). By extension, it is the marker for all subsurface reality—especially the reality disguised, distorted, concealed, or inadequately represented by language.

As his commitment to archaeology gradually gives way to an overmastering fascination with epigraphy, Owen begins obsessively studying inscriptions, traveling great distances and learning difficult languages the better to read and experience them. Epigraphy is one kind of "writing," one demonstration of language and how it works. Owen's grasp of writing goes from the literal characters of humanity's first commitment of words to clay tablets to the grammatological tenets embodied in epigraphy. Owen seems, then, to have arrived independently at Derrida's insight regarding the paradoxical anteriority of writing to speech. Derrida, one recalls, deconstructs the notion of writing as unnatural supplement to speech; in fact, he deconstructs the logic of supplementation in all its forms. The existence of supplements (and frames and parerga) argues against the completeness of the things supplemented. The distinction between text and commentary breaks down, along with such distinctions as work and frame or—more to the point—those invoked to defend the idea that speech, as self-sufficient vehicle of "presence," is superior to writing, supposedly doomed to rehearse "absence." Derrida shows that all language is writing. All language, that is, masks absence as presence and endlessly defers the encounter with the thing named. Critiquing the doctrine of writing's inferiority to speech, Derrida makes writing the umbrella concept for all language.

Owen's epigraphy—writing on the outside, on the surface—is a metaphor for language. Pursuing inscriptions, Owen comes to that insight of the postmodern *épistémè:* there is only surface, only language, only words, only "characters"—all of them in a fiendish conspiracy against fixed meanings, final signification, the very idea of depth. Owen's experience suggests a terrible irony in the famous opening of the Gospel of John: "En archê ên ho lógos." In the beginning was the word—and nothing else.

Insofar as these precepts militate against what one might call the archaeological or depth option, insofar as they endorse the epigraphical option, DeLillo resists them—as one sees when the connoisseur of surfaces, the man indifferent to what might lie at the bottom of the archaeological trench, undergoes a significant intellectual and moral collapse. Owen's fate presages that of a world wedded to the literally superficial, a world that has come to traffic only in images— giving up in despair the belief in the more substantial, three-dimensional things those images were once thought to stand for. Bound by steel-forged signifying links, doomed to an endless epistemology of surfaces, Owen is drawn powerfully to the cultists because he shares—half-consciously—their logic, nor does he demur convincingly when Singh hails him as *semblable* and *frère*. Owen becomes incapable of resisting the pull of depths that, paradoxically, his ontology denies. Like the cultists, he has stared into the abyss until, as Nietzsche says, he has become the abyss. But where the cultists may think they can recover, as with some alchemical formula, the absolute bond between word and thing, Owen is trapped in the opposite condition, where one lives only with epigraphy, writing on the surface, never with whatever exists under that surface. Owen in chains.

Owen's drawn-out anagnorisis has its blind complement in the almost obsessive work of Axton's wife, Kathryn, who labors ceaselessly to assemble a few sherds from an inconsequential archaeological site. Axton characterizes the trench she works as "a five-foot block of time abstracted from the system. Sequence, order, information" (133). An intuitive person traumatized not so much by her husband's infidelity (for she has perhaps been unfaithful with Volterra) as by the *casualness* of that infidelity, Kathryn has committed herself passionately to her trench, emblem of subsurfaces and all linear enterprises, all quests for knowledge in depth. When Kathryn becomes absorbed in the archaeological enterprise, she seeks, in her small way, to restore the shattered order and logic of past civilizations that have suffered, albeit on a grander scale, the same fate as her marriage. Manifestly engaged in the outmoded "modernist" enterprise of shoring fragments against her ruin, she strives to validate some anti-grammatological principle.

Though her estranged husband will eventually pursue his own version of this quest, he offers little understanding of her present efforts. His remarks on her pursuit of "order" and "logic" in the "linear" trench represent a phallocentric appropriation—a "naming," as it were—of her experience. As such, they continue the abusive pattern seen in the adultery and in the mocking compilation, by James, of the twenty-seven "depravities"—almost too obviously a patriarchal rewriting of his wife's anger and humiliation (the reader may recall David Bell, in *Americana,* who lists "exactly ten reasons for lying to" his ex-wife).[9] Flattening, schematizing, "alphabetizing" these real emotions, Axton denies them depth and validity. He transforms her subjectivity into the object of his own.[10]

Interestingly, however, Axton's twenty-seven depravities represent an attempt to devise a grammar—or rather, given the suggestive number, an alphabet— of one person's iniquity. Indeed, the number 27 seems palpably alphabetical, since most of the common writing systems operate with twenty-odd characters or letters: 22 in Hebrew, 24 in Greek, and 26 in English. (Modern orthographical practice often refines a few letters out of existence: English once had 30 letters, Greek 27.)[11] The twenty-seven-character alphabet of depravities, in any event, is "inscribed" early in a text that recurs often to the subject of writing, from Tap's novel to the inscription around the tomb Axton visits with Rowser, not to mention the abundant epigraphy that Owen Brademas seeks from Syria to Iraq to Persia to India. Even murder is *écriture:* in their bizarre compulsion violently to correlate sets of initials—those of prospective victims with those of the places where they are dispatched—the "abecedarian" (210) cult members at times resort to the sharp instrument that, as Owen has told Tap and Tap tells his father, is one of the original meanings of the word *character* (10). The twenty-seven depravities recur, in italics, from time to time, but they function centrifugally: that is, far from building blocks by which one may order experience and write wholeness, they appear as ironic, disjointed commentary on a life that, reeling from the break-up of a marriage, is moving toward yet greater dislocations. Moreover, the twenty-seven depravities allow the writing, the "inscribing," of only one kind of reality. *The Names* is, nonetheless, the story of one man's clumsy search for alternative alphabets—in his own life and in the life of his culture.

"Do you know the alphabet, James?" a friend asks ironically (63). Alphabets are supposed to be the phonetic signs by which we represent the world. Though alphabets enable us, by piecing things together, to arrive at whole texts, the painful truth—as world terrorism demonstrates—is that the world one makes by knowing "the correct order of letters" has no objective life outside of writing. It is rather the product of such writing. Thus the terrorists of the world operate according to an alphabet that can be used to write only a narrative of American iniquity. As Axton remarks more than once, terrorists have subscribed to the powerful "myth" of American evil (114, 317), the myth of America as the great Satan against whom any violence, any enormity, is justified. Axton and his nervous expatriate friends ask travelers who have been in regions of unrest, "Are they killing Americans?" (45, 95).

With considerable ingenuity, DeLillo makes the activities of his cultists an indirect commentary on real-world terrorism. Both of these elements are shadowy presences in the novel, and yet they occupy its thematic center. One element is very much a part of real public life, the other DeLillo's fabrication (a fabrication, nonetheless, that strains credulity not a whit). Instinctively, DeLillo allows neither to come fully into focus, but he provides some tentative answers regarding the cultists, who like terrorists respond to some perceived breakdown of cultural order. Cultist and terrorist are manifestations of a need for stable meanings (though only the terrorist imagines reliable categories of good and evil, just and unjust). Each turns to violence in a desperate attempt to restore a vanished center to life. Each acts out of a compulsion that has religious roots—or so the speculation runs regarding the cultists. Each is a sign of times popularly imagined to be apocalyptic. For each, the violence and its supposed ends become less and less related.

The cultists in particular remain pentecostal poseurs, amateurs of apocalypse. Closer to Borges than might seem initially apparent, the cult members pursue a radical simplification, a violent return to the Adamic state of language and primal writing. They strive desperately to force, to dislocate, minimalist signifiers (the initials) into absolute congruencies. "Through a terminal act of connection," observes Paula Bryant, they "attempt the binding of symbol and object into one-to-one correspondence." [12] But what is this symbol? What is this object? The murders in fact effect nothing so coherent. Dennis A. Foster more persuasively suggests that with the cult "reference is replaced by pattern and juxtaposition." [13] The point of the pattern, the gist of the juxtaposition, lies in mockery of the human need for system and order. "No sense," thinks Axton, "no content, no historic bond, no ritual significance. Owen and I . . . knew in the end we'd be left with nothing. Nothing signified, nothing meant" (216). Owen corroborates: "These killings mock us. They mock our need to structure and classify." Yet even "mockery" is too structured a concept. "They intended nothing, they meant nothing. They only matched the letters" (308).

Tower and Paraclete

The biblical myth that purports to account for the dizzying plenitude and mutual unintelligibility of humanity's languages condemns human presumption in building a tower to heaven, a tower threatening God with—if not naked rivalry—forms of petition more immediate than prayer. In the human aspiration to be as gods and in the divine commination, the story of Babel (Gen. 11) recapitulates (or extends) the Fall. Like the Fall, too, the curse of Babel has its New Testament countermyth: the descent of the paraclete at Pentecost (Acts 2), conferring upon the disciples the gift of tongues, wherewith they can undertake the proselytizing of all nations. Both of these myths—Babel and Pentecost—represent the postlapsarian struggle to compensate for the lost vision of language in its primal, Adamic purity. In the idea of prelapsarian language the mythographer projects a supreme order in human affairs at a time when the divine and the human had regular, casual intercourse.

This is not the relationship posited by Christian fundamentalists but something closer to what Walter Benjamin sketches in his magisterial essay "On Language As Such and on the Language of Man." Benjamin's subject is in large measure names and naming, and he addresses particularly the familiar stories about language in Genesis. Benjamin characterizes language as "an ultimate reality, perceptible only in its manifestation, inexplicable and mystical" (67).[14] *"In the name,"* moreover, *"the mental being of man communicates itself to God"* (65). Indeed, "The theory of proper names is the theory of the frontier between finite and infinite language. Of all beings, man is the only one who names his own kind" (69). Reading Genesis closely, Benjamin recognizes a motif: "the deep and clear relation of the creative act to language." Genesis "begins," he says, "with the creative omnipotence of language, . . . and at the end language, as it were, assimilates the created, names it. Language is therefore both creative and finished creation; it is word and name" (68). Benjamin is intrigued by the shift in the biblical account when God turns from the verbal creation of nature (by repeated "Let there be's") to the *making* of Adam. "God did not create man from the word, and he did not name him. He did not wish to subject him to language, but in man God set language, which had served *him* as medium of creation, free. God rested when he had left his creative power to itself in man." Nevertheless, "The infinity of all human language always remains limited and analytic in nature, in comparison to the absolutely unlimited and creative infinity of the divine word" (68). This last (sounding rather like eighteenth-century rationalizations of the existence of evil in God's perfect creation) allows Benjamin also to account for the myth of Babel—which he views as the extension specifically into language of the Fall. "Since the . . . naming word in the knowledge of man . . . must fall short of the creative word of God, there is reason for the multiplicity of languages" (70).

As noted before, DeLillo often arrives independently at philosophical insights paralleling those of linguistic and literary theory. One need not argue, then, that he has been influenced by Benjamin's essay. Benjamin serves, rather, to gloss ideas that may be fundamental to the DeLillo enterprise. Theistic formulation of these ideas would betray their subtlety, but surely the author senses in language (in *naming,* that synecdoche for language) something impervious to the clumsy reductions of pentecostalists and linguistic theorists alike. As

Frost once wrote, "We dance round in a ring and suppose, / But the Secret sits in the middle and knows."

The linguistic secret is commonly taken to be wholly synchronic. Though *The Names* suggests that one must exercise caution in projecting dreams of order and coherence onto any past, whether personal, historical, mythical, or linguistic, Owen Brademas may not err to hail "the deep past" as "the only innocence" (304). As a boy he had witnessed religious transport but had never been able to share it. Late in the book, in India, he moves toward mystical experience that proves disastrously abortive. Suffering a "ruinous inner life" (19), he remains, alas, a person completely of his age, a hollow man unable to connect with numinous experience at either the beginning or the end of his life. He symbolizes spiritually obtunded twentieth-century humanity, to whom only a memory of meaningful religion remains, a memory troubling those it touches with the idea of the numen, contact with which would transform barren lives, redeem a wasteland.

"How many languages do you speak?" is the recurrent, strangely compelling question the cultists ask of those they encounter. The more languages, presumably, the more one has compensated for or canceled out the curse of Babel. From the first time he hears this fateful question, Owen hints at having discovered in the cult something with which he has a deep affinity. Though nominally at odds with all forms of religious exaltation, the cult is as "pentecostal" as the members of the church in which Owen Brademas suffered as a child. Owen never quite calls to consciousness the connection between his childhood embarrassment at being unable to speak in tongues and his adult fascination with the cultists; yet he half understands that some relationship may exist between the pentecostalists who raised him and the people who, evidently training themselves to speak one language after another, seem to hail the polyglot other.

Significantly, Owen retreats into his glossolalia story at the time the cultists—in effect his fellow cultists now—carry out the murder of poor Hamir Mazmudar (303 ff.). Ultimately, the reader hears—never directly—the story of Owen's childhood encounters with glossolalia three different times. The first two times the narrator, James, recalls Owen's account. The last time it structures Tap's novel. The significance of Owen's story emerges only gradually: it represents the first phase of what will become a profound estrangement, a pervasive inner despair. Mastery of tongues, the link between the childhood frustration and the encounter with the adult horror, will reveal nothing of the numinous, so far as Owen himself can see. Eventually, the nihilistic romance with epigraphy will mirror and complete his frustration, in childhood, at the inability to connect with the supposedly divine reality so present to those around him in that prairie church.

Glossolalia is the dream of language that issues directly from the ecstatic contact with godhead—an absolute transcendence of Babel. Hawthorne, himself the author of a book named for a single letter of the alphabet, calls this visitation of the paraclete "not the power of speech in foreign and unknown languages, but that of addressing the whole human brotherhood in the heart's native language."[15] The desire for a definitive linguistic medium also lies behind Owen's discourse on "the evolution of letters. The praying-man shape from the Sinai. The ox pictograph. Aleph, alpha. From nature, you see. The ox, the house, the camel, the palm of hand, the water, the fish. From the external world. What men saw, the simplest things. Everyday objects, animals, parts of the body. It's interesting to me, how these marks, these signs that appear so pure and abstract to us, began as objects in the world, living things in many cases" (116). Owen never manages to recognize that writing—even, as here, at its most primitive—was always already the marker of absence masquerading as presence. His interest in ancient pictographic symbols, in which the thing and the writing of the thing seem closely joined, expresses a nostalgia for lost simplicity, for a lost language free from ambiguity, a lost language of directness and full presence.

Striving, in their bizarre game with initials, to reduce language to its barest essentials, the cultists seem to express their own nostalgia. From one point of view their attempt to inscribe at the zero degree seems to complement the rational interpretation of the phenomenon of glossolalia. Most twentieth-century people view "speaking in tongues" with what Axton calls the "rock-bound doubt" of profound skepticism (92). For the skeptic, glossolalia is language—by definition an intricately ordered vehicle of varied meanings—reduced to gibberish. As such, however, it reifies the terrible insight glimpsed by both Axton and Owen Brademas: that language at its most ordered and precise seems still to be the servant of absence, signifier of a larger, cosmic meaninglessness, the nothing at the heart of things.

DeLillo's novel resists such nihilism as a reprehensible misvaluation of language. Owen's term for speaking in tongues is "holy gibberish" (307), and the adjective seems still to carry weight for DeLillo. Discussing the references to glossolalia in this novel in an interview with Anthony DeCurtis, he observes, "It isn't just gibberish. It isn't language, but it isn't gibberish, either. . . . Glossolalia or speaking in tongues, you know, could be viewed as a higher form of infantile babbling. It's babbling which seems to mean something, and this is intriguing" (64).[16] DeLillo leaves open the possibility that a relationship persists between the linguistic and the divine. Thus when James Axton hears the many languages spoken on the Acropolis, he experiences an epiphany: "This is what we bring to the temple, not prayer or chant or slaughtered rams. Our offering is language" (331). One thinks here of the ram Odysseus slaughters for Tiresias in the underworld, the blood of which briefly restores to the seer the gift of language. From his later cultural vantage, DeLillo reimagines the gift: Axton, the modern Odysseus, recognizes language itself as the supreme offering, that which may yet quicken, or quicken into, fresh prophecy, fresh revelation.

Conversations with Madness

The promise, ultimately, concerns what Benjamin speaks of: the relationship of language to creation. But the crisis of representation has undermined that relationship. "In this century," says Owen, "the writer has carried on a conversation with madness" (118). Owen sets up a number of ironies with this remark, for several characters in *The Names* "write" in one sense or another— and all hold conversations with madness. They also—irony number one— have conversations with Owen, who, with no calling to create, cannot objectify or distance himself from experiences that, early and late, overwhelm him. Thus the book's central, hideous conspiracy draws him relentlessly into its web.

Those who have conversations with Owen, then—especially Volterra and the Axtons, father and son—encounter a moral passivity, an accelerating anomie or weltschmerz that is one of the forms madness takes in the twentieth century. Volterra and Axton have conversations with the cultist Andahl, too, and both respond (unlike Owen, who also meets Andahl) as artists. Volterra, as will be seen, is the more self-conscious but less responsible creator. Axton, who mocks himself as *"reluctant adulterer"* (17, 29), proves a reluctant artist as well—but a more enlightened one in the end. Perhaps, indeed, one recognizes a curious metaphor for art in the work he does as "risk analyst": ostensibly contributing to the security of Americans and their business interests abroad, he engages in acts of petty espionage and eavesdropping. As Hawthorne knew, the artist has, as artful eavesdropper and voyeur, much in common with the spy.

What Axton does not quite realize is that, in repeatedly processing the story of Owen's tormented childhood, he has made it part of a larger and different story—his own. But in one of his more alarming statements, Owen suggests, even as he admits his "likeness" to the cult members (293), that a special affinity exists between Axton and himself—that in time Axton will become him. Axton does not contradict this assertion; he sees the "likeness" as "plausible" (294). Much of the book's psychological drama, then, turns on Axton's moral fate. Will he become another Owen Brademas, another burnt-out case? Observing that Owen "lived with the consequences of self-discovery," James "suspected this was a more exacting hardship than anything the world might have worked out for him" (36). James, too, pursues self-discovery, and toward the end of his story, he makes a telling comment about his expatriate friends: "These are the people I've tried to know twice, the second time in memory and language. Through them, myself. They are what I've become, in ways I don't understand but which I believe will accrue to a rounded truth, a second life for me as well as for them" (329). One imagines Axton's moral drama continuing beyond the story's nominal end. He will always be impaired by his failed marriage, not to mention the venial failings of the twenty-seven depravities (a wonderfully deft index, albeit a negative one, to his character). But in moving toward self-knowledge, he does not move toward annihilation the way Owen does—Owen who lives with those chastening consequences of self-discovery, Owen who asks himself, "How else could men love themselves but in memory, knowing what they know?" (305).

One other character shares the epigrapher's sick fascination with the cult. Like Owen, Frank Volterra cannot resist its gravitational pull and ends up terribly compromised. The whole dynamic between Axton and Volterra is charged with a mutual ambivalence. Axton suspects Volterra with his wife, but declines Del's offer to tell him exactly what, if anything, took place between them. This is at once the courting of a willful ignorance or "lack of awareness"—and the necessary avoidance of encounters with a disabling reality. As such, it bears a certain intriguing resemblance to the plight of the contemporary writer, but not more emphatically than does Volterra's obsession with the cult. Volterra's storyboard for a film on the cult is the novel's central *mise en abîme:*

Look. You have a strong bare place. Four or five interesting and mysterious faces. A strange plot or scheme. A victim. A stalking. A murder. Pure and simple. I want to get back to that. It'll be an essay on film, on what film is, what it means. It'll be like nothing you know. Forget relationships. I want faces, land, weather. People speaking whatever languages. Three, four different languages. I want to make the voices part of a landscape of sound. The spoken word will be an element in the landscape. I'll use the voices as synchronous sound and as off-screen narration. The voices will be *filmed* voices. The wind, the donkeys braying, the hunting dogs. And then this line that moves through the film. A scant narrative line. Everything else gathers around this line, hangs from it. Somebody's being watched, he's being followed. There's a pattern, something inevitable and mad, some closed-in horrible logic, and this cult is locked into it, insane with it, but calm, very patient, faces, eyes, and the victim is off in the distance, he's always in the distance, among the stones. All the elements are here. Some strong and distinct like the towers. Some set back a ways like the victim, a crippled goatherd maybe, a vague figure, throwing stones at his flock, living in one of those tin-roof enclosures up in the hills. (199)

Volterra is really, of course, describing the book in which he appears as character. Moreover, when he says he wants to "get back to" the "pure and simple," he sounds like nothing so much as one of the cultists, pining for a lost simplicity. The movie he proposes to make is indeed "an essay on film" and "what it means." What it means, however, is the abrogation of depth, the full commitment to the superficial, the abnegation of *de profundis* ethics. DeLillo's own self-parody (down to the verbless sentences), Volterra is a travesty of the postmodern artist—or not a parody at all if one believes that the true art of our time is relentlessly nihilistic. Though appealing in his intensity and commitment to craft, he is clearly guilty of an unhealthy obsession with the cult. Axton has his reasons for not telling him what he and Owen have separately worked out: the system of linking the initials of the victim's name and the place of execution. Axton sees through the pose of Andahl and walks away from the prospect of further intimacy with the cultists. The reader may wish him more curious, but he is proved right not to believe in Andahl and the proffered meeting with the others. Volterra gets strung along. Ultimately, moreover, he betrays his calling in the name of a spurious disinterestedness. Specifically, as Del tells Axton, Volterra pursues the chimera of a reality, an actuality, nailed down at last. He has every intention of filming an actual cult murder, and he merits the reproach a character in *Great Jones Street* levels at Bucky Wunderlick: "You embraced the insanity you were telling us about." [17]

Volterra's powerful vision of images detached from meaning, detached even from sound—his mental *mise en scène,* that is, of the cult members in a circle (that signifying shape, that emblem of eternity and nothingness), the grass around them flattened by a helicopter's rotor wash—becomes something other than the honorable artistic attempt to exploit his medium in fresh ways and to achieve, perhaps, fresh insights. It becomes tainted with its own complicity in murder. Unlike such real cinematic artists as Godard (who experiments constantly with the coming and going of sound) or Kurosawa (who, in his 1986 film *Ran,* presents a stunning battle sequence in sudden, excruciating silence), he undermines an essential premise of the artistic storyteller: it is true, yet it never happened. The violence in *Ran* (as atavistic, in its way, as anything perpetrated by the cult) loses nothing for the film's fictionality. Volterra, on the other hand, embraces a species of totalitarian art. Like Owen, he is a candidate for membership in the cult. Realized, his own version of *The Names* would be only an elaborate snuff film.

Volterra, in other words, would discard a distinction preserved in the literary project that occupies Axton's son Tap. Tap works in a genre, the "nonfictional" novel, predicated on the universal fictiveness of any narrative into which one tries to shoehorn reality (a word, Nabokov reminds us, that means nothing without quotes). Though we can only apprehend the undifferentiated flux of the phenomenal world by telling stories about it, we often delude ourselves into thinking the stories objective. Stories are always colored by their tellers, their point of view. Almost paradoxically, the nonfiction novel forces a recognition that narrative, however ostensibly veracious, remains fictive.

Tap, then, remains free of the deference to actuality that any real artist must find disenabling. In his novel Tap creates a protagonist, "Orville Benton," whose initials coincide with those of his model, Owen Brademas. Like the cultists (or like his father at Jebel Amman), Tap evinces a certain sensitivity to such orthographic congruence; here the *O* and the *B* spell Ob, the playful pseudo-language that Axton finds curiously annoying. This element notwithstanding, Tap's father reads the story with near-ideal appreciation, understanding immediately that the real "subject" is the performative language and what it makes of the things that happened to Owen. He recognizes and applauds the artistic energy with which Tap, conscientiously rendering his protagonist's frustration, transforms a dispiriting narrative into a strangely "exhilarating" one. Though no doubt subjective in its way, Tap's version allows language itself to write, or speak, the Owen story, and therein lies its genius.

Tap has found, remarkably early, the one truly numinous calling. He remains in the sphere invoked by Bill Gray, the writer in *Mao II* who remarks, remembering his childhood pastime of making up baseball games (DeLillo tips his hat to Coover's J. Henry Waugh), "I've been trying to write toward that kind of innocence ever since. The pure game of making up."[18] Even as he composes nonfictional fiction, Tap immerses himself in that "pure game." Actuality remains malleable in Tap's hands. Thus the last (also first) of the book's artists is withal the most sane. Writing his novel with its extraordinary charm, naïveté, and energy, Tap seems to reinvent his medium from sentence to sentence—and without qualifying DeLillo's larger deconstruction of the myths of Babel, Pentecost, and Adamic language. In the DeCurtis interview DeLillo remarks, "I think we feel, perhaps superstitiously, that children have a direct route to, have direct contact to the kind of natural truth that eludes us as adults. In *The Names* the father is transported by what he sees as a kind of deeper truth underlying the language his son uses in writing his stories. He sees misspellings and misused words as reflecting a kind of reality that he as an adult couldn't possibly grasp."[19] For DeLillo, then, children are close to the perhaps redemptive mystery of language, and here as elsewhere he subverts the familiar idea—itself a myth, ripe for postmodernist deconstruction—of language as prison house. Language is a prison only for those without the ability to play with or in it. Owen and the cult members, incapable of this ludic vision, are destroyed by the terrifying fluidity of language.

Tap is the artist as child, his powerful language and vision a strange mirror—another *mise en abîme*—of the larger, less naive effort of DeLillo himself. The essence of his vision is that it concerns a boy who cannot "tap" into the "whole language of the spirit" (338). Yet a more authentic version of that spiritualized language seems to breathe through Tap's constantly suggestive spelling and syntax. "I found these mangled words exhilarating," says Axton. "He'd made them new again, made me see how they worked, what they really were. They were ancient things, secret, reshapable." How interesting that Axton sees malleability ("reshapable") as a positive feature of Tap's words—the very antithesis of the reductivism envisioned by the cult (and by Frank Volterra). They seek to embrace a mirage, for they have misunderstood the potential—the *play*—in the pliability of words. Certain of Tap's "misrenderings were wilder, freedom-seeking, and seemed to contain curious perceptions about the words themselves, second and deeper meanings, original meanings" (313).

DeLillo concludes, significantly, by juxtaposing aesthetic epiphanies. Axton's appreciation of his son's humane creativity seems to complement the revelation that awaits him when he finally visits the Acropolis. Both works of art, Tap's novel and the Acropolis complex, offer a final commentary on the book's themes of Babel, Pentecost, and the fantasy of Edenic perfection:

> This is what I mainly learned up there, that the Parthenon was not a thing to study but to feel. It wasn't aloof, rational, timeless, pure. I couldn't locate the serenity of the place, the logic and steady sense. It wasn't a relic species of dead Greece but part of the living city below it. This was a surprise. I'd thought it was a separate thing, the sacred height, intact in its Doric order. I hadn't expected a human feeling to emerge from the stones but this is what I found, deeper than the art and mathematics embodied in the structure, the optical exactitudes. I found a cry for pity. This is what remains to the mauled stones in their blue surround, this open cry, this voice we know as our own. (330)

Mauled stones: dressed with the maul, arranged as mall, mauled by time. The monuments of the Acropolis, looming above the aimless, inconsequential lives of the characters from the very beginning, are recognized only at the end as not that which we have rescued from the chaos, not as fragments of some richer and better and more coherent order of the past—but as an embodiment of humanity's limitless grief at imperfection and mortality. Another artist, also sore beset by life's vicissitudes, contemplated the fragmented friezes of the Parthenon and arrived at the painful knowledge that he would perish like a sick eagle, looking skyward. DeLillo, like Keats, sees in these honeyed stones an art commensurate with tragic human yearning. He hints, finally, that art in the age of mechanical reproduction—the absentee photographer's, Tap's, his own— must be as well prepared to withstand the mauling of time.

The author of *The Names,* then, develops the conceit of naming from less to more complex language-games. DeLillo represents a curious paradox in contemporary art: the more thoroughgoing and innovative the postmodern aesthetic, the more the artist, read thoughtfully, turns out to be a resister in the language wars—a version, even, of John Gardner's "moral artist." Thus DeLillo writes playful fiction that, seeming to rehearse the antifoundationalist gospel, yet enacts a search for some larger moral vision. As Vonnegut and Pynchon embrace pacifism, social justice, and an end to racism; as Nabokov, pursuing the free world of timelessness, eloquently condemns brutality in all its forms; as Abish (I am thinking of *How German Is It*) declines to allow the Nazi evil to disappear into postmodernity's ethical vacuum—so does DeLillo come to insist, over and over, on the something numinous and redemptive in language. DeLillo trusts the medium in which he works and has his creative life. Conceptualizing language at some frontier of the immutable and the ephemeral, DeLillo seems actually—in this matter and in others—to tease the reader with what one might call intimations of essentiality.

11   **"The Physics of Language"**   *Underworld*

In *Underworld* (1997) DeLillo's engagement with language reaches an apogee. Even before one recognizes the central importance of the discussion of language in which Nick Shay and Father Paulus engage, as well as the idea of the single mystical word that Nick takes away from his reading of *The Cloud of Unknowing,* one discovers that every scene seems to turn on or enact or illustrate some principle of language. From page to page it is almost wholly as language that the author realizes his project of a secret or "underworld" history of America in the Cold War years, America in the jaws of nuclear dread. Public or private, this history, as DeLillo explains in a *New York Times Magazine* article, finds its truest gauge in language. From the outset and throughout the labor of writing, the author observes, he thought of the submerged history he sought to realize as something embodied in a set of half-forgotten idiolects. Delighting in "the prospect of recovering a nearly lost language, the idiom and scrappy slang of the postwar period," he ranges from baseball's "quirky" demotic to "the glossy adspeak of Madison Avenue." He embraces, too, "the rich rude tang in the Italian-American vulgate" to render "the smatter language of old street games and the rhythms of a thousand street-corner conversations, adolescent and raw."[1] Language as performance, in other words, vies for importance with language as quasi-metaphysical principle.

Emphasizing the extent to which he sought to conceptualize history as language, the author cites *Ragtime* and *The Public Burning* as fictions in which "diverse human voices ultimately come into conflict with a single uninflected voice, the monotone of the state, the corporate entity, the product, the assembly line." Like Doctorow or Coover, DeLillo "sets his pleasure, his eros, his creative delight in language . . . against the vast and uniform Death that history tends to fashion as its most enduring work." Defining language as "a form of counterhistory," he speaks of "the primal clash—the tendency of the language to work in opposition to the enormous technology of war that dominated the era and shaped the . . . themes" of *Underworld*.[2]

As a writer, DeLillo embraces an "eros" of the word, a libidinal principle of artistic creation. Thus he qualifies what may seem a commitment to the standards of documentary realism (recovering those lost languages). Whatever the delights afforded by his archaeology of street discourse, in other words, "the writer wants to construct a language that will be the book's life-giving force. He wants to submit to it. Let language shape the world. Let it break the faith of conventional re-creation."[3] To keep that faith would involve an imaginative surrender to preestablished norms of representation—to allow the state or the media or some other coercive system to dictate one's picture of social, cultural, and historical reality. However persuasively detailed its picture of America from 1951 to the late 1990s, he suggests, one must not take simple mimesis as the animating principle in *Underworld*. In this complex idea of language that "breaks faith" with convention and "shapes" the world it ostensibly represents, DeLillo implies that realism may be secondary to some visionary quality in his text, a language-based rectification of the ills that Nick Shay and all in his generation are heir to.

Thus DeLillo is at pains constantly to characterize his subject matter in terms of the challenge it poses to language. In *Underworld* he contemplates, as always, the words that seem to provide a handle on reality as well as the reality beyond words. There is a kind of agon here between the wordable and the unwordable: experience tamed because named on one side, experience outside the established or sanctioned lexicon on the other.

The author shows particular sensitivity to whatever resists naming or goes unnamed. The scientists who came to New Mexico in the 1940s "worked on the thing with no name, the bomb."[4] When Oppenheimer called this linguistic black hole *merde,* says Klara Sax, he suggested a relationship between language and waste: "Something that eludes naming is automatically relegated . . . to the status of shit" (77). In the novel's closing pages the reader sees the mirror image of this calculus in remote Kazakhstan. Here the former history teacher Viktor Maltsev, that Russian Bronzini, observes sardonically that certain words—*radiation,* for example—were "banned" under the Soviets (801). But the unspeakable issues only in the yet more unspeakable: the horrors housed in the Museum of Misshapens, with its mutant fetuses, and in the clinic full of blind and disfigured children, victims of "unknown diseases." Like their counterparts who dwell beside the Wall in the South Bronx (or the American "downwinders" [405–6] that Matt Shay's "bombhead" colleague Eric Deming speculates about), such victims of "words that are . . . unknown" (800) are a part of an "underworld" of human waste—swept aside, buried, seldom faced or brought to consciousness.

Counterposed in barest adequacy against this linguistic *horror vacui* is the possibility of learning and understanding the world by naming it. It is a vision of language gradually forcing back the frontiers of ignorance. As more than one character in DeLillo's previous work observes, to live in the world one must "learn the names." Only *language* can free us from the unspeakable. DeLillo underscores this idea in *Underworld* by returning over and over again to the monologues—brilliantly mimicked, not transcribed—of hipster Lenny Bruce. Like DeLillo himself, Lenny exhibits "*Sprachgefühl,* a feel for language" (585). Like the author, too, he thinks of language as eroticized, an "eros," and on stage he tries, outrageously, to fit a condom over his tongue. DeLillo devotes considerable space to the monologues because the man who delivers them insists on putting all of the forbidden subject matter into verbal play. He devotes himself to the unspeakable and the obscene in all senses of those words, forcing into language all that comfortable middle-class America most fears and is least willing to confront: race, sexual anatomy, and, during the Cuban Missile Crisis, the terror of nuclear Armageddon. The authorities bust him repeatedly for his *language.*

The old Jesuit, Father Paulus, may seem an unlikely fellow traveler, but he, too, teaches the naming of parts. In a conversation with Albert Bronzini, Father Paulus speaks briefly of an educational experiment his order plans to undertake: "Latin as a spoken language," "mathematics as an art form like poetry or music," "subjects that people don't realize they need to know" (675). Presently established in remote Minnesota, the experimental school welcomes a chastened Nick Shay when he gains his release from the reformatory to which he was sent after the killing of George Manza. Though he drifts into anomie later in life, Nick remains always much influenced by what he learns from Father Paulus at the Jesuit school.

In an important scene Father Paulus catechizes Nick Shay on the words for parts of a shoe. The priest's real subject is "the physics of language" (542), especially the linguistic analogue to particle theory: what remains invisible because unworded or unwordable. "You didn't see the thing because you don't know how to look. And you don't know how to look because you don't know the names," says Father Paulus (540). "How everyday things lie hidden. Because we don't know what they're called" (541). Nick returns from his session with Father Paulus with a sense that some active engagement with language and its mechanics might be "the only way in the world you can escape the things that made you" (543). This insight is of immense importance to an aesthetic vision that, rooted in naturalism, seeks nonetheless to refute—or at least revisit—that movement's argument against free will. In interviews DeLillo has called the conversation between delinquent and Jesuit "theological," at least "in a sense." To Diane Osen he explained that the discussion "has a shaping effect on Nick. It occurs to him, as the perpetrator of a violent act, that what he needs to transcend this act, to un-invent and then remake himself, is a grip on language."[5]

And language, his story suggests, is a power greater than the inexorable forces of social decline, greater than history itself. As DeLillo's fictionalized Lenny Bruce says, "Never underestimate the power of language" (582). Language favors those who recognize its importance and imposes terrible penalties on those who neglect or betray it. This message figures in a number of ways, but especially in the "naming of parts" motif that recurs throughout the text. Becoming a connoisseur of accurate terminology, Nick learns the names: "A hawser is the thing you tie around a bollard" (103), the "crimp" lies "at the bottom of the toothpaste tube" (105). "This is the washer, this is the packing, this is the spout" (119). He knows what "spectator shoes" are (337), and he delights in etymologies, especially those "from the Latin" (102, 106, 120, 621, 805, etc.), which he studies "in school, then on my own, pretty intensively" (281). In later years he himself teaches both English and Latin.

Speaking with Gerald Howard, DeLillo notes that as with his character, so with any writer, like himself, who comes of age through a mastery of words: "It occurs to me that this is what a writer does to transcend the limitations of his background. He does it through language, obviously. He writes himself into the larger world. He opens himself to the entire culture. He becomes, in short, an American—the writer equivalent of his immigrant parents and grandparents. And so there are two sets of language in this book. The difference between them isn't very stark but in fact a sort of journey is detectable, solely in sentences and pacing and word choice, between the Bronx of Part Six and the larger environment that surrounds it."[6] The ontogeny of the writer recapitulates, as it were, the phylogeny of letters. Though one would err to think Nick Shay an autobiographical character, he shares with his creator a sensitivity to language, and in the relationship of word mastery to *Bildung* one recognizes an essential parallel between the two.

Like a writer, then, Nick transcends his background through language, but he has only mixed success in seeking the word of words that might deliver him from midlife *Weltschmerz*. The idea of such a word also dates, for Nick, from his season among the Jesuits in Minnesota. One of the books he read was the fourteenth-century mystical treatise *The Cloud of Unknowing* (which provides the title of part 3 of DeLillo's novel and also figures in *White Noise*), presumably put into his hands by Father Paulus, who may have thereby signaled the next stage in Nick's lifelong engagement with language. Years later, Nick will remember the book for an interpellation, a hailing, that seems almost personal: "Pause for a moment, you wretched weakling, and take stock of yourself" (295). But the context in which this recollection comes up is decidedly unsanctified: Nick is half-heartedly making a pass at a woman attending a swingers' conclave in the Mojave Desert. He is at once attracted to and repelled by her and her friends. What is remarkable is that he reveals his spiritual side to this stranger, tells her things about himself—not just what a fourteenth-century mystical work means to him but that he had, as a youth, killed a man—that he would not tell his wife or children, with whom he interacts only with emotional distance: "You withhold the deepest things from those who are closest and then talk to a stranger in a numbered room" (301). This "lontananza" lies at the heart of his mature alienation, and the book is to some degree the record of his struggle with an emotional reticence dictating, among other things, that one can affirm one's belief-system in the workplace or to a strange woman in a hotel room, but not at home (303).

He regales Donna, then, not his wife Marian, with the kernels he has gleaned from *The Cloud of Unknowing*. The book teaches him that he cannot apprehend God "through the intellect" alone, that he must find a single, mystical, prayer-like word of "naked intent" to pass into, if not dispel, the Cloud of Unknowing that surrounds the numen. This, we recognize, is a recurrent DeLillo ideal, Broch's word beyond speech, the pure *erworbenes Wort* of Rilke's ninth Duino elegy. But Nick cannot discover a suitable one-syllabled word: "I thought the problem is language, I need to change languages, find a word that is pure word" (296). Nick eventually settles for Saint John of the Cross's phrase

Todo y nada, the inadequacy of which seems manifest when, years later, he and the woman he is seducing agree that it defines what "two people share word-lessly more or less"—"the best sex" (297).

But the principle remains, the idea that there might be a numinous word that could, as the focus of meditation, bring one closer to the divine principle. At the end of this novel, of course, the word *peace* appears (827), a word of the requisite single syllable desiderated in *The Cloud of Unknowing.* Abandoning the Sanskrit of Owen Brademas and T. S. Eliot, DeLillo intimates the reply to travail such as theirs: not the limp exhaustion of *shantih, shantih, shantih* but the simple hope of a true shibboleth, one's "naked edge," one's "edging into darkness, into the secret of God" (297). Characterizing *peace* as "a word that spreads a longing" (827), the narrator invites a connection with "the sharp dart of longing love" (298) that motivates the mystic in *The Cloud of Unknowing* or the "mutilated yearning" (444) expressed in Eisenstein's *Unterwelt.* Indeed, the longing invoked on the last page of *Underworld* figures also on the first: "Longing on a large scale is what makes history" (11). "Don't underestimate our capacity for complex longings," remarks the former garbage guerilla Jesse Detweiler (285). But "most of our longings," as Nick Shay observes, "go un-fulfilled. That is the word's wistful implication—a desire for something lost or fled or otherwise out of reach" (803).

Nostalgie de la Boue

With its attention to mystical words and the "theological" significance of nam-ing, *Underworld* is in large measure a story of spiritual travail. Nick Shay, pro-tagonist and sometime narrator, apprentices himself to an onomastic master more venerable, even, that Father Paulus: in the names that he studies so as-siduously one discerns nothing less than the mythic legacy of Adam. Nick's lifelong alienation has its theological point as well, for his slaying of George Manza is a version of the fall, the primal transgression that can be fully expiated only in eternity. Some such absolutist frame may account for a curiously Janus-faced element in the narrative's unfolding affect. Throughout his story (but with increasing insistence as he gets older), Nick presents himself to the reader as a person who, though unable finally to transcend his past and what it has done to him, seems nonetheless to be moving toward a degree of equanimity. A pure product of the Bronx, Nick lives now in Phoenix, the city that David Bell, in *Americana,* never gets to in his odyssey through the American West. Here the city in the desert seems an appropriate home for a person subject to late-Christian yearnings for some ultimate recycling of what must otherwise rot in the rubbish pile of Gehenna.

In Nick's frequent references to the conscientiousness he and his family bring to recycling, one sees something more than the author's desire to equip his character with traits appropriate to his professional involvement with waste:

> At home we removed the wax paper from cereal boxes. We had a recycling closet with separate bins for newspapers, cans and jars. We rinsed out the used cans and empty bottles and put them in their proper bins. We did tin versus aluminum. On pickup days we placed each form of trash in its separate receptacle. . . . We used a paper bag for the paper bags. We took a large paper bag and put all the smaller bags inside and then placed the large bag alongside all the other receptacles on the sidewalk. We ripped the wax paper from our boxes of shredded wheat. There is no language I might formulate that could overstate the diligence we brought to these tasks. We did the yard waste. We bundled the newspapers but did not tie them in twine. (102–3)

This passage is itself recycled, a version of it having appeared earlier (89)—nor does it conclude the recycling, for at least two more variants will appear in the story (803–4, 806–7). Verbal recycling takes place, moreover, even within the brief confines of the present example (the repetition of the point about wax paper and cereal boxes, the repetition of individual words like *receptacles* and *paper bags*). The "no language" locution seems to come naturally to sustained evocations of waste. Freighted with dread, the affirmation of ecological "diligence" here frames and partly masks a half-conscious hunger for the larger recycling of spiritual waste. The speaker, that is, cannot disguise a deep disquiet that his recycling efforts (not to mention his almost obsessive recounting of them) do not keep at bay. Like Jack Gladney poking through the trash or Gary Harkness encountering the excrement in the desert, Nick fears that "what we excrete comes back to consume us" (791), that human beings must eventually become the garbage they generate in such quantities.

DeLillo is unsparing in his depiction of Nick's residual disquiet, which cannot be allayed by smoothing things out with Marian, by becoming a grandfather, or by savoring his professional success. One can never, it seems, leave altogether behind the loss of a father, the act of "criminal negligence" that resulted in a death, the marital betraying and being betrayed. In a way, Nick suffers the fate of the child touched, in his brother Matt's fantasy, by "Sister Skelly Bone" to become "*it* forever" (717). Profoundly suggestive, this condition of being "it" also fascinates Albert Bronzini, who recognizes "a fearsome power in the term" that renders one not just "separate from all the others" but "nameless" or "name-shorn" (677). Himself shorn of the paternal surname, the son of Jimmy Costanza seems to exemplify the pronouncement of Klara Sax regarding the disturbing connection between namelessness and waste.

"It" all his life, Nick may recognize an affinity with the children he sees in Kazakhstan. Always and irreversibly "it" in the gamesmanship of nuclear powers, these children play at versions of the amusements Albert Bronzini and Father Paulus reminisce about—amusements that have survived unchanged for centuries, as Father Paulus, recalling Bruegel's 1560 canvas *De Kinderspelen,* points out to Bronzini. But when the latter mentions the painting to his wife Klara, she not only characterizes it as "unwholesome," "sinister," and filled with some nameless "menace" (682), she links it to Bruegel's terrifying apocalyptic canvas *The Triumph of Death* (ca. 1562). The discussions of Albert, Klara, and Father Paulus take place in the same historical moment—1951—as the author's previous introduction of Bruegel: J. Edgar Hoover's encounter with *The Triumph of Death* floating from the upper stands at a baseball field (of course six hundred pages have intervened, with temporal settings throughout the latter part of the century, including the 1966 of Truman Capote's Black and White Ball, at which Klara—in another life and on the arm of another husband—actually crosses paths with Hoover). But much comes together in this long-delayed dropping of the second allusive shoe—especially when the subject of children's games recurs in the Kazakhstan sequence, where Nick observes a group of disfigured children "playing follow the leader. A boy falls down, gets up. They all fall down, get up" (802). This game and its cousin, Blindman's Bluff, figure in *De Kinderspelen,* but as the Kazakh children stumble over each other they momentarily act out another Bruegel painting, *The Parable of the Blind* (1568), which pictorializes the familiar biblical precept: "If the blind lead the blind, both shall fall into the ditch" (Matt. 15.14). In the mutual blindness of nuclear rivalry, a particularly fearsome ditch first yawned on that day in 1951 when, as the Soviets tested the bomb and as assorted innocents played a game—its antecedents also appear in Bruegel's 1560 painting—with stick and ball, the reproduction of that other Bruegel wafts earthward as gently as radioactive dew.

The Kazakh victims of radiation figure proleptically in DeLillo's imagined Sergei Eisenstein film *Unterwelt,* which supplies this novel's title with one of its important referents.[7] Thought to have been filmed in Kazakhstan some time in the thirties, *Unterwelt* concerns the horribly mutilated and crippled victims of a crazed scientist, the embodiment of Faustian desire and its consequences. DeLillo represents this film as the anticipation of a cinematic subgenre that would flourish during the first decade of the Cold War. A kind of cross between Fritz Lang's *Metropolis* (a screening of which DeLillo once saw at Radio City

Music Hall) and Wells's *The Island of Dr. Moreau, Unterwelt* parodies both "Japanese science fiction"[8] cinema (though less explicitly than Pynchon in *Vineland*) and the exercises in nuclear dread that proliferated in the 1950s— variously witting allegories of atom-bomb-engendered teratology and Communist infiltration (from *Them* to such aliens-among-us films as *Invasion of the Body Snatchers* and *Village of the Damned*). But this element of droll pastiche proves unstable. With an irony that has its own half-life, like some radioactive isotope, DeLillo imagines *Unterwelt* as modulating toward more sober augury. A Bruegel for the twentieth century, its director prophesies the atrocities committed on the human form at Auschwitz, at Hiroshima, and at Minamata, as well as the horrors witnessed by Nick.

In the epilogue Nick remains subject to feelings of loneliness, loss, and confusion: "I don't know what happened, do I?" (807). Set in the 1990s (but otherwise, as he told Peter Körte, "temporally unspecific"),[9] the novel's concluding section begins in Moscow, proceeds to Kazakhstan, and ends in Phoenix, where Nick may or may not be a candidate for rebirth from his own ashes. Only here does Nick himself engage in the present-tense narration that has hitherto been reserved for the Texas Highway Killer videotape and accounts of the mythic baseball's early career (i.e., all of the sections narrated from the point of view of Cotter Martin or his father, Manx). Nick comes to terms with Jimmy Costanza's desertion, concluding that his father simply "went under," without giving much thought to his abandoned family. But "the failure it brought down on us does not diminish" (809). Confronting Brian Glassic, another of DeLillo's reluctant adulterers, Nick momentarily threatens to become Jack Gladney redux, the cuckold who embraces atavistic violence (the reader may recognize in Nick a version, as well, of the Albert Bronzini who loses a mother to death and suffers—with Nick himself in the Brian Glassic role—a spouse's betrayal). On the verge of confrontation, Nick reflects on himself as some kind of impostor: "Brian thought I was the soul of self-completion. Maybe so. But I was also living in a state of quiet separation from all the things he might cite as the solid stuff of home and work and responsible reality. When I found out . . . I was hereby relieved of my phony role as husband and father, high corporate officer. Because even the job is an artificial limb. Did I feel free for just a moment, myself again, hearing the story of their affair? . . . None of it ever belonged to me except in the sense that I filled out the forms" (796). The last phrase suggests that one might switch roles (or identities) as one switches jobs: just fill out more application forms. It also suggests that one's roles in life merely approximate—fill out—certain ideals or "forms" of the Platonic variety. Nick had once helped the marginally literate George

Manza to fill out forms (690), and the figure, repeated, hints at a symbolic role for George as the shadow self that drifts into addiction and untimely death while another, more privileged self fills out other forms. More than the circumstance that shapes a naturalistic literary action, then, Nick's murder of George is a slaying of the double, the self that by rights Nick (a drop-out at sixteen) was destined to be.

But in the Jungian system one must integrate—not deny or destroy—the shadow self, and Nick's act takes a psychological toll throughout his life. His occasional experience of something like serenity at the end must vie with more durable feelings of incompleteness. Nick qualifies his sense of having survived most revealingly when he thinks, "I'll tell you what I long for, the days of disarray, when I didn't give a damn or a fuck or a farthing" (806). DeLillo told one interviewer that he considers this a "telling" admission. Nick "ultimately expresses his regret and longing for the days when he felt physically connected to the earth. The days when he had freedom to commit transgressive acts. And it's not a nostalgia for innocence, it's a nostalgia for guilt." [10] Nick's expression of yearning for the gutter encourages the reader to see the true psychological and sociological complexity of this story. It cannot end with some unqualified affirmation or renewal in the city named for an archetype of resurrection— for the conflicting perceptions and the heavy weight of history conspire to allow only the most fitful visitations of grace, only occasional reversals of the anomie that has grown unchecked through a century of weapons, waste, and woe. This tough-minded adherence to a postlapsarian reality principle makes of *Underworld* something greater than a simple *ubi sunt* elegy for the passion, the certainty, the simplicity of youth. It is the companion piece to those great documents of bitter reconciliation to a lost vitality—texts such as Willa Cather's *The Professor's House,* Frost's poem "The Oven Bird," and the Immortality Ode. "You used to have the same dimensions as the observable universe," remarks Marian Shay to Brian Glassic, her feckless lover; "Now you're a lost speck" (170).

"Everything Connects in the End"

A speck. The image is that of any homer but especially, of course, the single baseball that more than one character intuitively sees as the living vehicle of a whole culture's youth. Marvin Lundy understands, when he relinquishes the ball, that "there's men in the coming years they'll pay fortunes. . . . They'll pay unbelievable. Because this is desperation speaking" (182). A postmodern refinement of the familiar twentieth-century angst, this desperation cloaks a hunger for authentic experience, for the historically unique event that binds whole nations. Such was the Bobby Thomson home run, a "shot heard 'round the world" by which ordinary people might experience a moment of shared historical intensity (unlike remote "upperworld" events such as the contemporaneous Soviet bomb test). What Lundy—and DeLillo—sees is that we live more and more in a world incapable of such authenticity. All such experience is pithed as it becomes endlessly replicated as mass consumption image or soundbite. In his *New York Times Magazine* article, DeLillo speaks of "the debasing process of frantic repetition that exhausts a contemporary event before it has rounded into coherence." This is the point of the Texas Highway Killer videotape, repeated screening of which encapsulates our experience with all media spectacle and with a host of related simulacra in a "culture" that "continues its drive to imitate itself endlessly—the rerun, the sequel, the theme park, the designer outlet—because this is the means it has devised to disremember the past."[11] The paradox resembles the one Freud identified in repetition compulsion: ostensibly grounded in a desire to take control of a painful reality (the absence of the mother in the famous *fort/da* illustration of *Beyond the Pleasure Principle*), repetition presently reveals itself as a drive to recover a prior inorganic state. Some such "death wish," DeLillo intimates, lies behind the culture's sick love affair with repetition.

Television news routinely screens and re-screens footage of sensational crime or disaster: Ruby murdering Oswald, assassinations attempted and carried out, the Rodney King beating, the terrible fall of the *Challenger*. DeLillo's cautionary remarks about this media phenomenon make clear the way or ways in which his imaginary Texas Highway Killer videotape functions in *Underworld:*

> You're staring at the inside of a convenience store on a humdrum night in July. This is a surveillance video with a digital display that marks off the tenths of seconds. Then you see a shuffling man with a handgun enter the frame. The commonplace homicide that ensues is transformed in the image-act of your own witness. It is bare, it is real, it is live, it is taped. It is compelling, it is numbing, it is digitally microtimed and therefore filled with incessant information. And if you view the tape often enough, it tends to transform you, to make you a passive variation of the armed robber in his warped act of consumption. It is another set of images for you to want and need and get sick of and need nonetheless, and it separates you from the reality that beats ever more softly in the diminishing world outside the tape.[12]

Diminishing reality—like the home-run ball that dwindles to a "speck" as it sails out of the stadium. With instant replay, however, the diminishment is compounded—not, as one might think, reversed or arrested. The point of the Bobby Thomson baseball is that it embodies a wholly memorable piece of reality—of history, even—precisely because it could not be "replayed." It remains *un*diminished as an experience of reality because it was never transformed into media simulacrum. Though it can embody bad luck, it remains the story's grail, brimming with the redemptive blood of historical truth. A tiny speck of unique experience and real history, the baseball is in the car with Judson Rauch at the time of his fatal encounter with the Texas Highway Killer. If this detail goes unnoticed at a first reading, all the better for DeLillo's point: the simulacrum elbows aside its counterpart in reality, overwhelms the old model of experience (memorable because unique, literally unrepeatable).

The baseball is also a textual nexus, linking virtually all of the novel's themes and motifs—including the theme of connectedness itself. Knocked into the stands on the same day that the Russians tested an atomic device, it is at one point described as the size of a bomb's "radioactive core" (172). In the hand it seems fruitlike, as if one could "juice it or milk it" and thereby produce something like the orange juice that also figures motivically here (131). The authorities use orange juice to wash the subway trains tagged by Moonman 157 and others. Charlie Wainwright, who owns the baseball at one point, "wanted to pitch the Minute Maid account. He thought about orange juice all the time" (534). Present in the car of a victim of the Texas Highway Killer (indeed, the videotaped death may be that of Judson Rauch himself), the ball eventually passes into the hands of the novel's protagonist, for whom, in the watches of the night, it becomes an uncanny intermediary between the different world he once inhabited—a world before the diminution of reality—and the world of guilt in which he still lives. A fan of the defeated Dodgers, Nick knows the answer to his rhetorical question about Ralph Branca, the pitcher with whom he identifies: "What's it like to have to live with one awful moment?" (97). Perhaps, too, he half-consciously recognizes, in the vagaries of his own volition, a bond between himself and the Texas Highway Killer. Whether an example of the *acte gratuit* or of the minimal volition Father Paulus calls velleity (539), the "life-defining act" of Nick Shay's boyhood finds its terrible reflection in the senseless killings carried out by Richard Henry Gilkey, the psychopath. At one point Nick is jocularly taken for the killer (79).

In addition to the textual reticulation (the product, merely, of an author's forethought or craft), the baseball subsumes as well the idea of a more genuinely metaphysical—even religious—connectedness that remains indeterminate and often debased as superstition or paranoid delusion. Thus the desire to conceptualize cyberspace as heaven's gate, or the traditional fear—chiefly articulated by Nick—of the number thirteen, or the two Edgars' convictions regarding a universal grid of germs or communists alike embody the yearning for a rational principle, even if it take the form of paranoia. Matt Shay, in Vietnam, notices "black drums" that "resembled cans of frozen Minute Maid" (462, 463): "How can you tell the difference between orange juice and agent orange if the same massive system connects them at levels outside your comprehension?" (465). The "cans of Minute Maid" recur on the billboard in which Sister Edgar sees Esmeralda (820), and DeLillo suggests that indeed some massive system links advertising, Vietnam, and bogus miracles.

"Everything connects in the end" (465), thinks Matt Shay, and the text enacts this theme relentlessly. In the closing pages, Sister Edgar becomes its exemplar, her late passion suggesting the fragility of faith on the eve of the millennium. When she dies she goes not to heaven but to cyberspace, the contemporary secular world's often paranoid model of universal linkage where, again, "everything is connected" amid "intersecting systems" now virtualized (825, 826). One reads her fate as a kind of poetic justice for a person whose devotional commitment seems to have been corrupted by a faith in the endlessly seen—movie stars—and in nondivine forms of the unseen: germs, radiation, communists among us. Though she abandons the movie stars, Sister Edgar remains a committed anticommunist with a fervor little short of religious. "The faith of suspicion and unreality. The faith that replaces God with radioactivity, the power of alpha particles and the all-knowing systems that shape them, the endless fitted links" (251). The nun has in fact made of her obsessions a graven image, violated the first and second commandments. One way or another, she shares more than a name with the paranoid director of the FBI, whose company in the infinitely linkable spaces of the Internet will provide little comfort, for death is not user-friendly and admits no such easy navigation.

Though all around him are ranged the ones and zeroes of embattled belief and hardened despair, Nick Shay continues, curiously enough, a believer, and in the gross tonnage of secular ore this trace element of belief contributes to his survival. In the end Nick's emotional and psychological condition seems to approximate and perhaps surpass the state of achievable psychological equilibrium that Freud called "ordinary everyday unhappiness." Though still given to waking up in the middle of the night and clutching the baseball that may or may not retain a special meaning, he notes a renewed intimacy with his wife, from whom he no longer withholds the secrets of his past, and he finds bearable, at least, the longings that must go unfulfilled. He experiences moods of near tranquillity, the muted countercurrent flowing from the vision imparted by the old Jesuit's teachings and nurtured, perhaps, by Nick's lifelong habit of reading. "I . . . feel a quiet kind of power because I've done it and come out okay, done it and won, gone in weak and come out strong" (803). In a passage that follows and qualifies yet another description of the Shay family's conscientious recycling, he even experiences his dead mother as a spiritual presence:

> The long ghosts are walking the halls. When my mother died I felt expanded, slowly, durably, over time. I felt suffused with her truth, spread through, as with water, color or light. I thought she'd entered the deepest place I could provide, the animating entity, the thing, if anything, that will survive my own last breath, and she makes me larger, she amplifies my sense of what it is to be human. She is part of me now, total and consoling. And it is not a sadness to acknowledge that she had to die before I could know her fully. It is only a statement of the power of what comes after. (804)

One detects in this passage no trace of ironic reservation, and one notes, in passing, that DeLillo has dedicated *Underworld:* "To the memory of my mother and father."

The ironic reservation does, however, color the interestingly parallel language with which DeLillo evokes Sister Edgar's perception of the miraculous presence in the orange juice billboard: "She sees Esmeralda's face take shape under the rainbow of bounteous juice and . . . there is a sense of someone living in the image, an animating spirit" (822). Although DeLillo affirms that the generally mean-spirited Sister Edgar experiences a moment of exaltation, he simultaneously denies its ultimate validity. The nun has duped herself—as presently even she realizes. Her misguided transports concluded, "there is nothing left to do but die" (824), the author declares, perhaps meaning to echo, with Eliot, the lines from Goldsmith suggesting that only death remains "when lovely woman stoops to folly." Yet if DeLillo does not represent the billboard manifestation as a genuine miracle, he remains deeply sympathetic to the spiritual yearning it feeds. Thus he allows Lenny Bruce's mock-hagiographic story of the "illiterate sad-eyed virgin" who can blow smoke rings from her vagina gradually to become, with a kind of dwindling satirical malice, that of a girl "hiding in the empty lots" of the South Bronx, "where she lives with her junkie mother" (630, 632–33). Unnamed, she anticipates the Esmeralda martyred thirty years later.

Yet regardless of which miraculous story is under review, hagiography remains a narrative imperfectly sanctioned by metanarrative. However moving her story, in other words, one cannot seriously imagine Esmeralda a saint. She is the gauge, merely, of a widespread and poignant yearning for sanctity and its miraculous trappings. One can agree only up to a point, then, with critics who see DeLillo as a religious writer. According to Vince Passaro, for example, "the subdued religious sentiment that runs through all his work has never been more evident than in *Underworld*."[13] John A. McClure takes a similar view: "DeLillo's work . . . insistently interrogates secular conceptions of the real, both by focusing the reader's attention on events that remain mysterious or even 'miraculous,' and by making all sorts of room for religious or spiritual discourses and styles of seeing."[14] But one must simultaneously recognize De-Lillo's tough-minded disinclination to accept moments of spiritualized perception as grounds for a more structured faith. As he told a British interviewer, "I feel a drive toward some kind of transcendence, perhaps religious but not in traditional ways."[15]

Striving to keep the faith, Sister Edgar fears, late in life, "that all creation is a spurt of blank matter that chances to make an emerald planet here, a dead star there, with random waste between. The serenity of immense design is missing from her life, authorship and moral form" (817). Thus she embraces a false miracle. Perhaps she enjoys a moment of grace when she briefly recognizes in Esmeralda "her virgin twin who is also her daughter" (824), but this identification seems sharply qualified when the narrative shifts to Sister Edgar's continuing consciousness in cyberspace. The momentary nexus of the Internet's many connections, her consciousness finds, as hyperlink, the H-bomb web page corresponding to her obsession in life. Here she "feels the power of false faith, the faith of paranoia," and mistakes "fifty-eight megatons" for the Merkabah (825).

In the aftermath of her religious credulity the author shifts to second person address, as at the opening ("He speaks in your voice, American"), and the language here resonates powerfully with other meditations on belief in this text:

> And what do you remember, finally, when everyone has gone home and the streets are empty of devotion and hope, swept by river wind? Is the memory thin and bitter and does it shame you with its fundamental untruth—all nuance and wishful silhouette? Or does the power of transcendence linger, the sense of an event that violates natural forces, something holy that throbs on the hot horizon, the vision you crave because you need a sign against your doubt? (824)

The images of wind and sign have their complement in the weary yearning of Nick's mother, Rosemary Shay. "Sometimes faith needs a sign. There are times when you want to stop working at faith and just be washed in a blowing wind that tells you everything" (757). Emblem of terrifying vacuity for Sister Edgar, the wind embodies a Pentecostal hope for Nick's long-suffering mother. Yet neither receives the desiderated sign, for its absence in modern times has become, at least since Eliot's "Gerontion," a spiritual given. As background to his great poem of spiritual aridity, one recalls, Eliot invokes a Launcelot Andrewes sermon on the New Testament text in which the Pharisees demand of Christ, "Master, we would see a sign." Christ answers in words suited to what he repeatedly calls a "generation of vipers" (Matt. 12.34; the phrase also supplies the title of Philip Wylie's midcentury castigation of American shallowness): "An evil and adulterous generation seeketh after a sign; and there shall no sign be given unto it" (Matt. 12.39). But like the early Eliot, DeLillo may well feel that the sign is withheld not because the countenance divine remains averted but because it has long since fossilized and cracked.

12 **DeLillolalia** From *Underworld* to *The Body Artist*

The recycling theme of *Underworld* subsumes a vision of art that lends itself to conclusions about the entire DeLillo oeuvre. Early in the narrative Nick Shay visits his former lover Klara Sax, an artist whose "career had been marked at times by her methods of transforming and absorbing junk."[1] So given is Klara to using cast-off materials that she has been called "the Bag Lady" (70). Her recycling extends even to some hundreds of decommissioned B-52s. The author intimates that Klara is not unique. Like the Simon Rodia who created Watts Towers out of junk, she is somehow, surprisingly, an *archetypal* artist. Indeed, as Michiko Kakutani remarked in a review of this novel, DeLillo himself "has taken the effluvia of modern life, all the detritus of our daily and political lives, and turned it into a dazzling, phosphorescent work of art."[2] DeLillo may think of Pound's injunction to "make it new" as an enthymeme, a syllogism with an unstated premise—in this case the dereliction or desuetude of "it." As they transmute suffering into beauty, artists transmute "the great squalor of our lives" (810). Art, like religion, promises the redemption of human waste. It recycles.

Underworld embraces an aesthetic of recycling that complements the obsessions of its protagonist. "Perhaps in keeping with the novel's theme," as Jesse Kavadlo points out, "portions of *Underworld* are themselves recycled, having been published previously in a number of magazines and journals."[3] Moreover, the novel recycles elements of earlier DeLillo fictions, several of which, as I suggested in discussing *White Noise,* glance at the theme of waste. As DeLillo told Diane Osen at the time of *Underworld*'s publication, "I'd been thinking about garbage for twenty years."[4] This recycling ranges from small details to major themes to that favorite DeLillo device, the grail-like object of universal desire.

Indeed, the pursuit of *Underworld*'s baseball represents an especially artful reimagining of the pursuits that structure DeLillo's other fictions, for DeLillo shares with Thomas Pynchon a tendency to structure novels as quests. Pynchon favors the highly factitious grail—V., the Trystero, the Rocket—which becomes the emblem of humanity's need for order and coherence, however spurious. V. confers structure on Herbert Stencil's century, the Trystero offers to Oedipa Maas the promise of an exit from "the absence of surprise to life," and the Rocket holds the key to humanity's Faustian drive for knowledge and power. A DeLillo novel, on the other hand, though it often revolves around some fixed point of general yearning, favors the grail less than what Hitchcock called the McGuffin, the simple device that sets the plot in motion: a scientific formula, missing diamonds, a stolen warhead. Possessed, the McGuffin effects no paradigm shift: it often proves as literally valueless as the Maltese falcon in the familiar Hammett novel. Thus in *Great Jones Street* most of the characters seek either the mountain tapes or the mystery drug developed by the government and stolen by Happy Valley; in *Running Dog* virtually everyone pursues the Hitler film. Only occasionally do DeLillo's characters strive for something more genuinely grail-like or metaphysical, something that, like Dylar in *White Noise,* or the code that will explain the message from Ratner's star, or the rationale behind the cult in *The Names,* promises to transform our thinking in some radical way. *Underworld*'s baseball, however, is at once McGuffin and grail, and the author presents it with considerable ambiguity—as an object of yearning, yes, but also as an emblem of bad luck, perhaps even as vitiated relic, something like Chaucer's "shrine from which the seinte is oute."

One sees DeLillo's inspired recycling as a localized or self-bounded illustration of the principle of intertextuality. To speak of recycling, then, is not to reproach the artist for some creative failure. All discourse, after all, reconfigures prior discourse. Thus when DeLillo's Lenny Bruce mocks as "linguists" the "cops on special duty" in his audience (594), he echoes a phrase about the repressive "king's linguists" in *Great Jones Street*.[5] Similarly, when Nick Shay visits Frankie's Tropical Bar (617) one may recognize the establishment from *Running Dog*. *Underworld*'s theme of nuclear anxiety, by the same token, re-imagines that of *End Zone* at the same time that it recontextualizes the argument, in *Libra*, for the Kennedy assassination as *fons et origo* of the late-century decades of dread (the dread—of the bomb—was there already, part of the background to the Bay of Pigs, itself widely perceived as somehow linked to the killing of the president).[6] From *The Names* DeLillo recycles reluctant adulterers and the emphasis on onomastics. The lonely passion of Bill Gray, central to *Mao II*, seems to lie behind the sense, projected in the *Unterwelt* set piece, of the artist's oppression by the host of benighted attitudes that swell the wave of societal devolution. The deserts of *Underworld*—literal ones in Arizona and Kazakhstan, figurative ones in agent-oranged Vietnam and the blighted Bronx—are of course a familiar DeLillo motif. Opening in the desert and periodically returning there, the Nick Shay narrative ends in the wastes of Kazakhstan and the wilderness around Phoenix.

In Nick's story, finally, one returns to the Oedipal drama that informs both *Americana* and *Running Dog*. Seducing an older woman, an artist, Nick re-enacts David Bell's consummated desire for the artist-mother, Sullivan. As Glen Selvy defies a father in Earl Mudger, then flees Cao and Van, the murderous agents of Oedipal retribution, so does Nick—shooting George Manza (who tells him, paternally, "Stay in school" [693])—unconsciously take revenge on his absconding father. More Orestes, even, than Glen Selvy, Nick subsequently struggles with Furies that take the form of filial guilt, sexual remorse, and forces that make him live at a distance from those in his own household.

All of these forces do what advertising was said to do in *Americana*: they turn subjects into third-person automatons. In *Underworld*, as in his first novel, DeLillo explores the unmoored self so familiar to postmodernity. *Americana*'s David Bell, telling his story in first person yet objectifying himself as movie character, destabilizes the boundary between first person and third. In *Ratner's Star*, by the same token, as the world advances into the Mohole, a series of first-person headings complicates the otherwise third-person narration. These shifts may remind one of the effects in certain war fictions. In Steven Wright's 1983 Vietnam novel, *Meditations in Green*, for example, the narrator represents himself in first-person in the present, when he is a near derelict, suffering from war wounds both physical and mental. But over half of the novel is set in Vietnam during his service there—and these sections are narrated in third person, as if two wholly different people—notwithstanding their shared name and DNA—have had the experiences reported to the reader. Similarly, in Salinger's "For Esmé, with Love and Squalor" the narrator begins in first person but concludes in third. Salinger, too, reserves third person for his picture of combat fatigue, a state of profound disjunction from the happier, more integrated self of "Sergeant X" just before and long after the Normandy invasion. This example may be the clearest indicator of what DeLillo seeks to represent here—a sense of the divided or alienated self during a war that, however cold, threatens at any moment to become the hottest ever. Thus in *Underworld*, one of the formal elements of which is the shift between first-person, third-person, and (at certain moments) second-person narration for the story of Nick Shay (murderer, thief, sexual predator, waste executive, survivor), DeLillo goes well beyond his previous experiments with point of view. The novel's shifts of viewpoint, like its dislocations of temporality (seen in the scrambling of chronology as well as the mixing of present-tense and past-tense narration), hint at the self's lability, especially vis-à-vis memory, which ranges forward and backward in time, at once registering and qualifying the individual's alienation.

Underworld may also be said to incorporate and recycle artistic conventions and styles. As Philip Nel has argued, "DeLillo's recent fiction in general and *Underworld* in particular challenges the validity of the modern-postmodern binarism."[7] Part of the greatness of this novel is the way that, at the end of the nineties, it seems a compendium of literary fashion from turn-of-the-century naturalism, through modernist and postmodernist reaction, to hybridized millennial vision. In other words, it offers the insights of naturalism qualified by elements of that movement's successor styles: dislocated chronology; abundant, often conflicting perspectives; intricately motivic construction modeling a near-paranoid dream of universal connectedness; deconstructions of national and religious myth; a self-referring model of history; and a treatment of language that seems to map out contending views on the limits of referentiality.

Seldom formally allusive, DeLillo incorporates elements that have, as it were, pedigrees, and a brief tracing of these and other literary affinities in *Underworld* will round out a premise of the present study that, though often implied, has not previously been made explicit. Throughout this project I have suggested that DeLillo's work must not be read in a vacuum, for like any other body of writing it follows or coexists with a host of literary currents. As Martin Amis observes in his review of *Underworld*, "DeLillo has always been a literary writer; deeply literary, and also *covertly* literary."[8] Thus I have glanced at Hemingway in discussing *End Zone* and *Mao II*, adduced fictions about the Vietnam War to probe *Running Dog*, briefly juxtaposed *Players* against a Frost poem and a story from *Dubliners*, brought Whitman into a discussion of *White*

Noise, and often noted the general affinities between DeLillo and his exact contemporary, Thomas Pynchon. *Underworld,* too, benefits from judicious contextualization—necessarily judicious, since anything approaching a comprehensive canvassing of its intertexts would require a discussion of some hundreds of pages.

In a novel with waste as central metaphor one expects at least traces of *The Waste Land,* and, sure enough, *Underworld's* protagonist is a combination of Phlebas ("Residents of Phoenix," Nick notes, "are called Phoenicians" [120]) and the prophet who is asked, "Can these bones live?" (Ezek. 37.3). Both works feature a Belladonna and both glance, in passing, at abortion. Both ladle material from the cauldron of unholy loves described by St. Augustine. Both problematize the compulsion to art (the Matisse remark that Klara quotes, "painters must begin by cutting out their tongues" [78], may even remind the reader of Eliot's primal artist, the tongueless Philomela). Both invoke the shored fragments of a moribund Christianity (including the grail legend) to arrive at a vision of peace.

One's understanding of *Underworld* also benefits from an awareness of, not the influence, exactly, but the looming, fraternal presence of certain of the big novels DeLillo has mentioned reading, notably *Ulysses.* Thus one discerns something of Joyce's cuckolded *homme moyen sensuel,* Leopold Bloom, in DeLillo's similarly cuckolded, similarly curious, similarly sympathetic Albert Bronzini. Similarly peripatetic as well, both men walk the streets perpending odd words and their etymologies. But the assimilated Jew here is Klara Sax, DeLillo's Molly Bloom, and she—not the "consubstantial" son of spiritual kinship—is the artist whose work, which involves the recycling of cast-off or waste materials, reflexively mirrors that of the author. The ephebe in this family romance, though apparently not called to art, struggles like Joyce's Stephen with complexes of paternity, duty to the mother, and the remorse of conscience. Indeed, both Stephen Dedalus and Nick Shay muse on obscure works of the fourteenth century: *Agenbite of Inwit* and *The Cloud of Unknowing,* respectively.

Similarly, there are broad resemblances with the early work of James T. Farrell. The Catholic, baseball-loving protagonist of the *Studs Lonigan* trilogy survives a tough urban boyhood (Chicago, rather than the Bronx), becomes involved with "underworld" figures, and is eventually destroyed, in the classic naturalist manner, by social, economic, and biological forces that make him their hapless puppet. DeLillo, too, acknowledges the enormous forces ranged against individuals of the underclass—absentee fathers, poverty, biological urges, drugs, crime, racism. These are only the immediate or local forces. Beyond them are the powerful currents of history: the bomb, the Cold War, big business, the media, advertising, and so on. Yet in the end DeLillo presents, in Nick Shay, a protagonist sufficiently self-aware to hold his own against social, biological, and historical determinism. Nick exercises something like free will, and thus does the author himself resist doctrinaire naturalism's final, coercive argument. As John N. Duvall observes, "An awareness of one's alienation is the last best hope to construct an opposition to the forces of consumer culture."[9]

DeLillo's Bronx, finally, resembles the Newark of Philip Roth's *American Pastoral,* published the same year as *Underworld.* Both authors meditate on a once-vital immigrant community and its fate in the late decades of the twentieth century. Roth's central character, the brilliant and gifted Seymour Levov, known as "Swede," passes through—and survives—trials remarkably similar to those of Nick Shay. If Swede's father, unlike Nick's, remains a forceful presence in the protagonist's life, the vexed relationship with a younger brother and the infidelity of a wife are direct parallels. The pivotal taking of a life also figures—Swede's disturbed daughter sets a bomb to protest the war in Vietnam and kills an innocent man. Both authors refuse to soften the toll that survival takes on their protagonists, who are, nonetheless, spared the fate of McTeague, Clyde Griffiths, Jude Fawley, et al. Nick and the Swede diverge only in the price each pays: where Roth's character cannot finally restore the happiness and integrity of his family, DeLillo's can congratulate himself, late in his story, on having "gone in weak and come out strong" (803).

Language and Time in *The Body Artist*

DeLillo's covert allusiveness also manifests itself in *The Body Artist* (2001). At times, for example, as DeLillo evokes the remote, ramshackle, vacation rental near the sea that is his setting here, one thinks of another time-troubled house, another sea, another meditation on the temporal dimensions of consciousness. Like the Ramsays' house in the Hebrides, the house in DeLillo's story provides the spatial complement to a thematically foregrounded experience with time. In his first sentence, "Time seems to pass,"[10] DeLillo echoes the title of the lyrical middle section of *To the Lighthouse:* "Time Passes." As that Woolf novel moves toward the vision of Lily Briscoe, so does *The Body Artist* move toward description of an epiphanic work of art. Like the author of *To the Lighthouse, Mrs. Dalloway,* and *The Waves,* DeLillo grapples with time as it reveals itself in language and consciousness. Stylistically, too, there are affinities, and one hears the Woolf of *Monday or Tuesday* in certain DeLillo sentences: "When birds look into houses, what impossible worlds they see. Think. What shedding of every knowable surface and process. She wanted to believe the bird was seeing her, a woman with a teacup in her hand, and never mind the folding back of day and night, the apparition of a space set off from time" (22).

In the collocation of bird, window, and spatialized time DeLillo revises an ancient trope: Bede's comparison of a single human life span to a bird's flying in one opening of a great hall and out the other. The woman with the teacup is Lauren Hartke, the "body artist" of the title. In the course of her story Lauren must, like the bird she contemplates, deal with a phenomenon that violates "every knowable surface and process." She discovers an apparently retarded man hiding out in the vacation house she has—until his suicide—shared with her husband, the filmmaker Rey Robles. The nameless retarded man—she mentally dubs him "Mr. Tuttle"—turns out to be a human tape recorder. Evidently having been in the house for some time, he shocks Lauren by parroting conversations she has in recent days had with her husband. Even more shocking: Mr. Tuttle perceives the future as readily as the past. He reproduces conversations that have not yet taken place—at least according to Lauren's linear experience of time. "He said, 'Don't touch it' in a voice that wasn't quite his. 'I'll clean it up'" (81). The words—and the voice—are those of Lauren on the occasion, a few days later, when her strange lodger drops a glass of water in the kitchen (93). "This," seemingly, "is a man who remembers the future," who "violates the limits of the human" (100).

Lauren naturally resists thinking of Mr. Tuttle as the embodiment of a singularity in space-time: "It can't be true that he drifts from one reality to another, independent of the logic of time. This is not possible. You are made out of time" (91–92). "If you examine the matter methodically, you realize that he is a retarded man sadly gifted in certain specialized areas, such as memory retention and mimicry, a man who'd been concealed in a large house, listening" (100). But insofar as Mr. Tuttle's mimicry extends to the not-yet-uttered, one cannot accept such a comforting, no-nonsense view. More than "a retarded man sadly gifted," Mr. Tuttle seems a modern version of what, in primitive societies, is taken as a figure of great mystery—a being directly in touch, like the lunatic or epileptic, with what ordinary people cannot see, hear, experience.

Appearing out of nowhere to grapple with the complexities of the world, Mr. Tuttle resembles that great enigma of the early nineteenth century, Kaspar Hauser, subject of a 1908 Jakob Wassermann novel and—artistically closer to DeLillo—Werner Herzog's 1974 film, *Jeder für sich und Gott gegen alle*. Hauser appeared mysteriously in Munich in 1828, claiming to have spent the years of his childhood locked away in an oubliette. Only five years later he perished of knife wounds that may have been self-inflicted. As Herzog explores the famous story in a cinematic style that is dreamy, poetic, slow-moving, and silence-ridden, so does DeLillo seem, in his form, to invite his readers to recognize in Mr. Tuttle some emissary from beyond. Unlike his German predecessor, Mr. Tuttle never learns to function in ordinary society, nor does he exhibit anything like Kaspar's remarkable intelligence. But his origin and fate are every bit as puzzling as those of the antitype, and the mystery of this latter-day Kaspar Hauser goes beyond his perceptual scrambling of time. He materializes just after Rey's death, and toward the end he simply disappears, like the fool in *King Lear*. He vanishes in part because he has fulfilled his function as heteroclite muse: after his departure Lauren creates and performs the work of art that apparently gestates during the visitation.

Mr. Tuttle, that is, becomes an enabler of the highly original narrative embodied in the work that Lauren, stimulated by him, eventually shapes. But first she must overcome her own resistance to the idea of a narrative sans past, present, and future. Lauren regards "time" as "the only narrative that matters" (92), and she tries to imagine "a kind of time that had no narrative quality" (65). Mr. Tuttle seems to violate the symbiosis of time and narrative. Pondering the relationship of time to narrative, Lauren struggles toward a formulation such as the one proposed by DeLillo's fellow novelist Marilynne Robinson. "What is eternal," Robinson observes, "must always be complete. . . . So it is possible to imagine that time was created in order that there might be narrative—event, sequence and causation, ignorance and error, retribution, atonement. A word, a phrase, a story falls on rich or stony ground and flourishes as it can, possibility in a sleeve of limitation. Certainly time is the occasion for our strangely mixed nature, in every moment differently compounded, so that often we surprise ourselves, and always scarcely know ourselves, and exist in relation to experience, if we attend to it and if its plainness does not disguise it from us, as if we were visited by revelation."[11] Plunged into temporal enigma, DeLillo's protagonist is ripe for revelation but unsure as to its legitimate character.

Although she senses what Robinson would call the revelation embodied in her experience with Mr. Tuttle, Lauren cannot so easily grasp it. Indeed, she must deal, first, with the validity of perceptions grounded in her own mental and emotional vulnerability after the death of her husband. Has she deceived herself about the reality of Mr. Tuttle? So far as the reader of the present narrative knows, only Lauren ever lays eyes on or converses with her visitor. Though she calls regional asylums after he has disappeared, it is by no means clear that she actually admits to the immediate circumstances of her inquiries. Perhaps, like the neurasthenic governess of James's *Turn of the Screw* or the troubled housewife of Rachel Ingalls's *Mrs. Caliban,* Lauren merely projects a fantasy out of a traumatized unconscious. Like "Larry," the bizarre reptilian lover in the Ingalls novel, Mr. Tuttle can be read as the projection of a troubled mind, at once pet, child, and spouse. He is, first, a half-fantasized surrogate for the dead husband, and at one point Lauren even lies on top of him and puts her hand in his shorts, as with a lover (90). But another identification receives greater emphasis. Lauren feeds him (94, 95), bathes him (68), finds him befouled in his car restraints (64). She reads to him from a "text on the biology of childbirth," including "a passage about the embryo, half an inch long, afloat in body fluid" (60). "At night she stood outside his room and watched him sleep" (71). She treats him, in short, as a child.

This symbolism has an obvious bearing on the problems of language, time, and consciousness in this text. Paradoxically, someone whose speech and sense of time are "impaired" (97) becomes a vehicle of insight into the mysteries of language and temporality. As noted several times before in this study, DeLillo often flirts with the Wordsworthian conceit of the child as bridge between one world and the next, and he has commented more than once, in interviews, on his sense that infantile babbling is structured. In any event, the reader alert to this author's characteristic subversion of the concept *infans* has at least one handle on Mr. Tuttle's riddling speech. It is constantly echoic, as if, like a child, he were striving to learn from the locutions of the most proximate "adult."

In the present instance the adult may stand to learn more than the child, but what does she learn—about, most importantly, Mr. Tuttle's identity? She rightly hesitates to accept at face value his apparent violations of the temporal norm. The reader ought also to avoid hasty conclusions about just where the author locates any putative ability to see the future, for Mr. Tuttle is not unique in either his shuttling backward and forward in time or his ability to act as a recording device to replicate or reproduce the world's discourse. The literary artist can do these things as well—and in narrative that need not proceed in a linear fashion. Like Mr. Tuttle, an artist reproduces the world's speech and gesture. Such mimesis figures with particular prominence within the present text's own circumscribed boundaries: word and phrase and action and image constantly echo internally, in elaborate, contrapuntal repetition. The author weaves his motivic material like the strands of a carpet that may or may not conceal a Jamesian figure: the hair in the mouth (11, 69), the bumping of the lamp when taking off clothing (35, 112, 122), the unrolling of wax paper (34, 113), the "bottle with a pistol-grip attachment" (32, 114), the Japanese woman (35–36, 105, 115), the tricks of peripheral or hurried vision (76, 91), the Internet video camera in Finland (38, 72, 107, 113), the birds at the feeder (on nearly every page), and the automated voice on the answering machine, which Lauren listens to repeatedly, then incorporates into her performance piece. At the same time, the narrator constantly repeats problematic words such as "somehow" (56, 63, 83, 92) or phrases such as "a strong bright day after a storm" (7, 25), "It is not able" (43, 65), "talk to me" (twice on 46), and "Say some words" (55, 62, 65, 81)—not to mention conversations that unfold, like scenes in Jacobean drama, as echolalia. Lauren says "The way we are talking now" (62) or "Talk into the thing" (70, 75), and Mr. Tuttle will iterate, "We are talking now" and "Talk into the thing." In this weave of repetition-with-incremental-difference, DeLillo models Mr. Tuttle in the act of modeling language itself.

In this paragon of verbal mimesis Lauren may encounter some version of the artist who, creating her, has an uncanny ability to reproduce her speech, however intimate—and to know, from moment to moment, her future. If one resists identifying the damaged Mr. Tuttle with an artist fully in command of his faculties, one can say that in Mr. Tuttle Lauren encounters, as a projection of her own unconscious, the artist in herself, temporarily obtunded or disoriented by late catastrophe. This view helps one make sense of certain odd details in the story. On occasion Lauren knows the exact time before looking at watch or clock (112, 120). When her landlord, looming over her car, gives her a mild shock (117), he reifies a scene she has previously envisioned (78). Initially it seems as if acquaintance with Mr. Tuttle brings out a natural prescience in Lauren, but perhaps it would be more accurate to say that an unrecognized prescience in Lauren naturally conjures some such manifestation as Mr. Tuttle.

In time Lauren manages to transmute psychic distress and hallucination (if that is what it is) into conscious art. If she thereby ministers to a mind diseased (or at least profoundly traumatized by the violent circumstances of her husband's death), she does so through a discipline and an art less of the mind than of the body. She is, after all, "Lauren Hartke, the body artist" (29), and like current writers who scrutinize the body as the site on which trauma is inscribed (often quite literally, as in the case of Sethe, the whip-scarred heroine of Toni Morrison's *Beloved*), she insists on bodily representation and working through of such trauma. At the same time she constantly strives to surpass the limitations of her own body, which remains, nonetheless, the medium of performance, the instrument of an art at once unique and generic, an art so singular as to become, metaphorically, all art. In this she resembles Kafka's hunger artist—whose cage, one recalls, is furnished with only a clock.

Thus DeLillo emphasizes Lauren's view of time as a *bodily* experience. At thirty-six, she has recently passed the halfway mark of the biblical three score and ten. When the reader last sees her she is savoring "the flow of time in her body," which will "tell her who she was" (124). Earlier on this final day of the story, as on the four previous days, Lauren had watched seagulls in flight, "the slant carriers of all this rockbound time, taking it out of geology, out of science and mind, and giving it soar and loft and body, bringing it into their flight muscles and bloodflow, into their sturdy hammering hearts, their metronomic hearts" (113). As she imagines the heart, like the metronome, as a device that keeps time for the body's music, DeLillo revisits and conflates various modernist images of flesh's heroic but doomed breasting of time's gale: Fitzgerald's boats against the current, the gull against the wind of Eliot's "Gerontion," and the standing wave of "West-Running Brook," which Frost compares to "a bird / White feathers from the struggle of whose breast / Flecked the dark stream and flecked the darker pool." [12] From his postmodern perspective, DeLillo emphasizes the body—avian or human—in which time literally pulses. But the author of *White Noise* knows, as Frost says, that "Our life runs down in sending up the clock." [13]

As Lauren devises an artistic form to represent what she has begun to see about time and language and the body, one discerns parallels between her performance piece, *Body Time,* and DeLillo's novel. Most obviously, both works engage time and its representation as the central artistic problem. Each artist devises strategies whereby time's texture and duration may be perceived by the reader or viewer. In DeLillo's setting, that large old house on a remote coast, the solitary life unfolds with every second reliefed against larger blocks of time. In the opening chapter, as in *Players,* DeLillo reproduces the elliptical speech and gesture characteristic of married life. Other scenes display their own moment-by-moment temporality. Lauren, by the same token, is willing to fatigue or alienate an audience forced "to feel time go by, viscerally, even painfully" (104). The audience views *Body Time* rather as its creator views Kotka, Finland, on her computer, "in its hours, minutes and seconds" (38). "A place stripped of everything but a road that approaches and recedes, both realities occurring at once" (39), Kotka is the spatial emblem of a traditional view of time in which past and future—the road in, the road out—converge from different directions on the present. Electronic technology allows viewers in one time zone to share another time zone's present. In its remote, Nordic fastness, Kotka ultimately represents the idea of "another structure, another culture, where time is something like itself, sheer and bare, empty of shelter" (92).

The crossroads in Kotka models a different intersection as well: "There has to be an imaginary point, a nonplace where language intersects with our perceptions of time and space," thinks Lauren. Mr. Tuttle "is a stranger at this crossing, without words or bearings" (99). In such figures DeLillo frames his subject—time—in terms of language. What, he asks, is time to language? What is language *without* time? Is time itself a language that Mr. Tuttle simply "hasn't learned" (99), or do language and time complement each other, imbricated in the very texture of consciousness? Is there, then, beyond parrots and other speaking birds, such a thing as language without consciousness? Listening to Mr. Tuttle, Lauren hears what DeLillo in his first published novel calls "the river which is language without thought."[14] Indeed, the most extraordinary thing about Mr. Tuttle is not that he reproduces conversations verbatim or hears the future—it is that he is capable of language even though one discerns in his eyes "no stirrings of tremulous self" (85). Lacking a self, he lacks the "consciousness" that Eddington characterizes as "self-knowing," the consciousness that, as Sir William Dampier explains, "enable[s] us to distinguish between past and future."[15] Nor can he answer Lauren's simplest question: "What's your name?" (46).

Both author and character see rhythm—aural time—as an essential quality of language. In *Mao II* and in propria persona DeLillo has spoken of the labor to capture, in prose, a living rhythm. Bill Gray speaks of "the swing of the sentence, the beat and poise,"[16] and in an interview DeLillo emphasizes how, in every "sentence" that he himself writes, he strives to preserve "the rhythm, the syllable beat."[17] By the same token, listening to Mr. Tuttle, Lauren perceives an absence of the "beat" (65) that characterizes the special quality of living speech. This arrhythmia compounds the unanchored temporality of his words: "Their talks had no time sense" (66). At the same time, the artificiality of composite phrases such as one hears from automated telephone messages strikes Lauren as a kind of revelation (67, 71). Here, too, one hears no rhythm, no beat, and one such message, with its false-sounding, cobbled syllables, figures in Lauren's performance piece as aural backdrop.

At the end, Lauren has a moment in which she thinks she may circle back on time, intervene in the sequence of events that culminates in Rey's suicide. When she pauses outside the bedroom door, momentarily certain that behind it she will reenter the past and clasp a living Rey Robles, one thinks, perhaps, of other such liminal moments in literature—"The Fall of the House of Usher," for example, or James's "The Jolly Corner," which ultimately turns on an encounter with a version of the self that has taken a different track on life's journey (has, that is, passed through time differently). But perhaps "The Monkey's Paw" provides the nearer analogue. What Lauren risks encountering, of course, is not some grisly revenant but some irremediable descent into solipsism, for the exemption from time that is a cerebral accident in Mr. Tuttle will be, in her, only madness. "The prison of time is spherical and without exits," observes the Nabokov of *Speak, Memory;* "the free world of timelessness" is not for the living.[18] Thus in DeLillo's narrative the moment on the threshold passes, at once real and imagined. Lauren Hartke enters a room merely empty and opens a window to smell the salt air, to feel, like those gulls, alive in time.

"What," wonders St. Augustine, "is time? If no one asks me, I know: if I wish to explain to one that asketh, I know not." [19] In *The Body Artist* DeLillo makes a story of considerable immediacy and pathos out of the abstruse reality of time—a reality that, seemingly so available to direct experience and perception, remains difficult to get a handle on. Indeed, after centuries of reflections on time on the part of philosophers, poets, physicists, and cosmologists, time remains, as DeLillo's heroine realizes, "the thing you know nothing about" (98, 99), "the thing no one understands" (100). Relativity theory shows time accelerating or decelerating as a function of mass and velocity (it slows as one approaches the speed of light), but it does not sanction the reversal of what Eddington calls time's arrow. Indeed, from Eddington to Stephen Hawking, the flight of that arrow remains unidirectional. But not in the mind and not in art, where one easily and routinely transcends the linear, arrow-vectored, and immutable character of physical time. In *The Body Artist* DeLillo ponders clock time, body time, mental time, and, with predictable emphasis, time in language.

From *Americana* to *The Body Artist* DeLillo has problematized language, and I should like briefly to recapitulate my arguments or discoveries in this book with a final point or two about this all-important theme. "For me," DeLillo told David Remnick, "the crux of the whole matter is language." [20] DeLillo takes a poet's interest in concision, cobbling clauses at once elfin and granitic, and he has been saluted as "the best writer of sentences in America." [21] He cares passionately about the rhythms of word and phrase, and he is at pains always to hold up a sound-mirror to the speech of the Americans he eavesdrops on and ventriloquizes. When Ben Jonson says, "Speak, that I may see thee," he implies that language can be an index to one's class and character and intellect. DeLillo concurs, but he seems to conceive of language more broadly as culture's mirror of mirrors.

The DeLillo model of language subsumes (often in highly personal or idiosyncratic forms) everything from traditional notions of referentiality to deconstruction and *écriture*—with side-trips into Saussurean linguistics, Heidegger's word-thresholds of Being, and the logicism of Frege, Russell, and Wittgenstein. But as should be obvious by now (though I will admit that it was slow to become obvious to me), DeLillo is a writer whose valuation of language has placed him at odds with what Nick Shay would call the contemporary *Weltanschauung.* To be sure, DeLillo invites his readers to recognize, with poststructuralist theory, the inadequacy of the old model of things and their word-labels. But he is impatient of the reductive thinking that makes language some kind of gossamer film, some completely depthless word-gauze between world and cognition. Such thinking, he would say, misvalues and belies a system that subsumes virtually all human experience. DeLillo's engagement with the postmodern, then, at least as it is commonly defined, is or has come to be adversarial. In particular, the putative postmodern depthlessness has come to seem restrictive, and DeLillo's career has taken him into deeper history, deeper psychology, deeper representation, deeper spirituality, and the deeper imagining that he himself characterizes as "fiction's role." [22] But deepest of all has been the DeLillo model of language.

Over thirteen novels, numerous stories, and a handful of plays, DeLillo has developed ideas about language that confound the scholarly desire to label and pigeonhole. To call his conception of language "romantic" or "sublime"— indeed, even to speak of something as formal as a "theory"—seems patently inadequate. Unencumbered by the heavy baggage of such terms, DeLillo's thinking about language is resolutely eclectic and creative. Language, for DeLillo, is the ground of all making, and no conceit is too extravagant to be essayed. He looks with unfailing, sympathetic attention at linguistic practices—glossolalia, for example—that others dismiss as psychopathology or simple fraud. Similarly, like Joyce, he can momentarily imagine language as a link to conceptual origins and human ontogeny, something like the omphalic telephone that Stephen Dedalus muses on: "Hello. Kinch here. Put me on to Edenville." [23] Nor should one wonder that more than once in his fictions the author represents the word as strangely eroticized and even divine, for language and sex share with deity the capacity to create. Programmed into the human cortex, language actualizes a universe of discrimination, shaping its speakers and answering their desire for unified and universal structure.

Notes

Introduction

1. John Updike, "Layers of Ambiguity," review of *Players, New Yorker,* 27 March 1978, 128.

2. McHale's two books, *Postmodernist Fiction* and *Constructing Postmodernism,* are important contributions to the ongoing definition of postmodernist literature.

3. Jean Baudrillard, "The Precession of Simulacra," in *Simulations,* trans. Paul Foss, Paul Patton, and Philip Bleitchman (New York: Semiotext[e], 1983), 12, 11.

4. Don DeLillo, *Running Dog* (New York: Knopf, 1978), 197, 31.

5. Don DeLillo, *Great Jones Street* (Boston: Houghton Mifflin, 1973), 31, 24, 89.

6. John Johnston, "Generic Difficulties in the Novels of Don DeLillo," *Critique* 30 (summer 1989), 268.

7. Paul Maltby, "The Romantic Metaphysics of Don DeLillo," *Contemporary Literature* 37.2 (1996), 258–77. Though like Maltby I will recur, from time to time, to the

Wordsworthian paradigm, I find myself somewhat resistant to the specifics of his argument, which seems to underestimate the degree of irony with which DeLillo occasionally invokes visionary or sublime experience. See, for example, note 5 (on the supposedly "transcendent" phrase "Toyota Celica") in chapter 5, on *White Noise* (below).

8. Tom LeClair, *In the Loop* (Urbana: Univ. of Illinois Press, 1987), 177.

9. Glen Scott Allen, "The End of Pynchon's Rainbow: Paranoid Spectres and Postmodern Spectra in *Ratner's Star*," *Postmodern Culture* 4, no. 2 (1994), paragraphs 2, 28.

10. Don DeLillo, *Americana* (New York: Houghton Mifflin, 1971), 189.

11. See Thomas Pynchon, *Gravity's Rainbow* (New York: Viking, 1973), 622.

12. Adam Begley, "Don DeLillo: The Art of Fiction CXXXV," *Paris Review* 35 (fall 1993), 284.

13. Charles Molesworth, "Don DeLillo's Perfect Starry Night," in Frank Lentricchia, ed., *Introducing Don DeLillo* (Durham: Duke Univ. Press, 1991), 143.

14. DeLillo, *Americana*, 7.

15. Anthony DeCurtis, "'An Outsider in This Society': An Interview with Don DeLillo," in Lentricchia, ed., *Introducing Don DeLillo,* 57.

16. Noel King, "Reading *White Noise:* Floating Remarks," *Critical Quarterly* 33.3 (autumn 1991), 66, 69. Hereafter cited parenthetically.

17. DeCurtis, "'An Outsider,'" 61.

18. Fredric Jameson, *Postmodernism, or the Cultural Logic of Late Capitalism* (Durham: Duke Univ. Press, 1991), 9, 12.

Football and *Unsäglichkeit: End Zone*

1. Don DeLillo, *End Zone,* 16, 18. Hereafter cited parenthetically.

2. For another critic this structure "resembles a nuclear disaster novel: Part 1 builds to a confrontation, the middle section details the 'war,' and Part 3 describes the aftermath." See Mark Osteen, *American Magic and Dread: Don DeLillo's Dialogue with Culture* (Philadelphia: Univ. of Pennsylvania Press, 2000), 44.

3. Rainer Maria Rilke, "Die neunte Elegie," in *Duineser Elegien, Gesammelte Gedichte* (Frankfurt: Insel-Verlag, 1962), 473–76. The other quotations here are all from this text.

4. Tom LeClair, "An Interview with Don DeLillo," in *Anything Can Happen: Interviews with Contemporary American Novelists,* conducted and edited by LeClair and Larry McCaffery (Urbana: Univ. of Illinois Press, 1983), 84.

5. In "Extraphilosophical Instigations in Don DeLillo's *Running Dog*," *Contemporary Literature* 26, no. 1 (1985), 74, Stuart Johnson pauses over this scene to point out the source of Harkness's allusion in a remark Wittgenstein made in a letter. "My work consists of two parts: the one presented here plus all that I have *not* written. And it is precisely this second part that is the important one." Johnson cites Garth Hallett, who quotes the letter in *A Companion to Wittgenstein's "Philosophical Investigations"* (Ithaca: Cornell Univ. Press, 1977), 233.

6. DeLillo, *Running Dog,* 229.

Pharmaceutical Philomela: *Great Jones Street*

1. DeLillo, *Great Jones Street,* 90. Hereafter cited parenthetically.

2. Osteen, *American Magic and Dread,* 24. See also Michael Oriard, "Don DeLillo's Search for Walden Pond," *Critique* 20 (1978), 5–24.

3. Anthony DeCurtis, "The Product: Bucky Wunderlick, Rock 'n Roll, and Don DeLillo's *Great Jones Street,"* in *Introducing Don DeLillo,* ed. Lentricchia, 140. As a writer for *Rolling Stone,* DeCurtis is good at spotting certain actual rock personalities behind the book's allusions. He sees Watney, for example, as "a kind of Alice Cooper figure" (138), Bucky as a composite of Mick Jagger and Bob Dylan (139). He sees Bucky's mountain tapes as "based on the 'basement tapes' Dylan made in Woodstock after his motorcycle accident in 1966" (137). Interestingly, this novel has been discussed by an actual rock musician, Luna's Dean Wareham, who sees Bucky as "a sort of Jagger/Barrett/Morrison/Cobain figure." See "My Favorite Rock & Roll Novel," in *Rolling Stone's Alt. Rock-a-Rama*, edited by Scott Schinder (New York: Delta, 1996), 384.

4. Ludwig Wittgenstein, *Philosophical Investigations,* trans. G. E. M. Anscombe (Oxford: Basil Blackwell, 1953), part 1, section 38, 19e.

5. Both DeCurtis (137–38) and Osteen (50–52) argue cogently that Fenig's wishful remarks about fame and success, not to mention his obsession with finding and exploiting a market for his work, reveal him, too, as a mindless cog in the machinery of consumption. But it should be noted that unlike Globke, Hanes, Azarian, Watney, Bohack, Dr. Pepper, and even Opel, he is not involved in any of the attempts to possess and exploit either the mountain tapes or the new drug.

6. Don DeLillo, *Mao II* (New York: Viking, 1991), 41.

Mortal Stakes: *Players*

1. Don DeLillo, *Players* (New York: Knopf, 1977), 3. Hereafter cited parenthetically.

2. As Eugene Goodheart has suggested in *Desire and Its Discontents* (New York: Columbia Univ. Press, 1991), DeLillo might "object to the theatrical metaphor" (164). His character Lyle, who likes television and movies, is bored by the theater, with its "three-dimensional bodies." But Lyle's spatial aesthetic founders on the notion of "manipulated depth" in film (100), and DeLillo has in fact used theatrical space—notably in his play *The Day Room*—to subvert the idea of subjective substance and depth. (The DeLillo phrases here are also cited by Goodheart.)

3. This film recalls DeLillo's story "The Uniforms" (*Carolina Quarterly* 22, no. 1 [1970]: 4–11), a gruesome take-off on Godard's *Weekend.* The story concerns the bloody predations—notably at a country club—of a band of terrorists whose ideology is expressed entirely in cinematic terms.

4. LeClair, "An Interview with Don DeLillo," 82. See also Begley, "Don DeLillo: The Art of Fiction CXXXV," 286.

5. Linda Hutcheon, *Narcissistic Narrative: The Metafictional Paradox* (New York: Methuen, 1984), 55.

6. Lucien Dällenbach, *The Mirror in the Text,* trans. Jeremy Whiteley with Emma Hughes (Chicago: Univ. of Chicago Press, 1989), 98–101.

7. LeClair, "An Interview with Don DeLillo," 81.

8. LeClair, "An Interview with Don DeLillo," 82.

9. This and the following quotations are from Robert Frost, *The Poetry of Robert Frost,* ed. Edward Connery Lathem (New York: Holt, Rinehart and Winston, 1969), 275–77.

10. Mervyn Rothstein, "A Novelist Faces His Themes on New Ground," *New York Times,* 20 December 1987, 19.

11. LeClair, "An Interview with Don DeLillo," 84. The ellipses, the codes, the oddly compelling banality of talk between spouses would, however, continue to interest DeLillo, as one sees in the desultory breakfast chat of Lauren Hartke and Rey Robles in *The Body Artist.* It also figures in DeLillo's "The Mystery at the Middle of Ordinary Life" (*Zoetrope: All-Story* 4.4 [winter 2000]: 70), a dramatic scene in which a man and a woman wonder out loud about conversations between long-married couples. "What do people say over a lifetime?" It is not clear how long the two characters have been together, but their own conversation ironically modulates from interesting to banal.

12. LeClair, "An Interview with Don DeLillo," 82.

13. John W. Aldridge, *The American Novel and the Way We Live Now* (New York: Oxford Univ. Press, 1983), 59.

14. The dildo may be DeLillo's reply to a much-quoted line from *Gravity's Rainbow*: "The real fucking is done on paper."

The Naive and Sentimental Reader: *Running Dog*

1. DeLillo, *Running Dog,* 60. Hereafter cited parenthetically.

2. DeCurtis, "'An Outsider,'" 64.

3. Begley, "Don DeLillo: The Art of Fiction CXXXV," 302.

4. Patrick O'Donnell, "Engendering Paranoia in Contemporary Narrative," *boundary 2* 19, no. 1 (spring 1992), 193.

5. Begley, "Don DeLillo: The Art of Fiction CXXXV," 286–87.

6. D. H. Lawrence, *Studies in Classic American Literature* (1923; New York: Viking, 1961), 62.

7. Patrick O'Donnell, "Obvious Paranoia: The Politics of Don DeLillo's *Running Dog,*" *Centennial Review* 34 (winter 1990), 65. Arguing that DeLillo masterfully subverts the conventions of the genre as a means to explore and debunk the social, political, and psychological dimensions of paranoia, O'Donnell rightly contests LeClair's characterization of *Running Dog* as DeLillo's "least subtle" or "least achieved" novel (see *In the Loop,* 145, 167). In his review for the *New Republic* (7 October 1978), LeClair is even harder on the novel: "A transistorized potboiler," it "reads too much like some compacted version of the literary waste—the intrigue—from which DeLillo has presumably meant to separate it with artful reduction" (34, 33). For a further defense of DeLillo's exploitation of the thriller, see Johnston, "Generic Difficulties," especially 271–72.

8. John Frow, *Marxism and Literary History* (Oxford: Basil Blackwell, 1986), 141.

9. Ellie Ragland-Sullivan, *Jacques Lacan and the Philosophy of Psychoanalysis* (Urbana: Univ. of Illinois Press, 1986), 43.

10. Not all of DeLillo's cops are so straight. One of his most bizarre stories concerns "Lady Madonna," a transvestite cop who muses on "the fecal confluence of many cultures" as he patrols a surreal cityscape. See "In the Men's Room of the Sixteenth Century," *Esquire*, December 1971, 175.

11. Donald Barthelme, *The Dead Father* (New York: Farrar, Straus and Giroux, 1975), 3.

12. "We hear more about and see more of Selvy than any other character in the novel," observes Stuart Johnson, "yet it is incongruous to think of him as the 'main character' because he is so little *there*. He is an extreme version of what DeLillo often gives us: a site at which various lines and pressures converge." See "Extraphilosophical Instigations in Don DeLillo's *Running Dog,*" *Contemporary Literature* 26, no. 1 (1985), 76, 79. John Johnston makes a similar point: this author's "characters remain immanent to their perceptions, and seem to have no other life—mental or otherwise—outside of the images that define them, and to which they react with private and ritualized reorderings." See "Generic Difficulties," 269, or "Post-Cinematic Fiction: Film in the Novels of Pynchon, McElroy, and DeLillo," *New Orleans Review* 17, no. 2 (summer 1990), 94.

13. Jacques Lacan, *The Seminar of Jacques Lacan, Book II. The Ego in Freud's Theory and in the Technique of Psychoanalysis, 1954–1955,* trans. Sylvana Tomaselli (1978; New York: Cambridge Univ. Press, 1988), 87.

14. Friedrich Nietzsche, *The Joyful Wisdom [La Gaya Scienza],* trans. Thomas Common, vol. 10 of *The Complete Works of Friedrich Nietzsche,* ed. Oscar Levy (New York: Macmillan, 1909–13), 270 (aphorism 341). For my understanding of Nietzsche, I am indebted to the notes and introductions in Walter Kaufman, ed. *The Portable Nietzsche* (New York: Viking, 1954).

15. Friedrich Nietzsche, *Ecce Homo,* trans. Anthony M. Ludovici, vol. 17 of *The Complete Works of Friedrich Nietzsche,* ed. Oscar Levy (New York: Macmillan, 1909–13), 96.

16. Friedrich Nietzsche, *Also Sprach Zarathustra,* trans. Thomas Common, vol. 11 of *The Complete Works of Friedrich Nietzsche,* ed. Oscar Levy (New York: Macmillan, 1909–13), 268.

17. Norman N. Holland, *The Dynamics of Literary Response* (New York: Oxford Univ. Press, 1968), 45, 110–14.

18. Ragland-Sullivan, *Jacques Lacan,* 60.

Timor Mortis Conturbat Me: White Noise

1. Mark Osteen, introduction to White Noise: *Text and Criticism,* by Don DeLillo, ed. Osteen (New York: Viking, 1998), xii–xiv. See John Frow, "The Last Things before the Last: Notes on *White Noise,*" in *Introducing Don DeLillo,* ed. Lentricchia, 175–91; John N. Duvall, "The (Super)Marketplace of Images: Television as Unmediated Media-

tion in DeLillo's *White Noise,*" *Arizona Quarterly* 50, no. 3 (autumn 1994), 127–53; Leonard Wilcox, "Baudrillard, DeLillo's *White Noise,* and the End of Heroic Narrative," *Contemporary Literature* 32 (1991), 346–65; Paul Maltby, "The Romantic Metaphysics of Don DeLillo," *Contemporary Literature* 37, no. 2 (summer 1996), 258–77; Lou F. Caton, "Romanticism and the Postmodern Novel: Three Scenes from Don DeLillo's *White Noise,*" *English Language Notes* 35 (September 1997), 38–48; Joseph Dewey, *In a Dark Time: The Apocalyptic Temper in the American Novel of the Nuclear Age* (West Lafayette, Ind.: Purdue Univ. Press, 1990), 205–29; and LeClair, *In the Loop,* 207–36. With the exception of Wilcox, Caton, and Dewey, all of these critics are represented in Osteen's selections for the Penguin casebook. Osteen opts to include Lentricchia's brief discussion of the visit to the most photographed barn in America as a DeLillo "primal scene," no doubt wanting to avoid undue duplication of Lentricchia's own volume, *New Essays on "White Noise";* however, one should note that Lentricchia's analysis of first-person narration in *White Noise* ranks with the LeClair chapter as one of the most helpful articles on this book. In the Lentricchia collection, see "Tales of the Electronic Tribe" (New York: Cambridge Univ. Press, 1991), 87–113.

2. Cornel Bonca, "Don DeLillo's *White Noise:* The Natural Language of the Species," *College Literature* 23, no. 2 (June 1996), 40, 27.

3. Bonca, "Don DeLillo's *White Noise,*" 31.

4. The phrases quoted are from Don DeLillo, *White Noise* (New York: Viking, 1985), 9, 41, 289, and 326. Hereafter cited parenthetically.

5. Arthur M. Saltzman, "The Figure in the Static: *White Noise,*" *Modern Fiction Studies* 40, no. 4 (winter 1994), 819.

6. See Saltzman, "The Figure in the Static," 811, and Nicoletta Pireddu, who in "Il Rumore dell'Incertezza: Sistemi Chiusi e Aperti in *White Noise* di Don DeLillo," *Quaderni di Lingue e Letterature* 17 (1991–1992), insists that Jack's "search for 'signs and hints' (154) in the mumbled words that Steffie articulates in dream reveal . . . not some 'splendid transcendence' (155) but only the monotonous succession of automobile names" (135). In "L'Amérique de Don DeLillo ou l'empire des signes," *Europe* 68 (May 1990), François Happe observes that Steffie's words document the "advertising litany that vampirizes our dreams" (56). For the argument that "the tenor of this passage is not parodic," see Maltby, 260 ff., and Bonca, 36–37. DeLillo himself, asked about the scene, was noncommittal. See Begley, "Don DeLillo: The Art of Fiction CXXXV," 290–91. This scene may have received more attention than it deserves.

7. Dewey, *In a Dark Time,* 220–21. Dewey reframes, with considerable originality, the poststructuralist or deconstructive premises regarding the way language estranges us from reality, but in his emphasis on the ways that "language—its artificiality, randomness, illusions, dangers" (206)—fails Jack Gladney (who "cowers behind the flimsy artifice of language" [208]), he seems to imply that DeLillo himself distrusts or despises the medium in which he works. Repeatedly declaring that "language fails" (211), repeatedly deploring the "manipulation of language" (218, 223), observing that "language is finally . . . powerless" (211), and lamenting "the banal categorizations of language" (222), Dewey paints with too broad a brush.

8. Arnold Weinstein, *Nobody's Home: Speech, Self, and Place in American Fiction from Hawthorne to DeLillo* (New York: Oxford Univ. Press, 1993), 306.

9. Horst Ruthrof, "Narrative and the Digital: On the Syntax of the Postmodern," AUMLA no. 74 (November 1990), 195. In his reading of *White Noise*, Ruthrof argues that "the digital" must be understood as more than technology: it is also recognizable "as a style of social practice," the "all-pervasive narrative syntax of present-day culture" (186) that includes a number of features familiar from other critiques of postmodernism, for example, "discursivity as constitutive of world," "seriality/replaceability/iterability," "reversal of the actual and the fictive," and so on (193).

10. DeLillo, *Americana*, 114 (106).

11. Don DeLillo, *Libra* (New York: Viking, 1988), 221.

12. Don DeLillo, *End Zone*, 88.

13. DeLillo, *End Zone*, 89.

14. William Dunbar, "[Timor Mortis conturbat me]," in *The Poems of William Dunbar* (Oxford: Oxford Univ. Press, 1979), 178–81. The subsequent quotation is also from this text.

15. For an account of the intersections between Jack's calling as historian and his precarious hold on a narrational "ici-maintenant," see Maurice Couturier, "L'histoire et la refiguration de l'instant: *White Noise* de Don DeLillo," *Revue française d'études américaines* no. 62 (November 1994), 387. Couturier adduces Ricoeur (specifically *Time and Narrative*) to shift the discussion of this novel from the "communicational" to the "philosophical, indeed, metaphysical" (385). Like Lentricchia, Couturier looks closely at the book's narrational strategy, but with particular emphasis on the self's discovery of its relation to time and death.

16. Begley, "Don DeLillo: The Art of Fiction CXXXV," 298. Pynchon makes a similar point in the introduction to his stories, *Slow Learner* (New York: Little, Brown, 1984): "When we speak of 'seriousness' in fiction ultimately we are talking about an attitude toward death—how characters may act in its presence, for example, or how they handle it when it isn't so immediate" (5).

17. Thomas Nashe, "In Time of Pestilence," in *Works*, ed. Ronald B. McKerrow, rev. F. Wilson (Oxford: B. Blackwell, 1958), 3:283.

18. DeLillo revealed this source in a letter to Tom LeClair (see *In the Loop*, 213 and 236 n. 7).

19. Mark Conroy, "From Tombstone to Tabloid: Authority Figured in *White Noise*," *Critique* 35, no. 2 (winter 1994), 103.

20. Begley, "Don DeLillo: The Art of Fiction CXXXV," 286.

21. Norman Mailer, *An American Dream* (New York: Dial, 1965), 159. DeLillo is likely to know more of Mailer's work than the one title for which he has mentioned an admiration, *Harlot's Ghost* (Begley 290).

22. Mailer, *An American Dream*, 8.

23. Begley, "Don DeLillo: The Art of Fiction CXXXV," 304.

24. John Winthrop, "A Modell of Christian Charity," in *Winthrop Papers*, ed. Stewart Mitchell, vol. 2 (New York: Russell & Russell, 1968), 295.

25. E. M. Forster, *Howards End* (1910; New York: Vintage, 1921), 239.

26. Walt Whitman, "Out of the Cradle Endlessly Rocking," in *Leaves of Grass: Comprehensive Reader's Edition,* ed. Harold W. Blodgett and Sculley Bradley (New York: New York Univ. Press, 1963), 252–53.

27. Ellen Pifer, *Demon or Doll: Images of the Child in Contemporary Writing and Culture* (Charlottesville: Univ. Press of Virginia, 2000), 230–32.

28. Paula Bryant, "Extending the Fabulative Continuum: DeLillo, Mooney, and Federman," *Extrapolation* 30, no. 2 (summer 1989), 159.

29. Yves-Charles Grandjeat, in an article exploring the ways in which the crisis depicted in this novel "is repeated at the level of its representation" (74), sees Wilder on the expressway not only as "the image of a preserved innocence" but as the counterentropic "image . . . of an imperturbable principle of perturbation that the narrative would attempt to preserve against the temptations of a deadly order" (83). My translation from "Le Sens de la crise dans *White Noise* de Don DeLillo," in *Éclats de voix: crises en représentation dans la littérature nord-américaine,* ed. Christine Raguet-Bouvart (La Rochelle: Rumeur des Ages, 1995).

30. Anonymous, *The Cloud of Unknowing and Other Works,* trans. Clifton Wolters (Harmondsworth: Penguin, 1961), 61–62.

31. Michel Serres, *Genesis,* trans. Geneviève James and James Nielson (1982; Ann Arbor: Univ. of Michigan Press, 1995), 119. Hereafter cited parenthetically. I am not the first to bring Serres to a reading of *White Noise.* Tom LeClair found support for his systems analyses in Serres's *The Parasite* and *Hermes: Literature, Science, Philosophy.* See *In the Loop,* 221, 231, 236.

32. Weinstein, *Nobody's Home,* 303.

33. DeLillo, *Great Jones Street,* 166.

34. Patti White, *Gatsby's Party: The System and the List in Contemporary Narrative* (West Lafayette, Ind.: Purdue Univ. Press, 1992), 15, 14.

35. N. Katherine Hayles, "Postmodern Parataxis: Embodied Texts, Weightless Information," *American Literary History* 2, no. 3 (fall 1990), 411.

36. DeLillo, *Great Jones Street,* 93.

37. Paul A. Cantor, "Adolf, We Hardly Knew You," in *New Essays on "White Noise,"* 60. N. H. Reeve and Richard Kerridge, in "Toxic Events: Postmodernism and DeLillo's *White Noise,"* *Cambridge Quarterly* 23 (1994), link "the German nun who treats Jack and Mink after the shooting" to the novel's other "specialised authority figures"—especially Winnie Richards—"who are expected to put an end to the cycle of rumour and deferral, but who express instead varying degrees of skepticism about the faith invested in them" (316). Reeve and Kerridge are especially good at tracing the possibilities here that "foundationalism, the ground of certainty, ha[s] been rather repressed and exiled from the contemporary world than abolished altogether" (318).

38. David E. Nye, "The Emergence of Photographic Discourse: Images and Consumption," in *Consumption and American Culture,* ed. Nye and Carl Pedersen, vol. 21 of *European Contributions to American Studies* (Amsterdam: VU Univ. Press, 1991), 34.

39. Walker Percy, "The Loss of the Creature," in *The Message in the Bottle: How Queer*

Man Is, How Queer Language Is, and What One Has to Do with the Other (New York: Farrar, Straus and Giroux, 1975), 47.

40. Bertrand Gervais, "Les murmures de la machine: Lire à travers le *Bruit de fond de* Don DeLillo," *Surfaces* 4, no. 203 (1994), 9. The sentence in English is my translation. Gervais makes this point in discussing the "convergence" of DeLillo's art here with its critical reception and the theory behind it—which he explains with reference to Stanley Fish's idea of an interpretive community. Among the critics who discuss this passage, Gervais includes Noel King, who notes a number of theories one might bring to bear on the passage were it not that "Murray . . . pre-empts any such interpretative turn." See Noel King, "Reading *White Noise:* Floating Remarks," *Critical Quarterly* 33, no. 3 (autumn 1991), 71.

41. Frow, "Last Things," 185.

42. The most astute readings of Murray avoid pronouncing on his pretensions to insight and wisdom. Thomas Peyser, for example, emphasizes Murray's status as cultural amphibium, whether as Jew or academic outsider: "He occupies the disturbingly unlocatable position of the stranger." See "Globalization in America: The Case of Don DeLillo's *White Noise,*" *Clio* 25, no. 3 (spring 1996), 263. Other critics, like Gérard Cordesse, note that Murray is as much Mephistopheles as "guru of modernity." See "Bruits et paradoxes dans *White Noise* de Don DeLillo," *Revue française d'études américaines,* no. 76 (March 1998), 60.

43. In "Whole Families Shopping at Night!" Ferraro analyzes the tangled bloodlines of the Gladney clan to probe the novel's picture of the American family in the age of divorce.

44. Allen Ginsberg, "A Supermarket in California," in *Collected Poems, 1947–1980* (New York: Harper & Row, 1984), 136.

45. Peyser, "Globalization in America," 269.

Convergence of the Twain: *Libra*

1. Begley, "Don DeLillo: The Art of Fiction CXXXV," 304.

2. Don DeLillo, "The Power of History," *New York Times Magazine,* 7 September 1997, 63.

3. For a comparison of selections from Marguerite Oswald's actual words, as recorded and transcribed, and those of the DeLillo character, see Douglas Keesey, *Don DeLillo* (New York: Twayne, 1993), 194–96.

4. DeCurtis, "'An Outsider,'" 55.

5. See the materials submitted to the Warren Commission by journalist William Stuckey, U.S. President's Commission on the Assassination of President John F. Kennedy, *Investigation on the Assassination of President John F. Kennedy, Hearings before the President's Commission on the Assassination of President Kennedy,* vol. 21 (Washington, D.C.: GPO, 1964).

6. Michel Foucault, "Orders of Discourse," trans. Rupert Swyer, *Social Science Information* 10 (April 1971), 17.

7. DeLillo, *Libra,* 418. Hereafter cited parenthetically.

8. Freud borrows this phrase from Goethe. See Sigmund Freud, *Totem and Taboo* (1913), trans. James Strachey, in *The Standard Edition of the Complete Psychological Works of Sigmund Freud,* ed. Strachey (London: Hogarth Press, 1953–74), 13: 161.

9. Lacan makes the observation a number of times. See, for example, Jacques Lacan, *Écrits: A Selection,* trans. Alan Sheridan (London: Tavistock, 1977), 50, 59, 234.

10. David Cowart, *History and the Contemporary Novel* (Carbondale: Southern Illinois Univ. Press, 1989).

11. Lion Feuchtwanger, *The House of Desdemona* (Detroit: Wayne State Univ. Press, 1963).

12. Thomas Carmichael, "Lee Harvey Oswald and the Postmodern Subject: History and Intertextuality in Don DeLillo's *Libra, The Names,* and *Mao II," Contemporary Literature* 34 (summer 1993), 207.

13. Christopher M. Mott, "*Libra* and the Subject of History," *Critique* 35 (spring 1994), 131. Mott's essay is helpful in relating DeLillo's vision to the "postmodern historiography" of Hayden White and Michel Foucault. White, he notes, "foregrounds the narrativization of history," while Foucault examines "subject positions initiated and maintained through the power of ideological imposition and manifested in discursive practices" (133). These theoretical perspectives facilitate a recognition that "*Libra* achieves what few other accounts of the assassination even attempt: a narrative that suggests that the bickering to establish the truth of the event is moot, especially in contrast to the possibility of learning something significant about our cultural orientation and ourselves" (145).

14. Ann Arensberg, "Seven Seconds," *Vogue,* August 1988, 338.

15. William Goldstein, "Don DeLillo," *Publishers Weekly,* 19 August 1988, 55, 56. "It's possible I wouldn't have become the kind of writer I am if it weren't for the assassination," DeLillo told Anthony DeCurtis. "Maybe it invented me" (DeCurtis, "'An Outsider,'" 48, 47).

16. See Max Holland, "After Thirty Years: Making Sense of the Assassination," *Reviews in American History* 22 (1994), 205. This is an especially sensible overview of perspectives on the assassination. I would also recommend Dale Carter, "Beyond the Grassy Knolledge: Conspiratorial Variations on the Kennedy Assassination," *Odense American Studies International Series* no. 11 (August 1994), 1–31.

17. Glen Thomas, "History, Biography, and Narrative in Don DeLillo's *Libra," Twentieth Century Literature* 43 (spring 1997), 121. Another critic remarks that *Libra* "finally makes the same case for history that chaos theory has clarified about weather forecasting: the impossibility of grasping the plurality of details inherent in initial conditions renders any human attempt at understanding the present or forecasting the future proportionally deficient"; see Stephen Bernstein, "*Libra* and the Historical Sublime," *Postmodern Culture* 4 (January 1994), paragraph 25. Jonathan Brent notes that the present historiographical task is further complicated by the tangled web of "plausible deniability" built into the original plot by Everett and Parmenter: "At every step of the assassination plot, each participant is 'protected' from knowledge and, in the end, events occur

for which no coherent epistemology of cause and effect is possible. No one individual can know because Everett's plan produces so many counterplans and points of unpredictability. . . . Everett produces probabilities, not designs, tendencies, not intentions. Once set in motion, his elaborate pattern of tendencies cannot be controlled, nor can its outcome be foreseen." As a result, "probability replaces causation; facticity replaces existence; indeterminacy replaces chance; events replace acts; 'the power and momentum of mass feelings' (DeLillo 445) replace intention; and . . . a collage of clichéd gestures and habits replaces the self." See "The Unimaginable Space of Danilo Kiš and Don DeLillo," *Review of Contemporary Fiction* 14 (spring 1994), 183.

18. Philip E. Simmons, *Deep Surfaces: Mass Culture and History in Postmodern American Fiction* (Athens: Univ. of Georgia Press, 1997), 81.

19. Don DeLillo, *Underworld* (New York: Scribner, 1997), 156. The other quotations here come from pages 155–60.

20. Don DeLillo, *Valparaiso* (New York: Scribner, 1999), 30. Hereafter cited parenthetically.

21. DeLillo, "The Power of History," 62.

22. John Johnston, "Superlinear Fiction or Historical Diagram? Don DeLillo's *Libra*," *Modern Fiction Studies* 40 (summer 1994), 329. In this article Johnston covers a great deal of ground, discussing, among other things, the way *Libra* "confirms the crucial significance of genre by focusing attention on the way genre delimits and governs the boundaries between fiction and history, above all through such regulative notions as character and plot" (319). Johnston also analyzes with great subtlety the story's "convergent double plot structure" (322) as both Branch and DeLillo conceptualize it: "Everett, Oswald, Branch, and by extension DeLillo the author form a series of men in small rooms who are both aligned and differentiated through a series of variously embedded assumptions about the difference between fiction and reality" (331).

23. Begley, "Don DeLillo: The Art of Fiction CXXXV," 302

24. Brigitte Desalm, "Masses, Power and the Elegance of Sentences" (interview), trans. Tilo Zimmermann, *Kölner Stadt-Anzeiger,* 27 October 1992 <http://perival.com/delillo/desalm_interview.html>.

25. Frank Lentricchia, "*Libra* as Postmodern Critique," in *Introducing Don DeLillo,* 201. Lentricchia provides a strong analysis of how "the social environment of the typical naturalist character is displaced in DeLillo by the charismatic environment of the image" (210). He draws attention to such moments as Marina Oswald's seeing herself on a shop-window video monitor or, at Love Field, the crowd's discovering "that Kennedy looked like himself, that he must therefore be himself because he looked like the photographs of himself" as key moments in a vision of "life lived totally inside the representations generated in the print and visual media" (206).

26. DeCurtis, "'An Outsider,'" 56.

27. Arensberg, "Seven Seconds," 339.

28. Don DeLillo, "American Blood: The JFK Assassination," *Rolling Stone,* 8 December 1983, 27.

29. "American Blood," 27.

30. DeCurtis, "'An Outsider,'" 53.

31. The quotations here are from Thomas Hardy, "Convergence of the Twain," *The Complete Poems* (London: Macmillan, 1976), 306–7.

32. Bill Millard, "The Fable of the Ants: Myopic Interactions in DeLillo's *Libra*," *Postmodern Culture* 4 (January 1994), paragraph 14. A number of critics have characterized this novel as, in the words of Joseph Kronick, "a self-organizing system bound by the binary opposition between chance and necessity." Millard ingeniously adduces scientific observations of ant trails, whose straightness proves to be the product of meandering motion on the part of individuals, to conceptualize how the individual machinations of the CIA, Alpha, and the mob can eventuate in what looks like a clockwork piece of conspiracy. Kronick, citing Ilya Prigogine and Isabel Stengers's *Order out of Chaos* (New York: Bantam, 1984), suggests something similar in his consideration of "the condition of intrinsically random systems. . . . In their study of open systems, as opposed to the closed systems of classical dynamics, Prigogine and Stengers propose that randomness can be derived from determinism and irreversibility: the universe is a deterministic system evolving in a stochastic (probabilistic) process out of chance"; see "*Libra* and the Assassination of JFK: A Textbook Operation," *Arizona Quarterly* 50 (spring 1994), 115, 116. For a discussion of DeLillo's handling of chance and nonlinear causality here as a "rework[ing of] the naturalistic leitmotif of the self caught within a universe of force" (33), see Paul Civello, "Undoing the Naturalistic Novel: Don DeLillo's *Libra*," *Arizona Quarterly* 48 (summer 1992), 33–56. Magali Cornier Michael also analyzes the tension between coincidence and cause and effect—but with more attention to the pathos of Oswald's failed or impaired or miscarried constructions of subjectivity. Michael offers one of the more thorough discussions of the novel's women characters, including Marguerite, Marina, Mary Frances Everett, and Beryl Parmenter. See "The Political Paradox within Don DeLillo's *Libra*," *Critique* 35 (spring 1994), 146–55.

33. DeLillo, *Underworld*, 496.

34. Freud, *Totem and Taboo*, 141.

35. Freud, *Totem and Taboo*, 154, 153.

36. Sigmund Freud, *Moses and Monotheism* (1939), trans. James Strachey, in *The Standard Edition of the Complete Psychological Works of Sigmund Freud*, ed. Strachey (London: Hogarth Press, 1953–74), 23: 88–89.

37. Norman Mailer, *Oswald's Tale: An American Mystery* (New York: Random House, 1995), 784. "Any concerted plan that placed Oswald in the gunner's seat," says Mailer, "would have had to have been built on the calculation that he would miss. That, indeed, was the thesis of the CIA men in Don DeLillo's fine novel *Libra*" (779). "If one's personal inclination would find Oswald innocent, or at least part of a conspiracy, one's gloomy verdict, nonetheless, is that Lee had the character to kill Kennedy, and that he probably did it alone" (778). Like DeLillo, however, Mailer is intrigued by the possibility that Jack Ruby acted on orders from the mob.

38. Warren Commission, *Investigation*, 3: 14.

39. Jean-François Lyotard, *The Postmodern Condition: A Report on Knowledge*, trans. Geoff Bennington and Brian Massumi (Minneapolis: Univ. of Minnesota Press, 1984), 60.

40. George Will, "Shallow Look at the Mind of an Assassin," *Washington Post*,

22 September 1988, A-25. See also Jonathan Yardley, "Appointment in Dallas," *Washington Post Book World*, 31 July 1988, 3.

41. DeLillo insists on the distinction between embracing paranoia and representing it as historical reality. In the interview with Brigitte Desalm, he dismisses Oliver Stone's tendentious film *JFK* as "Disneyland for paranoids."

"Our Only Language Is Beirut": *Mao II*

1. "If I were a writer," says Owen Brademas in *The Names* (New York: Knopf, 1982), "how I would enjoy being told the novel is dead. How liberating to work in the margins, outside a central perception" (77). DeLillo told Ann Arensberg: "American writers ought to stand and live in the margins" ("Seven Seconds," 340). In "Don DeLillo: *Americana, Mao II*, and *Underworld*," Adam Begley observes that "if everything in the culture argues against the novel, that's what DeLillo's going to make. If celebrity is the expected path, he'll find a detour. He chooses to set up shop on the far periphery, in the shadows—out of sight, but with a clear view of the center" (490). In the LeClair interview, DeLillo speaks sympathetically of the "writer . . . working against the age," the writer who "feels some satisfaction at not being widely read," the writer "diminished," even, "by an audience" (see LeClair, "An Interview with Don DeLillo," 87).

2. Mark Osteen, *American Magic and Dread*, 193. Osteen's is one of the more satisfying discussions of *Mao II*—even if one resists his view of Brita as the author's proposed new model of authorship. Though he is not the first to read this novel against Guy Debord's "society of the spectacle," Osteen turns the connection to particularly good use.

3. Street people, DeLillo told LeClair, "speak a kind of broken language. It's part of the language of cities, really. . . . In the subway arcades under Fourteenth Street you hear . . . this strange broken language. The language of the insane is stronger than all the others. It's the language of the self, the pain of self" (88).

4. Vince Passaro, "Dangerous Don DeLillo," *New York Times Magazine*, 19 May 1991, 77.

5. Don DeLillo, "The Artist Naked in a Cage," *New Yorker*, 26 May 1997, 6.

6. Steffen Hantke, "'God Save Us from Bourgeois Adventure': The Figure of the Terrorist in Contemporary American Conspiracy Fiction," *Studies in the Novel* 28, no. 2 (1996), 237. Hantke also sees DeLillo as "eclectically raiding the realm of modernist iconography" to create "a portrait of Gray that consists of aspects from different manifestations of modernism" (234). There is some critical agreement that Bill Gray represents a kind of holdover from an earlier model of the literary artist. Margaret Scanlan sees him as a Romantic survival ("Writers among Terrorists: Don DeLillo's *Mao II* and the Rushdie Affair," *Modern Fiction Studies* 40, no. 2 [summer 1994]: 236–37, 242, 244); Richard Levesque speaks of him as both Romantic and modernist ("Telling Postmodern Tales: Absent Authorities in Didion's *Democracy* and DeLillo's *Mao II*," *Arizona Quarterly* 54, no. 3 [autumn 1998]: 79–81); and Osteen discovers a kind of elegy for what he calls "the Romantic or Dedalian model of authorship" (192). I agree with these charac-

terizations up to a point, but it remains important to recognize in Bill Gray's story something more than a belated lament for artistic fashions out of date by half a century or more. The harrowing power of Bill's fate lies, I think, in his *not* being a literary anachronism, Miniver Cheevy as novelist. As Joseph Tabbi points out in *Postmodern Sublime: Technology and American Writing from Mailer to Cyberpunk* (Ithaca: Cornell Univ. Press, 1995), Bill is the true contemporary and literary partner of the age's least backward-looking artists: "Pynchon, Salinger . . . Gaddis . . . McElroy, and DeLillo himself" (195).

7. Ezra Pound, "Homage to Sextus Propertius," in *Selected Poems of Ezra Pound* (New York: New Directions, 1957), 78.

8. DeLillo, *The Names*, 118.

9. In a postcolonialist critique, Peter Baker tentatively faults DeLillo for an "imaginative 'failure' . . . to attempt to render any kind of satisfactory counterpart to the Western novelist in the figure of the terrorist leader." Baker also suggests that Bill Gray's failure to confront Abu Rashid may be DeLillo's illustration of "a certain reality, a division between world views and systems of thinking." But this is not such an uncrossable divide—indeed, it is the perennial task of literary artists to make such imaginative leaps. See "The Terrorist as Interpreter: *Mao II* in Postmodern Context," *Postmodern Culture* 4.2 (1994), paragraph 27.

10. Brigitte Desalm, "Masses, Power and the Elegance of Sentences" (interview) trans. Tilo Zimmermann, *Kölner Stadt-Anzeiger*, 23 July 2001 <http://perival.com/delillo/desalm_interview.html>. Compare Warhol's remark: "I never read. I just look at pictures" (Andy Warhol, Kasper König, Pontus Hultén, and Olle Granath, eds., *Andy Warhol* [Stockholm: Moderna Museet, 1968], n.p.; quoted in *Andy Warhol: A Retrospective*, ed. Kynaston McShine [New York: Museum of Modern Art, 1989], 463).

11. Keesey, *Don DeLillo*, 190.

12. Norman Mailer, *Advertisements for Myself* (New York: Berkley Medallion, 1959), 20, 15. DeLillo has indicated his awareness of Mailer's remarks. See David Streitfeld, "Don DeLillo's Gloomy Muse," *Washington Post*, 14 May 1992, C4, col. 3.

13. Desalm, "Masses, Power."

14. Søren Kierkegaard, "'That Individual': Two 'Notes' Concerning My Work as an Author," in *The Point of View*, trans. Walter Lowrie (Oxford: Oxford Univ. Press, 1939), 116.

15. Peter Brooker, *New York Fictions: Modernity, Postmodernity, and the New Modern* (London: Longman, 1996), 231.

16. Louis Althusser, "Ideology and Ideological State Apparatuses (Notes Towards an Investigation)," in *Lenin and Philosophy and Other Essays*, trans. Ben Brewster (London: New Left Books, 1971), 127–86. Though he invokes Bakhtin rather than Althusser, Ryan Simmons argues ("What Is a Terrorist? Contemporary Authorship, the Unabomber, and *Mao II*," *Modern Fiction Studies* 45, no. 3 [fall 1999], 675–95) that "Bill Gray is part of a social consciousness, not an individual one," that "acts of 'authorship' correspond to all other social acts, that authorship itself is, at once, a paradigm for society and just another element within it" (682), and that DeLillo, in the end, "points out the degree

to which the binaries by which authorship is defined—especially the binary between individual and mass consciousness—are untenable" (693). Simmons's argument is wonderfully subtle, but in deconstructing the binary of terrorist vs. author (partly through the example of Unabomber Theodore Kaczynski, who was both) it seems to me to embrace agency-and-consciousness-denying theories that DeLillo, however distanced from his character Bill Gray, would surely find abhorrent.

17. "To me," DeLillo told Brigitte Desalm, "audience means a small group of interested people, not a large number of consumers" ("Masses, Power").

18. See Bradford Collins and David Cowart, "Through the Looking-Glass: Reading Warhol's *Superman,*" *American Imago* 53 (summer 1996), 107–37.

19. One realizes here the extent to which, in his novel *Plowing the Dark* (2000), Richard Powers rewrites *Mao II*, revisiting the year 1989 and its upheavals as background to a story contrasting the experience of a hostage in Beirut and the travail of a burnt-out artist.

20. Margaret Roberts, "'D' is for Danger—and for Writer Don DeLillo," *Chicago Tribune,* 22 May 1992, sec. 5, 5.

21. Marco Livingstone, "Do It Yourself: Notes on Warhol's Technique," in *Andy Warhol,* ed. McShine, 74.

22. Tabbi, *Postmodern Sublime,* 198, 203–4.

23. James Joyce, *A Portrait of the Artist As a Young Man* (1916; New York: Viking, 1964), 214. The subsequent quotation in this paragraph is from the same passage in *Portrait.*

24. Arthur O. Lovejoy, *The Great Chain of Being: A Study of the History of an Idea* (Cambridge: Harvard Univ. Press, 1936).

25. Passaro, "Dangerous Don DeLillo," 77

26. Jonathan Franzen quotes from a personal letter in "Perchance to Dream," *Harper's Magazine,* April 1996, 54.

27. Laura Barrett, "'Here But Also There': Subjectivity and Postmodern Space in *Mao II,*" *Modern Fiction Studies* 45, no. 3 (fall 1999), 801.

28. Willa Cather, "The Novel Démeublé," in *Not under Forty* (New York: Knopf, 1936), 50.

For Whom Bell Tolls: *Americana*

1. Though *Americana* remains the least discussed of DeLillo's major novels, an Oedipal dimension has been noted by both Tom LeClair, in *In The Loop,* and Keesey, in *Don DeLillo.* Neither, however, foregrounds this element. LeClair, in his magisterial chapter on this novel (which he names, along with *Ratner's Star* and *The Names,* as one of DeLillo's "primary achievements" [33]), represents the Oedipal theme as largely ancillary to the proliferating "personal, cultural, and aesthetic . . . schizophrenia" that he sees as pervasive in the life of David Bell and in the culture of which he is a part (34). Thus LeClair explores the dynamics of what Gregory Bateson and R. D. Laing call the "double bind" in "the system of communication in Bell's family," which, "understood

in Bateson's terms, establishes the ground of Bell's character and presents a microcosm of the larger cultural problems manifested in *Americana*" (35–36). Keesey, by contrast, takes a feminist view of Bell's personality and life problems. Keesey is especially interesting on the Oedipal relationship between Bell and his father, and on the idea that Bell, in his film, is striving unsuccessfully to recover the mother's "way of seeing" the world—a way lost to him when he embraced the values expressed in his father's "ads for sex and violence" (23).

2. Don DeLillo, *Americana* (New York: Houghton Mifflin, 1971; rev. ed., New York: Penguin, 1989). In preparing the Penguin edition, DeLillo made numerous small cuts in the text, and, generally speaking, the gains in economy improve the novel. For the most part, the author simply pares away minor instances of rhetorical overkill. For example, he deletes a gratuitously obscene remark about the spelling of "mothercountry," and he reduces the space devoted to the relationship of Bell and his ex-wife, Meredith. The cuts afford glimpses of a gifted writer's maturing sense of decorum and understatement. Thus a minor motif like that of the woman ironing (it contributes to the reader's grasp of Bell's Oedipal obsession) becomes a little less extravagant in the longer of the two passages in which it appears. Elsewhere, one applauds the excision of the syntactically tortured and the merely pretentious (e.g., unsuccessful descriptions of film's epistemological and ontological properties). At no point, however, does the author add material or alter the novel's original emphases, and I have only occasionally found it necessary or desirable to quote material that does not appear in both versions of the text. Except in these instances, I give page numbers for both editions—the 1971 Houghton Mifflin version first, the 1989 Penguin version second.

3. "The Heart Is a Lonely Craftsman," *Los Angeles Times Calendar,* 29 July 1984, 7.

4. Thomas Pynchon, *The Crying of Lot 49* (Philadelphia: Lippincott, 1966), 180.

5. Rainer Maria Rilke, *Gesammelte Gedichte* (Frankfurt: Insel-Verlag, 1962), 313. Rilke's "Der Panther," by the same token, may lie behind Pike's desire to encounter a mountain lion face to face.

6. The only substantial discussion of the *Ikiru* allusions is that of Mark Osteen, in *American Magic and Dread,* 26–27. Osteen acutely suggests that Bell sees himself in the film's moribund main character, Watanabe, and "fears his own living death." The recurrent references to the scene on the swing represent "David's attempt to generate the kind of retrospective epiphany that Watanabe undergoes" (26).

7. The author describes the genesis of this novel in a positive evocation of *Americana*:

> I was sailing in Maine with two friends, and we put into a small harbor on Mt. Desert Island. And I was sitting on a railroad tie waiting to take a shower, and I had a glimpse of a street maybe fifty yards away and a sense of beautiful old houses and rows of elms and maples and a stillness and wistfulness—the street seemed to carry its own built-in longing. And I felt something, a pause, something opening up before me. It would be a month or two before I started writing the book and two or three years before I came up with the title *Americana,* but in fact it was all implicit in that moment—a moment in which nothing happened, nothing ostensibly changed, a

moment in which I didn't see anything I hadn't seen before. But there was a pause in time, and I knew I had to write about a man who comes to a street like this or lives on a street like this. And whatever roads the novel eventually followed, I believe I maintained the idea of that quiet street if only as counterpoint, as lost innocence. (Begley, "Don DeLillo: The Art of Fiction CXXXV," 279)

This recollection dictates not only the scene off Mt. Desert Island but also and more clearly the scene in picturesque Millsgate, the little town on Penobscot Bay where the travelers pick up Brand. Here, at the end of part 1, Bell conceives the idea for his film—just as DeLillo, in a similar setting, conceived the idea of *Americana.*

8. *Great Jones Street,* 1.

"More Advanced the Deeper We Dig": *Ratner's Star*

1. Don DeLillo, *Ratner's Star* (New York: Knopf, 1976), 432. Hereafter cited parenthetically.

2. Ludwig Wittgenstein, *Tractatus Logico-Philosophicus,* trans. D. F. Pears and B. F. McGuinness (1922; London: Routledge & Kegan Paul, 1961), proposition 4.12. DeLillo interestingly views Wittgenstein himself as being "outside the world." In the LeClair interview, the author remarks, "I like the way he uses the language. Even in translation, it's very evocative. It's like reading Martian. . . . Wittgenstein is the language of outer space, a very precise race of people" (LeClair, "An Interview with Don DeLillo," 85).

3. The breakdown of Softly, as of Endor and perhaps Billy Twillig as well, prefigures that of Eric Lighter, the mathematician protagonist of DeLillo's first published play, *The Engineer of Moonlight* (*Cornell Review* 1 [1979], 21–47). Now fifty-five years old, Lighter has become a mental case after early achievements in his field. Indeed, he is the mysterious "engineer of moonlight" invoked in the title—a man who has become a strange mix of the rational (as engineers and mathematicians are supposed to be) and the dreamy or mad (the traditional "lunar" qualities). Though the source of his problem remains obscure, Lighter seems troubled by the world's endless resistance to his attempt to represent it in mathematical or other language. This inability to pierce the "veil" of reality is underscored in the naming of Lighter's third and fourth wives, who are part of the play's small cast. Their names—one is Diana Vail, the other is Maya—suggest Eric Lighter's career-long professional failure to close with the real. In Hindu philosophy, Maya is the veil of illusion that perennially cloaks the real, and in the course of this drama the marital Maya teaches her troubled husband to count in Sanskrit. Perhaps in other ways she will be able to minister to his Western itch to seek objective truth in quantification.

4. Sir Charles Percy Snow, *The Two Cultures; and, A Second Look: An Expanded Version of The "Two Cultures and the Scientific Revolution"* (New York: Cambridge Univ. Press, 1964), 4.

5. Jacob Bronowski and Bruce Mazlish, *The Western Intellectual Tradition: From Leonardo to Hegel* (New York: Harper & Row, 1960), vii.

6. Voltaire, *Candide,* trans. Lowell Bair (1759; New York: Bantam, 1959), 18–19. Vol-

taire seems also to hover in the background of *Amazons,* the 1980 novel on which DeLillo collaborated anonymously. Certainly there is considerable similarity between the sexual infantilism that figures in *Ratner's Star* and the omnivorous sexuality of Cleo Birdwell, the narrator (and ostensible author) of *Amazons.* "First woman ever to play in the National Hockey League," Cleo is a female Candide—a picara who chronicles a series of experiences on the ice and in the boudoir. Her innocence, however, is not sexual—like Barthelme's Snow White, in fact, she sleeps with all seven of the major male characters, including the same Murray Jay Siskind who plays so prominent a role in *White Noise.* What she says of him applies as well to her other lovers in this comedy of sexual stereotyping: "Too much innocence" (Cleo Birdwell, *Amazons* [New York: Holt, Rinehart and Winston, 1980], 297). Cleo encounters picaresque experience of vice and folly in the form of certain advertising accounts, including a breakfast-food company called Kelloid (an artful blend of Kellogg, cheloid, and Filboid, suggesting corn flakes with the consistency of scar tissue and at the same time saluting H. H. Munro's "The Mouse That Helped," an early satire on consumerism featuring a breakfast cereal named Filboid Studge).

7. Jonathan Swift, *Gulliver's Travels,* ed. Herbert Davis (1726; Oxford: Basil Blackwell, 1962), 163. Hereafter cited parenthetically.

8. LeClair, "An Interview with Don DeLillo," 86.

9. LeClair, "An Interview with Don DeLillo," 85.

10. LeClair, "An Interview with Don DeLillo," 83–84.

11. Glen Scott Allen, "Raids on the Conscious: Pynchon's Legacy of Paranoia and the Terrorism of Uncertainty in Don DeLillo's *Ratner's Star,*" *Postmodern Culture* 4, no. 2 (January 1994), paragraph 17.

"The Deepest Being": Language in *The Names*

1. DeLillo, *The Names,* 52. Hereafter cited parenthetically.

2. "Preface 1855—*Leaves of Grass,* First Edition," in *Leaves of Grass: Comprehensive Reader's Edition,* ed. Harold W. Blodgett and Sculley Bradley (New York: New York Univ. Press, 1963), 714.

3. Wittgenstein, *Philosophical Investigations,* part 1, section 19, 8e.

4. Unless otherwise noted, the quotations in this paragraph are from Martin Heidegger, *An Introduction to Metaphysics,* trans. Ralph Manheim (New Haven: Yale Univ. Press, 1959).

5. Martin Heidegger, "Hölderlin and the Essence of Poetry," trans. Douglas Scott, in *Existence and Being,* 3rd ed., ed. Werner Broch (London: Vision, 1968), 298. Hereafter cited parenthetically.

6. The quotations in this paragraph are from Jacques Derrida, "The Supplement of Copula: Philosophy before Linguistics," in *Margins of Philosophy,* trans. Alan Bass (Chicago: Univ. of Chicago Press, 1982), 175–205.

7. DeLillo, *Underworld,* 542, 540.

8. DeLillo, *Ratner's Star,* 264.

9. DeLillo, *Americana* (1971), 63–64.

10. Though he does not take up the twenty-seven depravities, Matthew J. Morris sees similar patriarchal gestures here as mirroring and complementing DeLillo's concern with colonialism. "Both colonialism and sexism . . . stem from a desire to exclude or appropriate alterity" (114). Morris seems to imply, though, a kind of standard reproach to Western colonialism on DeLillo's part—and thereby misses or underestimates a much broader indictment of political myth-making on all sides. See "Murdering Words: Language in Action in Don DeLillo's *The Names,*" *Contemporary Literature* 30 (spring 1989), 113–27.

11. DeLillo may have read Alexander and Nicholas Humez's books on the alphabet (e.g., *Alpha to Omega: The Life and Times of the Greek Alphabet*), which include accounts not only of the three discarded letters of the Greek alphabet but also of the boustrophedon script that Owen Brademas remarks on. I have elsewhere availed myself of their transliteration of the Greek opening of the Gospel of John.

12. Paula Bryant, "Discussing the Untellable: Don DeLillo's *The Names,*" *Critique* 29 (fall 1987), 19.

13. Dennis A. Foster, "Alphabetic Pleasures: *The Names,*" in *Introducing Don DeLillo,* ed. Lentricchia, 168.

14. The quotations in this paragraph are taken from Walter Benjamin, "On Language As Such and on the Language of Man," trans. Edmund Jephcott, in *Selected Writings, Volume 1: 1913–1926,* ed. Marcus Bullock and Michael W. Jennings (Cambridge: Harvard Univ. Press, 1996), 62–74.

15. Nathaniel Hawthorne, *The Scarlet Letter,* vol. 1 of *The Centenary Edition of the Works of Nathaniel Hawthorne,* ed. William Charvat et al. (Columbus: Ohio State Univ. Press, 1962), 142. Hawthorne's phrase "native language" echoes that of Milton describing the Tower of Babel in *Paradise Lost* (12:54).

16. DeCurtis, "'An Outsider,'" 64.

17. DeLillo, *Great Jones Street,* 88.

18. Don DeLillo, *Mao II* (New York: Viking, 1991), 46.

19. Anthony DeCurtis, "'An Outsider,'" 64.

"The Physics of Language": *Underworld*

1. DeLillo, "The Power of History," 60, 63.

2. DeLillo, "The Power of History," 63.

3. DeLillo, "The Power of History," 63.

4. DeLillo, *Underworld,* 422. Hereafter cited parenthetically.

5. Diane Osen, "Window on a Writing Life: A Conversation with National Book Award Winner Don DeLillo," Book-of-the-Month Club, last accessed 23 July 2001 <http://www.pubweekly.com/NBF/docs/wwl_curri_DeLillo.htm>

6. Gerald Howard, "The American Strangeness: An Interview with Don DeLillo," *Hungry Mind Review* 43 (1997), 16. DeLillo makes the same point in an interview in the Austrian paper *Der Standard:* "Language," he says, "is the only escape. A young writer

with a specific social background makes himself through language, which he develops, what else has he?" (Peter Körte, "Sprache ist der Einzige Fluchtweg," *Der Standard*, 30 October 1998, A1; my translation).

7. No one has described the density of this title better than Tom LeClair, who notes that it packs together "Dante, the Mafia, hollowed earth, humankind's sediment, ghetto life, underground politics, the subconscious, and linguistic roots" ("An Underhistory of Mid-Century America," *Atlantic*, October 1997, last accessed 4 March 2001 <http://www.theatlantic.com/issues/97oct/delillo.htm>). To LeClair's enumeration one might add the idea of an artistic underworld as represented in such works as *Unterwelt* and the literally subterranean graffiti of Moonman 157. Both homosexual, Eisenstein and Muñoz dwell also in sexual underworlds.

8. Osen, "Window on a Writing Life."

9. Körte, "Sprache ist der Einzige Fluchtweg," A1.

10. Osen, "Window on a Writing Life."

11. DeLillo, "The Power of History," 62, 63.

12. DeLillo, "The Power of History," 63.

13. Vince Passaro, "The Unsparing Vision of Don DeLillo," *Harper's Magazine*, November 1997, 74.

14. John A. McClure, "Postmodern/Post-Secular: Contemporary Fiction and Spirituality," *Modern Fiction Studies* 41 (1995), 142–43. In a thoughtful review of *Underworld*, the novelist Thomas Mallon seconds Passaro and McClure, characterizing DeLillo's novel as "finally, if tentatively, a religious book" ("The Bronx, with Thonx," *GQ*, September 1997, 196).

15. Andrew Billen, "Up from the Underworld," *London Evening Standard*, 28 January 1998, last accessed 5 April 2001 <http://www.thisislondon.co.uk/dynamic/lifestyle/bottom_review.html?in_review_id=26802&in_review_text_id=20603>.

DeLillolalia: From *Underworld* to *The Body Artist*

1. DeLillo, *Underworld*, 102. Hereafter cited parenthetically.

2. Michiko Kakutani, "'Underworld': Of America as a Splendid Junk Heap," *New York Times*, 16 September 1997, last accessed 4 March 2001 <http://www.nytimes.com/books/97/09/14/daily/underworld-book-review.html>.

3. Jesse Kavadlo, "Celebration and Annihilation: The Balance of *Underworld*," *Undercurrent*, no. 7 (spring 1999), note 4, Univ. of Oregon, last accessed 4 March 2001 <http://darkwing.uoregon.edu/~ucurrent/uc7/7-kava.html>.

4. Osen, "Window on a Writing Life."

5. DeLillo, *Great Jones Street*, 68.

6. As Peter Knight has persuasively argued, "*Underworld* revises the anatomy of popular American paranoia that DeLillo has conducted in his previous novels, pushing back the inquiry before the assassination of President John F. Kennedy, which had previously served as the watershed event in his work, and reaching ahead into the as yet unconfigured world beyond the end of the Cold War"; see "Everything Is Connected:

Underworld's Secret History of Paranoia," *Modern Fiction Studies* 45, no. 3 (fall 1999), 812. Knight contrasts what he calls the "secure paranoia" of the Cold War with the more recognizably postmodern "insecure paranoia" that began on the fateful November day in Dallas (817). He is also an especially able cataloger of *Underworld*'s many connections, but where I have emphasized the purely textual or modernist element in these connections (with consideration of the way they buttress worldviews now superstitious, now metaphysical or religious), Knight underscores the picture of world capital's emergent and progressive connectedness. He makes the telling point that this secret history of the Cold War pays virtually no attention to its end: the fall of the Berlin Wall and the New World Order. Rather, the Cold War's secure paranoia gradually gives way to "an underground current of increasing awareness and consternation that slowly everything is becoming connected" as "social and economic relationships within a global economy" (825).

7. Philip Nel, "'A Small Incisive Shock': Modern Forms, Postmodern Politics, and the Role of the Avant-garde in *Underworld*," *Modern Fiction Studies* 45, no. 3 (fall 1999), 737. This important article "argues that *Underworld* complicates traditional distinctions between modern and postmodern by drawing on both a high modernist aesthetic and those residual elements of the historical avant-garde that characterize certain postmodernisms" (725–26).

8. Martin Amis, "Survivors of the Cold War," *New York Times Book Review*, 5 October 1997, 12.

9. John N. Duvall, "Introduction: From Valparaiso to Jerusalem: DeLillo and the Moment of Canonization," *Modern Fiction Studies* 45, no. 3 (fall 1999), 561. For the argument that Nick "has neither historical nor aesthetic self-consciousness," see Timothy L. Parrish, "From Hoover's FBI to Eisenstein's *Unterwelt*: DeLillo Directs the Postmodern Novel," *Modern Fiction Studies* 45, no. 3 (fall 1999), 719. Parrish is especially good on DeLillo's conceptualization of the J. Edgar Hoover character as another of the novel's postmodern artists, but one resists his attempt to read the Dodgers-Giants game as an event that is as "apprehended through the media" as the Texas Highway Killer's "murdering spree" (709). In another article (on "Pafko at the Wall" and written before the story's reappearance as part of *Underworld*), Duvall makes the similar argument that "the mediation of radio, both for Hodges and his listeners, has become as invisible as an FBI wiretap. When a media form comes to seem transparent, when its role in the construction of aura is experienced paradoxically as an unmediated mediation, then we have entered, the novella suggests, the realm of the postmodern, technological sublime" ("Baseball As Aesthetic Ideology: Cold War History, Race, and DeLillo's 'Pafko at the Wall,'" *Modern Fiction Studies* 41 [1995], 303). Such arguments are intrinsically valuable, but they fail (for obvious reasons, in Duvall's case) to take sufficiently into account DeLillo's patent contrasting, in "The Power of History," of the past and its low-tech media with the present and its Möbius-strip journalism. In one, an idea of the historical survives; in the other it is vitiated.

10. Don DeLillo, *The Body Artist* (New York: Scribner, 2001), 7. Hereafter cited parenthetically.

11. Marilynne Robinson, "Psalm Eight," in *The Death of Adam: Essays on Modern Thought* (Boston: Houghton Mifflin, 1998), 242–43.

12. Robert Frost, "West-Running Brook," in *The Poetry of Robert Frost,* 258.

13. Robert Frost, "West-Running Brook," 259.

14. DeLillo, *Americana* (1971), 189.

15. Sir William Dampier, *A History of Science and Its Relations with Philosophy and Religion* (New York: Macmillan, 1930), 480. Dampier quotes and glosses A. S. Eddington, *The Nature of the Physical World* (Cambridge: Cambridge Univ. Press, 1928).

16. DeLillo, *Mao II,* 48.

17. Begley, "Don DeLillo: The Art of Fiction CXXXV," 283.

18. Vladimir Nabokov, *Speak, Memory: An Autobiography Revisited* (New York: Putnam's, 1966), 20.

19. Augustine, *The Confessions of Saint Augustine,* trans. Edward B. Pusey (New York: Collier, 1961), 194.

20. David Remnick, "Exile on Main Street: Don DeLillo's Undisclosed Underworld," *New Yorker,* 15 September 1997, 47.

21. Andrew O'Hagan, "National Enquirer: Don DeLillo Gets under America's Skin," *Voice Literary Supplement,* 16 September 1997, 8.

22. DeLillo's actual words are: "It is fiction's role to imagine deeply" ("The Power of History," 62).

23. James Joyce, *Ulysses* (1922; Paris: Shakespeare and Co., 1924), 38.

Works by Don DeLillo

This list is not intended to be exhaustive, only to include novels, drama, major non-fiction, and short fiction not incorporated into book-length works. The most comprehensive bibliography in print at the time this book went to press was that of Joseph S. Walker in the special DeLillo number of *Modern Fiction Studies* 45.3 (fall 1999): 837–51. Both Curt Gardner and Philip W. Nel maintain excellent running bibliographies on websites devoted to this author: *Don DeLillo's America* <http://perival.com/delillo/delillo.html> and the website of the Don DeLillo Society <http://www.ksu.edu/english/nelp/delillo/>, respectively (last checked 4 March 2001).

"The River Jordan." *Epoch* 10, no. 2 (winter 1960): 105–20.
"Take the 'A' Train." *Epoch* 12, no. 1 (spring 1962): 9–25.
"Spaghetti and Meatballs." *Epoch* 14, no. 3 (spring 1965): 244–50.
"Coming Sun. Mon. Tues." *Kenyon Review* 28, no. 3 (June 1966): 391–94.
"Baghdad Towers West." *Epoch* 17 (1968): 195–217.

"The Uniforms." *Carolina Quarterly* 22, no. 1 (1970): 4–11.

Americana. New York: Houghton Mifflin, 1971; rev. ed., New York: Penguin, 1989.

"In the Men's Room of the Sixteenth Century." *Esquire,* December 1971, 174–77, 243–44.

End Zone. New York: Houghton Mifflin, 1972.

"Total Loss Weekend." *Sports Illustrated,* 27 November 1972, 98–120.

Great Jones Street. Boston: Houghton Mifflin, 1973.

Ratner's Star. New York: Knopf, 1976.

Players. New York: Knopf, 1977.

Running Dog. New York: Knopf, 1978.

"Creation." *Antaeus* 33 (spring 1979): 32–46.

The Engineer of Moonlight. Cornell Review 1 (1979): 21–47.

Amazons: An Intimate Memoir of the First Woman to Play in the National Hockey League. New York: Henry Holt, 1980. (DeLillo and anonymous collaborator, under joint pseudonym Cleo Birdwell.)

The Names. New York: Knopf, 1982.

"Human Moments in World War III." *Esquire,* July 1983, 118–26.

"American Blood." *Rolling Stone,* 8 December 1983, 21–22, 24, 27–28, 74.

White Noise. New York: Viking, 1985.

The Day Room. New York: Knopf, 1987.

Libra. New York: Viking, 1988.

"The Runner." *Harper's,* September 1988, 61–63.

"The Ivory Acrobat." *Granta* 25 (fall 1988): 199–212.

"Silhouette City: Hitler, Manson, and the Millennium." *Dimensions: A Journal of Holocaust Studies* 4, no. 3 (1988): 29–34.

"The Rapture of the Athlete Assumed into Heaven." *The Quarterly* 15 (fall 1990). Reprint, *Harper's,* December 1990, 44.

Mao II. New York: Viking, 1991.

"The Artist Naked in a Cage." *New Yorker,* 26 May 1997, 6–7.

"The Power of History." *New York Times Magazine,* 7 September 1997, 60–63.

Underworld. New York: Scribner, 1997.

Valparaiso. New York: Scribner, 1999.

"The Mystery at the Middle of Ordinary Life." *Zoetrope: All-Story* 4, no. 4 (winter 2000): 70. Reprint, *Harper's,* January 2001, 37

The Body Artist. New York: Scribner, 2001.

Bibliography

Aldridge, John W. *The American Novel and the Way We Live Now.* New York: Oxford Univ. Press, 1983.

Allen, Glen Scott. "Raids on the Conscious: Pynchon's Legacy of Paranoia and the Terrorism of Uncertainty in Don DeLillo's *Ratner's Star.*" *Postmodern Culture* 4, no. 2 (1994): 28 paragraphs.

Althusser, Louis. "Ideology and Ideological State Apparatuses (Notes Towards an Investigation)." In *Lenin and Philosophy and Other Essays,* trans. Ben Brewster, 127–86. London: New Left Books, 1971.

Amis, Martin. "Survivors of the Cold War." *New York Times Book Review,* 5 October 1997, 12–13.

Anonymous. *The Cloud of Unknowing and Other Works.* Trans. Clifton Wolters. Harmondsworth: Penguin, 1961.

Arensberg, Ann. "Seven Seconds." *Vogue,* August 1988.

Baker, Peter. "The Terrorist as Interpreter: *Mao II* in Postmodern Context." *Postmodern Culture* 4, no. 2 (1994): 34 paragraphs.

Barrett, Laura. "'Here But Also There': Subjectivity and Postmodern Space in *Mao II.*" *Modern Fiction Studies* 45, no. 3 (fall 1999): 788–810.

Barthelme, Donald. *The Dead Father.* New York: Farrar, Straus and Giroux, 1975.

Baudrillard, Jean. "The Precession of Simulacra." In *Simulations,* trans. Paul Foss, Paul Patton, and Philip Bleitchman, 1–79. New York: Semiotext(e), 1983.

Begley, Adam. "Don DeLillo: *Americana, Mao II,* and *Underworld.*" *Southwest Review* 82, no. 4 (1997): 478–505.

———. "Don DeLillo: The Art of Fiction CXXXV." *Paris Review* 35 (fall 1993): 274–306.

Benjamin, Walter. "On Language As Such and on the Language of Man," trans. Edmund Jephcott. In *Selected Writings, Volume 1: 1913–1926.* Ed. Marcus Bullock and Michael W. Jennings, 62–74. Cambridge: Harvard Univ. Press, 1996.

Bernstein, Stephen. "*Libra* and the Historical Sublime." *Postmodern Culture* 4 (1994): 25 paragraphs.

Billen, Andrew. "Up from the Underworld." *London Evening Standard,* 28 January 1998, last accessed 4 March 2001 <http://www.thisislondon.co.uk/dynamic/lifestyle/bottom_review.html?in_review_id=26802&in_review_text_id=20603>

Bonca, Cornel. "Don DeLillo's *White Noise:* The Natural Language of the Species," *College Literature* 23, no. 2 (June 1996): 25–44.

Brent, Jonathan. "The Unimaginable Space of Danilo Kiš and Don DeLillo." *Review of Contemporary Fiction* 14 (spring 1994): 180–88.

Bronowski, Jacob, and Bruce Mazlish. *The Western Intellectual Tradition: From Leonardo to Hegel.* New York: Harper & Row, 1960.

Brooker, Peter. *New York Fictions: Modernity, Postmodernity, and the New Modern.* London: Longman, 1996.

Bryant, Paula. "Discussing the Untellable: Don DeLillo's *The Names.*" *Critique* 29 (fall 1987): 16–29.

———. "Extending the Fabulative Continuum: DeLillo, Mooney, and Federman." *Extrapolation* 30, no. 2 (summer 1989): 156–65.

Burke, William. "Football, Literature, Culture." *Southwest Review* 60 (1975): 391–98.

Cantor, Paul A. "'Adolf, We Hardly Knew You.'" In *New Essays on "White Noise,"* ed. Frank Lentricchia, 39–62. New York: Cambridge Univ. Press, 1991.

Carmichael, Thomas. "Lee Harvey Oswald and the Postmodern Subject: History and Intertextuality in Don DeLillo's *Libra.*" *Contemporary Literature* 34 (summer 1993): 204–18.

Carter, Dale. "Beyond the Grassy Knolledge: Conspiratorial Variations on the Kennedy Assassination." *Odense American Studies International Series* no. 11 (August 1994), 1–31.

Cather, Willa. "The Novel Démeublé." In *Not under Forty,* 43–51. New York: Knopf, 1936.

Caton, Lou F. "Romanticism and the Postmodern Novel: Three Scenes from Don DeLillo's *White Noise*." *English Language Notes* 35 (September 1997): 38–48.

Champlin, Charles. "The Heart Is a Lonely Craftsman." *Los Angeles Times Calendar,* 29 July 1994, 7.

Civello, Paul. "Undoing the Naturalistic Novel: Don DeLillo's *Libra.*" *Arizona Quarterly* 48 (summer 1992): 33–56.

Collins, Bradford, and David Cowart. "Through the Looking-Glass: Reading Warhol's *Superman.*" *American Imago* 53 (summer 1996): 107–37.

Conroy, Mark. "From Tombstone to Tabloid: Authority Figured in *White Noise.*" *Critique* 35, no. 2 (winter 1994): 97–110.

Cordesse, Gérard. "Bruits et paradoxes dans *White Noise* de Don DeLillo." *Revue française d'études américaines* no. 76 (March 1998): 54–60.

Couturier, Maurice. "L'histoire et la refiguration de l'instant: *White Noise* de Don DeLillo," *Revue française d'études américaines* no. 62 (November 1994): 383–92.

Cowart, David. *History and the Contemporary Novel.* Carbondale: Southern Illinois Univ. Press, 1989.

Dällenbach, Lucien. *The Mirror in the Text.* Chicago: Univ. of Chicago Press, 1989.

Dampier, Sir William. *A History of Science and Its Relations with Philosophy and Religion.* New York: Macmillan, 1930.

DeCurtis, Anthony. "'An Outsider in This Society': An Interview with Don DeLillo." In *Introducing Don DeLillo,* ed. Lentricchia, 43–66.

———. "The Product: Bucky Wunderlick, Rock 'n Roll, and Don DeLillo's *Great Jones Street.*" In *Introducing Don DeLillo,* ed. Lentricchia, 131–41.

Derrida, Jacques. "The Supplement of Copula: Philosophy before Linguistics." In *Margins of Philosophy,* trans. Alan Bass, 175–205. Chicago: Univ. of Chicago Press, 1982.

Desalm, Brigitte. "Masses, Power and the Elegance of Sentences," trans. Tilo Zimmermann. *Kölner Stadt-Anzeiger,* 27 October 1992, last accessed 23 July 2001 <http://perival.com/delillo/desalm_interview.html>.

Dewey, Joseph. *In a Dark Time: The Apocalyptic Temper in the American Novel of the Nuclear Age,* 205–29. West Lafayette, Ind.: Purdue Univ. Press, 1990.

Dunbar, William. *The Poems of William Dunbar.* Ed. James Kinsley. Oxford: Oxford Univ. Press, 1979.

Duvall, John N. "Baseball as Aesthetic Ideology: Cold War History, Race, and DeLillo's 'Pafko at the Wall.'" *Modern Fiction Studies* 41 (1995): 285–313.

———. "Introduction: From Valparaiso to Jerusalem: DeLillo and the Moment of Canonization." *Modern Fiction Studies* 45, no. 3 (fall 1999): 559–68.

———. "The (Super)Marketplace of Images: Television as Unmediated Mediation in DeLillo's *White Noise.*" *Arizona Quarterly* 50, no. 3 (autumn 1994): 127–53.

Eddington, A. S. *The Nature of the Physical World.* Cambridge: Cambridge Univ. Press, 1928.

Feuchtwanger, Lion. *The House of Desdemona.* Detroit: Wayne State Univ. Press, 1963.

Foster, Dennis A. "Alphabetic Pleasures: *The Names.*" In *Introducing Don DeLillo,* ed. Lentricchia, 157–73.

Foucault, Michel. "Orders of Discourse," trans. Rupert Swyer. *Social Science Information* 10 (April 1971): 7–30.

Franzen, Jonathan. "Perchance to Dream." *Harper's Magazine,* April 1996, 35–54.

Freud, Sigmund. *Moses and Monotheism.* Vol. 23 of *The Standard Edition of the Complete Psychological Works of Sigmund Freud.* Ed. and trans. James Strachey. 24 vols. London: Hogarth Press, 1964.

———. *Totem and Taboo.* Vol. 13 of *The Standard Edition of the Complete Psychological Works of Sigmund Freud.* Ed. and trans. James Strachey. London: Hogarth Press, 1955.

Frost, Robert. *The Poetry of Robert Frost.* Ed. Edward Connery Lathem. New York: Holt, Rinehart and Winston, 1969.

Frow, John. "The Last Things before the Last: Notes on *White Noise.*" In *Introducing Don DeLillo,* ed. Lentricchia, 175–91.

———. *Marxism and Literary History.* Oxford: Basil Blackwell, 1986.

Gardner, John. *Grendel.* New York: Knopf, 1971.

Gervais, Bertrand. "Les murmures de la machine: lire à travers le *Bruit de fond* de Don DeLillo." *Surfaces* 4, no. 203 (1994): 1–26.

Ginsberg, Allen. "A Supermarket in California." In *Collected Poems, 1947–1980.* New York: Harper & Row, 1984.

Goldstein, William. "Don DeLillo." *Publishers Weekly,* 19 August 1988, 55–56.

Goodheart, Eugene. *Desire and Its Discontents.* New York: Columbia Univ. Press, 1991.

Grandjeat, Yves-Charles. "Le Sens de la crise dans *White Noise* de Don DeLillo." In *Éclats de voix: crises en représentation dans la littérature nord-américaine,* ed. Christine Raguet-Bouvart, 73–83. La Rochelle: Rumeur des Ages, 1995.

Hallett, Garth. *A Companion to Wittgenstein's "Philosophical Investigations."* Ithaca: Cornell Univ. Press, 1977.

Hantke, Steffen. "'God Save Us from Bourgeois Adventure': The Figure of the Terrorist in Contemporary American Conspiracy Fiction." *Studies in the Novel* 28, no. 2 (1996): 219–43.

Happe, François. "L'Amérique de Don DeLillo ou l'empire des signes." *Europe* 68 (May 1990): 55–58.

Hardy, Thomas. *The Complete Poems.* Ed. James Gibson. London: Macmillan, 1976.

Hawthorne, Nathaniel. *The Scarlet Letter.* Vol. 1 of *The Centenary Edition of the Works of Nathaniel Hawthorne.* Ed. William Charvat et al. Columbus: Ohio State Univ. Press, 1962.

Hayles, N. Katherine. "Postmodern Parataxis: Embodied Texts, Weightless Information." *American Literary History* 2, no. 3 (fall 1990): 394–421.

Heidegger, Martin. "Hölderlin and the Essence of Poetry," trans. Douglas Scott. In *Existence and Being.* Ed. Werner Broch, 291–315. London: Vision, 1968.

———. *An Introduction to Metaphysics.* Trans. Ralph Manheim. New Haven: Yale Univ. Press, 1959.

Holland, Max. "After Thirty Years: Making Sense of the Assassination." *Reviews in American History* 22 (1994): 191–209.

Holland, Norman N. *The Dynamics of Literary Response.* New York: Oxford Univ. Press, 1968.

Howard, Gerald. "The American Strangeness: An Interview with Don DeLillo." *Hungry Mind Review* 43 (1997): 13–16.

Humez, Alexander and Nicholas. *Alpha to Omega: The Life and Times of the Greek Alphabet.* Boston: David R. Godine, 1981.

Hutcheon, Linda. *Narcissistic Narrative: The Metafictional Paradox.* New York: Methuen, 1984.

———. *A Poetics of Postmodernism: History, Theory, Fiction.* New York: Routledge, 1988.

Jameson, Fredric. *Postmodernism, or the Cultural Logic of Late Capitalism.* Durham: Duke Univ. Press, 1991.

Johnson, Stuart. "Extraphilosophical Instigations in Don DeLillo's *Running Dog.*" *Contemporary Literature* 26, no. 1 (1985): 74–90.

Johnston, John. "Generic Difficulties in the Novels of Don DeLillo." *Critique* 30 (summer 1989): 261–75.

———. "Post-Cinematic Fiction: Film in the Novels of Pynchon, McElroy, and DeLillo." *New Orleans Review* 17, no. 2 (summer 1990): 90–97.

———. "Superlinear Fiction or Historical Diagram? Don DeLillo's *Libra.*" *Modern Fiction Studies* 40 (summer 1994): 319–42.

Joyce, James. *A Portrait of the Artist As a Young Man.* 1916. New York: Viking, 1964.

———. *Ulysses.* 1922. Paris: Shakespeare and Co., 1924.

Kakutani, Michiko. "'Underworld': Of America as a Splendid Junk Heap." *New York Times,* 16 September 1997, last accessed 4 March 2001 <http://www.nytimes.com/books/97/09/14/daily/underworld-book-review.html>

Kaufman, Walter, ed. and trans. *The Portable Nietzsche.* New York: Viking, 1954.

Kavadlo, Jesse. "Celebration and Annihilation: The Balance of *Underworld.*" *Undercurrent* no. 7 (spring 1999), University of Oregon, last accessed 4 March 2001 <http://darkwing.uoregon.edu/~ucurrent/uc7/7-kava.html>.

Keesey, Douglas. *Don DeLillo.* New York: Twayne, 1993.

Kierkegaard, Søren. "'That Individual': Two 'Notes' Concerning My Work As an Author." In *The Point of View,* trans. Walter Lowrie, 105–40. Oxford: Oxford Univ. Press, 1939.

King, Noel. "Reading *White Noise:* Floating Remarks." *Critical Quarterly* 33, no. 3 (autumn 1991): 66–83.

Knight, Peter. "Everything Is Connected: *Underworld*'s Secret History of Paranoia." *Modern Fiction Studies* 45, no. 3 (fall 1999): 811–36.

Körte, Peter. "Sprache ist der Einzige Fluchtweg." *Der Standard,* 30 October 1998, A1.

Kronick, Joseph. "*Libra* and the Assassination of JFK: A Textbook Operation." *Arizona Quarterly* 50 (spring 1994): 109–32.

Kucich, John. "Postmodern Politics: Don DeLillo and the Plight of the White Male Writer." *Michigan Quarterly Review* 27 (spring 1988): 328–41.

Lacan, Jacques. *Écrits: A Selection.* Trans. Alan Sheridan. London: Tavistock, 1977.

———. *The Seminar of Jacques Lacan, Book II: The Ego in Freud's Theory and in the Technique of Psychoanalysis, 1954–1955.* Trans. Sylvana Tomaselli. New York: Cambridge Univ. Press, 1988.

LeClair, Tom. "An Interview with Don DeLillo." In *Anything Can Happen: Interviews with Contemporary American Novelists.* Cond. and ed. LeClair and Larry McCaffery, 79–90. Urbana: Univ. of Illinois Press, 1983.

———. *In the Loop: Don DeLillo and the Systems Novel.* Urbana: Univ. of Illinois Press, 1987.

———. Review of *Running Dog,* by Don DeLillo. *New Republic* 7 (October 1978): 33–34.

———. "An Underhistory of Mid-Century America." *Atlantic,* October 1997, last accessed 4 March 2001 <http://www.theatlantic.com/issues/97oct/delillo.htm>.

LeClair, Tom, and Larry McCaffery, eds. *Anything Can Happen: Interviews with Contemporary American Novelists.* Urbana: Univ. of Illinois Press, 1983.

Lentricchia, Frank. "*Libra* as Postmodern Critique." In *Introducing Don DeLillo,* ed. Lentricchia, 193–215.

———. "Tales of the Electronic Tribe." In *New Essays on "White Noise,"* ed. Lentricchia, 87–113.

———, ed. *Introducing Don DeLillo.* Durham: Duke Univ. Press, 1991.

———, ed. *New Essays on "White Noise."* New York: Cambridge Univ. Press, 1991.

Levesque, Richard. "Telling Postmodern Tales: Absent Authorities in Didion's *Democracy* and DeLillo's *Mao II,*" *Arizona Quarterly* 54, no. 3 (autumn 1998): 69–87.

Livingstone, Marco. "Do It Yourself: Notes on Warhol's Technique." In *Andy Warhol: A Retrospective,* ed. McShine, 63–78.

Lovejoy, Arthur O. *The Great Chain of Being: A Study of the History of an Idea.* Cambridge: Harvard Univ. Press, 1936.

Lyotard, Jean-François. *The Postmodern Condition: A Report on Knowledge.* Trans. Geoff Bennington and Brian Massumi. Minneapolis: Univ. of Minnesota Press, 1984.

Mailer, Norman. *Advertisements for Myself.* New York: Berkley Medallion, 1959.

———. *An American Dream.* New York: Dial, 1965.

———. *Oswald's Tale: An American Mystery.* New York: Random House, 1995.

Mallon, Thomas. "The Bronx, with Thonx." *GQ,* September 1997, 193–96.

Maltby, Paul. "The Romantic Metaphysics of Don DeLillo." *Contemporary Literature* 37, no. 2 (summer 1996): 258–77.

McClure, John A. "Postmodern/Post-Secular: Contemporary Fiction and Spirituality." *Modern Fiction Studies* 41 (1995): 141–63.

McHale, Brian. *Constructing Postmodernism.* New York: Routledge, 1992.

———. *Postmodernist Fiction.* New York: Methuen, 1987.

McShine, Kynaston, ed. *Andy Warhol: A Retrospective.* New York: Museum of Modern Art, 1989.

Michael, Magali Cornier. "The Political Paradox within Don DeLillo's *Libra.*" *Critique* 35 (spring 1994): 146–55.

Millard, Bill. "The Fable of the Ants: Myopic Interactions in DeLillo's *Libra*." *Postmodern Culture* 4 (January 1994): 29 paragraphs.

Molesworth, Charles. "Don DeLillo's Perfect Starry Night." In *Introducing Don DeLillo*, ed. Lentricchia, 381–94.

Morris, Matthew J. "Murdering Words: Language in Action in Don DeLillo's *The Names*." *Contemporary Literature* 30 (spring 1989): 113–27.

Moses, Michael Valdez. "Lust Removed from Nature." In *New Essays on "White Noise*," ed. Lentricchia, 63–86.

Mott, Christopher M. "*Libra* and the Subject of History." *Critique* 35 (spring 1994): 131–45.

Nabokov, Vladimir. *Speak, Memory: An Autobiography Revisited*. New York: Putnam's, 1966.

Nashe, Thomas. *Works*. Ed. Ronald B. McKerrow, rev. F. P. Wilson. 5 vols. Oxford: B. Blackwell, 1958.

Nel, Philip. "'A Small Incisive Shock': Modern Forms, Postmodern Politics, and the Role of the Avant-garde in *Underworld*." *Modern Fiction Studies* 45, no. 3 (fall 1999): 724–52.

Nietzsche, Friedrich. *Also Spake Zarathustra*. Trans. Thomas Common. Vol. 11 of *The Complete Works of Friedrich Nietzsche*. Ed. Oscar Levy. 18 vols. New York: Macmillan, 1910.

———. *Ecce Homo*. Trans. Anthony M. Ludovici. Vol. 17 of *The Complete Works of Friedrich Nietzsche*. Ed. Oscar Levy. 18 vols. New York: Macmillan, 1911.

———. *The Joyful Wisdom*. Trans. Thomas Common. Vol. 10 of *The Complete Works of Friedrich Nietzsche*. Ed. Oscar Levy. New York: Macmillan, 1910.

Nye, David E. "The Emergence of Photographic Discourse: Images and Consumption." In *Consumption and American Culture*. Ed. Nye and Carl Pedersen, 34–48. European Contributions to American Studies, vol. 21. Amsterdam: VU Univ. Press, 1991.

O'Donnell, Patrick. "Obvious Paranoia: The Politics of Don DeLillo's *Running Dog*." *Centennial Review* 34 (winter 1990): 56–72.

O'Hagan, Andrew. "National Enquirer: Don DeLillo Gets under America's Skin," *Voice Literary Supplement*, 16 September 1997, 8–10.

Oriard, Michael. "Don DeLillo's Search for Walden Pond." *Critique* 20 (1978): 5–24.

Osen, Diane. "Window on a Writing Life: A Conversation with National Book Award Winner Don DeLillo." Book-of-the-Month Club. Last accessed 23 July 2001 <http://www.pubweekly.com/NBF/docs/wwl_curri_DeLillo.htm>

Osteen, Mark. *American Magic and Dread: Don DeLillo's Dialogue with Culture*. Philadelphia: Univ. of Pennsylvania Press, 2000.

———. Introduction to *"White Noise": Text and Criticism*, by Don DeLillo. Ed. Osteen. New York: Viking, 1998. vii–xv.

Parrish, Timothy L. "From Hoover's FBI to Eisenstein's *Unterwelt*: DeLillo Directs the Postmodern Novel." *Modern Fiction Studies* 45, no. 3 (fall 1999): 696–723.

Passaro, Vince. "Dangerous Don DeLillo." *New York Times Magazine*, 19 May 1991, 34–36, 38, 76–77.

————. "The Unsparing Vision of Don DeLillo." *Harper's Magazine,* November 1997, 72–75.

Percy, Walker. "The Loss of the Creature." In *The Message in the Bottle: How Queer Man Is, How Queer Language Is, and What One Has to Do with the Other,* 46–65. New York: Farrar, Straus and Giroux, 1975.

Peyser, Thomas. "Globalization in America: The Case of Don DeLillo's *White Noise.*" *Clio* 25, no. 3 (spring 1996): 255–71.

Pifer, Ellen. *Demon or Doll: Images of the Child in Contemporary Writing and Culture.* Charlottesville: Univ. Press of Virginia, 2000.

Pireddu, Nicoletta. "Il Rumore dell'Incertezza: Sistemi Chiusi e Aperti in *White Noise* di Don DeLillo." *Quaderni di Lingue e Letterature* 17 (1991–92): 129–40.

Pound, Ezra. *Selected Poems.* New York: New Directions, 1957.

Powers, Richard. *Plowing the Dark.* New York: Farrar, Straus and Giroux, 2000.

Pynchon, Thomas. *The Crying of Lot 49.* Philadelphia: Lippincott, 1966.

————. *Gravity's Rainbow.* New York: Viking, 1973.

————. *Slow Learner.* New York: Little, Brown, 1984.

Ragland-Sullivan, Ellie. *Jacques Lacan and the Philosophy of Psychoanalysis.* Urbana: Univ. of Illinois Press, 1986.

Reeve, N. H., and Richard Kerridge. "Toxic Events: Postmodernism and DeLillo's *White Noise.*" *Cambridge Quarterly* 23 (1994): 303–23.

Remnick, David. "Exile on Main Street: Don DeLillo's Undisclosed Underworld." *New Yorker,* 15 September 1997, 42–48.

Rilke, Rainer Maria. *Gesammelte Gedichte.* Frankfurt: Insel-Verlag, 1962.

Roberts, Margaret. "'D' is for Danger—and for Writer Don DeLillo." *Chicago Tribune,* 22 May 1992, sec. 5, pp. 1, 5.

Robinson, Marilynne. "Psalm Eight." In *The Death of Adam: Essays on Modern Thought,* 227–43. Boston: Houghton Mifflin, 1998.

Rothstein, Mervyn. "A Novelist Faces His Themes on New Ground." *New York Times,* 20 December 1987, H5, 19.

Ruthrof, Horst. "Narrative and the Digital: On the Syntax of the Postmodern." *AUMLA* no. 74 (November 1990): 185–200.

Saltzman, Arthur M. "The Figure in the Static: *White Noise.*" *Modern Fiction Studies* 40, no. 4 (winter 1994): 807–26.

Scanlan, Margaret. "Writers among Terrorists: Don DeLillo's *Mao II* and the Rushdie Affair." *Modern Fiction Studies* 40, no. 2 (summer 1994): 229–52.

Serres, Michel. *Genesis.* Trans. Geneviève James and James Nielson. Ann Arbor: Univ. of Michigan Press, 1995.

Simmons, Philip E. *Deep Surfaces: Mass Culture and History in Postmodern American Fiction.* Athens: Univ. of Georgia Press, 1997.

Simmons, Ryan. "What Is a Terrorist? Contemporary Authorship, the Unabomber, and *Mao II.*" *Modern Fiction Studies* 45, no. 3 (fall 1999): 675–95.

Snow, Sir Charles Percy. *The Two Cultures; and, A Second Look: An Expanded Version* of *"The Two Cultures and the Scientific Revolution."* New York: Cambridge Univ. Press, 1964.

Streitfeld, David. "Don DeLillo's Gloomy Muse." *Washington Post,* 14 May 1992, C1, 4.

Swift, Jonathan. *Gulliver's Travels.* Ed. Herbert Davis. Oxford: Basil Blackwell, 1962.

Tabbi, Joseph. *Postmodern Sublime: Technology and American Writing from Mailer to Cyberpunk.* Ithaca: Cornell Univ. Press, 1995.

Thomas, Glen. "History, Biography, and Narrative in Don DeLillo's *Libra." Twentieth-Century Literature* 43 (spring 1997): 107–24.

Updike, John. "Layers of Ambiguity." Review of *Players,* by Don DeLillo. *New Yorker,* 27 March 1978, 127–28.

U.S. President's Commission on the Assassination of President John F. Kennedy. *Investigation on the Assassination of President John F. Kennedy. Hearings before the President's Commission on the Assassination of President Kennedy.* 26 vols. Washington, D.C.: GPO, 1964.

Wareham, Dean. "My Favorite Rock & Roll Novel. In *Rolling Stone's Alt. Rock-a-Rama.* Ed. Scott Schinder, 384–85. New York: Delta, 1996.

Warhol, Andy, Kasper König, Pontus Hultén, and Olle Granath, eds. *Andy Warhol.* Stockholm: Moderna Museet, 1968.

Weinstein, Arnold. *Nobody's Home: Speech, Self, and Place in American Fiction from Hawthorne to DeLillo.* New York: Oxford Univ. Press, 1993.

White, Patti. *Gatsby's Party: The System and the List in Contemporary Narrative.* West Lafayette, Ind.: Purdue Univ. Press, 1992.

Whitman, Walt. *Leaves of Grass: Comprehensive Reader's Edition.* Ed. Harold W. Blodgett and Sculley Bradley. New York: New York Univ. Press, 1963.

Wilcox, Leonard. "Baudrillard, DeLillo's *White Noise,* and the End of Heroic Narrative." *Contemporary Literature* 32 (1991): 346–65.

Will, George. "Shallow Look at the Mind of an Assassin." *Washington Post,* 22 September 1988, A25.

Winthrop, John. "A Modell of Christian Charity." In *Winthrop Papers.* Ed. Stewart Mitchell. Vol. 2. New York: Russell & Russell, 1968.

Wittgenstein, Ludwig. *Philosophical Investigations.* Trans. E. M. Anscombe. Oxford: Basil Blackwell, 1953.

———. *Tractatus Logico-Philosophicus.* Trans. D. F. Pears and B. F. McGuinness. London: Routledge and Kegan Paul, 1961.

Yardley, Jonathan. "Appointment in Dallas." *Washington Post Book World,* 31 July 1988, 3.

Index

Troilus and Criseyde (Chaucer), quoted, 198

Trotsky, Leon, 103

Tuchman, Barbara, 94

Turn of the Screw, The (James), 204

"Two Tramps in Mud Time" (Frost), 46

Ulysses (Joyce), 47, 201

"Under the Rose" (Pynchon), 101–2

Underworld (DeLillo), 5, 7, 9, 71, 75, 76, 82, 96; allusiveness and literary affinities, 200–203; art and the artist in, 197–98, 231 (n. 9); baseball, 189, 190–91, 191–92, 193, 198; formal and stylistic elements, 200, 231 (n. 6, n. 7); George Manza as double, 190; identity and point of view, 199–200; language in, 166, 181–86; religious feelings in, 186, 192, 193–96, 230 (n. 14); Texas Highway Killer videotape, 98–100; 189, 191, 192; title, 188, 230 (n. 7); waste and recycling, 186–87, 197–99

Unification Church, 122

"Uniforms, The" (DeLillo), 213 (n. 3)

Universal Baseball Association, The (Coover), 3, 18, 178

"University Days" (Thurber), 19

Updike, John: reviews *Players*, 2

V. (Pynchon), 198

Valparaiso (DeLillo), 98, 100–101

Vargas Llosa, Mario, 7

Vico, Giambattista, 135

Vietnam War, 95, 133, 193, 199. See also *Running Dog*

Village of the Damned (Rilla), 189

Vineland (Pynchon), 61, 153, 189

Virilio, Paul, 10

Voltaire, 153, 154, 227–28 (n. 6)

Vonnegut, Kurt, 22, 180

Walker, General Edwin, 104, 105

Wallace, George, 95

Warhol, Andy, 3, 123, 124, 125, 126, 127, 224 (n. 10)

Warren Commission Report, 60, 75. See also *Libra*

Wassermann, Jakob, 203

Waste Land, The (Eliot), 40, 201. See also *End Zone*

Watergate scandal, 95

Watts Towers, 197

Waves, The (Woolf), 202

Weekend (Godard), 213 (n. 3)

Weinstein, Arnold, 73, 84

Weir, Peter, 85

Wellington, Duke of, 150

Wertmuller, Lina, 30

"West-Running Brook" (Frost), 207

White, Curtis, 11

White, Hayden, 220 (n. 13)

White Noise (DeLillo), 7, 9, 11, 52, 93, 110, 140, 143, 185, 187, 198, 200–201, 207; blood relations within Gladney family, 219 (n. 43); character of Murray, 88, 219 (n. 42); death theme, 72, 73, 76–8, 79–82, 84, 85, 89, 90; the Gladney garbage, 74–76; language in, 72–73, 74, 85–88, 89, 216 (n. 7); and Michel Serres, 73, 79, 83–84, 89; "most photographed barn in America," 86–87; narrative technique and point of view, 216 (n. 1), 217 (n. 15); neo-Romantic elements in, 4, 71; postmodernism of, 10; religious elements in, 71, 77–78; simulacra in, 4, 71; *Toyota Celica* crux, 73, 212 (n. 7), 216 (n. 6); white noise, 72, 73, 83, 84; Wilder and his tricycle, 81, 89–90, 143, 158, 218 (n. 29)

White, Patti, 85

Whitman, Walt, 80, 81, 82, 89, 164, 200

Wilcox, Leonard, 71

Wilde, Oscar, 152

Will, George, 110

Winthrop, John, 79